SHORTLIST

London
2011

WHAT'S NEW | WHAT'S ON | WHAT'S BEST

www.timeout.com/london

London

Contents

Don't Miss: 2011

Sights & Museums	8
Eating & Drinking	14
Shopping	21
Nightlife	26
Arts & Leisure	31
Calendar	36

Itineraries

Looking at London 2012	48
The Wren Route	51
The City by Night	54

London by Area

The South Bank 58
  Map 60
Westminster & St James's 74
  Map 75
South Kensington & Chelsea 84
  Map 86
The West End 98
  Map 99
  Map 114
  Map 128
The City 149
  Map 150
Neighbourhood London 170

Essentials

Hotels 194
Getting Around 211
Resources A-Z 217
Index 220

Published by Time Out Guides Ltd
Universal House
251 Tottenham Court Road
London W1T 7AB
Tel: + 44 (0)20 7813 3000
Fax: + 44 (0)20 7813 6001
Email: guides@timeout.com
www.timeout.com

Managing Director Peter Fiennes
Editorial Director Ruth Jarvis
Business Manager Daniel Allen
Editorial Manager Holly Pick
Assistant Management Accountant Ija Krasnikova

Time Out Guides is a wholly owned subsidiary of Time Out Group Ltd.

© Time Out Group Ltd
Director & Founder Tony Elliott
Chief Executive Officer David King
Group Financial Director Paul Rakkar
Group General Manager/Director Nichola Coulthard
Time Out Communications Ltd MD David Pepper
Time Out International Ltd MD Cathy Runciman
Time Out Magazine Ltd Publisher/Managing Director Mark Elliott
Group Commercial Director Graeme Tottle
Production Director Mark Lamond
Group IT Director Simon Chappell

Time Out and the Time Out logo are trademarks of Time Out Group Ltd.

This edition first published in Great Britain in 2010 by Ebury Publishing
A Random House Group Company
Company information can be found on www.randomhouse.co.uk
Random House UK Limited Reg. No. 954009
10 9 8 7 6 5 4 3 2 1

Distributed in the US and Latin America by Publishers Group West (1-510-809-3700)
Distributed in Canada by Publishers Group Canada (1-800-747-8147)

For further distribution details, see www.timeout.com

ISBN: 978-1-84670-162-7

A CIP catalogue record for this book is available from the British Library.

Printed and bound in Germany by Appl.

The Random House Group Limited supports The Forest Stewardship Council (FSC), the leading international forest certification organisation. All our titles that are printed on Greenpeace approved FSC certified paper carry the FSC logo. Our paper procurement policy can be found at www.rbooks.co.uk/environment.

Time Out carbon-offsets all its flights with Trees for Cities (www.treesforcities.org).

London Shortlist

The **Time Out London Shortlist 2011** is one of a series of annual guides that draws on Time Out's background as a magazine publisher to keep you current with everything that's going on in town. As well as London's key sights and the best of its eating, drinking and leisure options, it picks out the most exciting venues to have opened in the last year and gives a full calendar of events running from September 2010 to December 2011. It also includes features on the important news, trends and openings, all compiled by locally based editors and writers. Whether you're visiting for the first time in your life or the first time this year, you'll find the *Time Out London Shortlist* contains all you need to know, in a portable, easy-to-use format.

The guide divides central London into six areas, each containing listings for Sights & Museums, Eating & Drinking, Shopping, Nightlife and Arts & Leisure, and maps pinpointing their locations. At the front of the book are chapters rounding up these scenes city-wide, and giving a shortlist of our overall picks. We also include itineraries for days out, plus essentials such as transport information and hotels.

Our listings give phone numbers as dialled in London. To dial them from elsewhere in the UK, preface them with 020. From abroad, use your country's exit code followed by 44 (the country code for the UK), 20 and the number given.

We have noted price categories by using one to four pound signs (**£-££££**), representing budget, moderate, expensive and luxury. Major credit cards are accepted unless otherwise stated. We also indicate when a venue is **NEW**, and give **Event highlights**.

All our listings are double-checked, but places do sometimes close or change their hours or prices, so it's a good idea to call a venue before visiting. While every effort has been made to ensure accuracy, the publishers cannot accept responsibility for any errors that this guide may contain.

Venues are marked on the maps using symbols numbered according to their order within the chapter and colour-coded as follows:

- ❶ Sights & Museums
- ❶ Eating & Drinking
- ❶ Shopping
- ❹ Nightlife
- ❶ Arts & Leisure

Map key	
Major sight or landmark	▢
Railway or coach station	▢
Underground station	⊖
Park	▢
Hospital	▢
Casualty unit	✚
Church	✚
Synagogue	✡
District	MAYFAIR
Theatre	●

Time Out **London** Shortlist 2011

EDITORIAL
Editor Simon Coppock
Proofreader Kieron Corless

DESIGN
Art Director Scott Moore
Art Editor Pinelope Kourmouzoglou
Senior Designer Kei Ishimaru
Group Commercial Designer Jodi Sher

Picture Editor Jael Marschner
Deputy Picture Editor Lynn Chambers
Picture Desk Assistant/Researcher Ben Rowe

ADVERTISING
New Business & Commercial Director
 Mark Phillips

Magazine & UK Guides Commercial Director
 St.John Betteridge
Magazine & UK Guides Account Managers
 Jessica Baldwin, Michelle Daburn, Ben Holt

MARKETING
Sales & Marketing Director, North America
 & Latin America Lisa Levinson
Senior Publishing Brand Manager Luthfa Begum
Group Commercial Art Director Anthony Huggins
Marketing Co-ordinator Alana Benton

PRODUCTION
Production Manager Brendan McKeown
Production Controller Damian Bennett

CONTRIBUTORS
This guide was researched and written by Simone Baird, Joe Bindloss, Simon Coppock, Maggie Davis, Guy Dimond, Rachel Halliburton, Dan Jones, Peter Watts and the writers of *Time Out London* and *Time Out* magazine.

PHOTOGRAPHY
Photography by pages 7, 11, 62, 74, 80, 91 (top right, bottom left), 106, 176 (bottom) 200 Jonathan Perugia; page 8 Richard Bryant/Arcaid courtesy of the Whitechapel Gallery; pages 13, 30, 57, 67, 98, 134, 190, 193, 194 Michelle Grant; pages 14, 15 Jitka Hynkova; page 16; Michael Franke; pages 17, 21, 25, 26, 29, 91 (top left, bottom right), 131, 176 (Top), 210 Rob Greig; page 19; Britta Jaschinski; pages 24, 137 Ed Marshall; page 31, 36 Belinda Lawley; page 39 Scott Wishart; pages 41, 47, 77, 126 Heloise Bergman; page 44 Claire Nash; page 46 Linda Nylind; pages 48, 49 London 2012; pages 51, 71, 84 Britta Jaschinski; page 52 Kenneth Yau; page 54 Olivia Rutherford; pages 55, 62 (bottom); pages 123, 154, 166 Alys Tomlinson; pages 58, 149 Simon Leigh; page 68 (left) Morley von Sternberg; page 68 (right) Marc Coudrais; page 94 Richard Lea-Hair; page 102 Jean Goldsmith; page 111 Tom Baker; page 118 Britta Jaschinski; page 143 Susannah Stone; page 147 RUG/Catherine Ashmore; page 153 (top) Jason Lowe; page 153 Jefferson Smith; page 163 Tove K Breitstein; page 170 Ben Rowe; page 175 Elisabeth Blanchet; page 178 Christina Theisen; page 181 Abigail Lelliott; page 187 Warren King; page 204 Emma Wood; page 208 Heike Bohnstengel.

The following images were provided by the featured establishments/artists: pages 34, 42, 160, 198, 207.

Cover photograph: London Eye. Credit: Getty.

MAPS
JS Graphics (john@jsgraphics.co.uk).

About **Time Out**

Founded in 1968, Time Out has expanded from humble London beginnings into the leading resource for those wanting to know what's happening in the world's greatest cities. As well as our influential what's-on weeklies in London, New York and Chicago, we publish nearly 30 other listings magazines in cities as varied as Beijing and Mumbai. The magazines established Time Out's trademark style: sharp writing, informed reviewing and bang up-to-date inside knowledge of every scene.

Time Out made the natural leap into travel guides in the 1980s with the City Guide series, which now extends to over 50 destinations around the world. Written and researched by expert local writers and generously illustrated with original photography, the full-size guides cover a larger area than our Shortlist guides and include many more venue reviews, along with additional background features and a full set of maps.

Throughout this rapid growth, the company has remained proudly independent, still owned by Tony Elliott four decades after he started Time Out London as a single fold-out sheet of A5 paper. This independence extends to the editorial content of all our publications, this Shortlist included. No establishment has been featured because it has advertised, and no magazine has influenced any of our reviews. And, for our critics, there's definitely no such thing as a free lunch: all bars and restaurants are visited and reviewed anonymously, and Time Out always picks up the bill.

For more about the company, see www.timeout.com.

Don't Miss 2011

What's best: **Sights & Museums**   8

What's best: **Eating & Drinking**   14

What's best: **Shopping**   21

What's best: **Nightlife**   26

What's best: **Arts & Leisure**   31

What's on: **Calendar**   36

Whitechapel Gallery p11

Sights & Museums

One effect of London winning the 2012 Olympic Games and Paralympic Games back in 2005 has been that the year tends now to occupy the minds of planners as an ultimate deadline: the blockbuster expansion begun this year at **Tate Modern** (p65), the pod-by-pod refurbishment of the **London Eye** (p63) and the renovations at **Kensington Palace** (p94) are all due for completion by 2012.

There's also a huge amount of new stuff open already: the **Museum of London** (see box p160), **Discover Greenwich** (see box p187) and the **Jewish Museum** (p171) are all impressive, balancing with real flair the desire to entertain and the obligation to inform. We're also loving the new galleries at the **V&A** (p85) and awestruck by the shiny space-age white Cocoon at the **Natural History Museum** (p85).

Serious explorers of London will have a lot of fun at the city's biggest building sites. Large areas of **King's Cross** are barely recognisable these days, as the numerous redevelopments in this once drug-addled part of London near completion. You can also chart the progress of the **Olympic Stadium**, **Aquatics Centre** and **VeloPark** in the east of the city; our London 2012 itinerary (pp48-50) is a good route round the key sites.

The **South Bank** remains London's key tourist destination. The principal attractions are well established – Tate Modern, **Shakespeare's Globe** (p65) and **Borough Market** (p70), the **Sea Life London Aquarium** (p65) and the **London Eye**, the **Southbank**

Centre (p73) – but take the time to explore some minor highlights: the **Garden Museum** (p59), the **Topolski Century** mural (p66) and the rejuvenated **Florence Nightingale Museum** (p59), which reopened in time for the pioneering nurse's centenary.

Across the river, the **City** authorities have been making a concerted effort to alter the reputation of the most ancient part of London as a place for bankers rather than pleasure-seekers. It should be an easy sell, given the number of wonderful historic attractions here – the **Tower of London** (p162) and **St Paul's** (p162) are only the best known – and easy access from the South Bank over the Millennium Bridge. St Paul's and the **Monument** (p161) have been vividly refurbished in the last couple of years. Don't neglect the strangely disregarded **Museum of London**, which should gain its proper, central place in visitors' affections with four amazing new galleries and inviting street-level windows, through which you can see the Lord Mayor's golden coach. Close by, starchitect Jean Nouvel's new shopping centre, **One New Change** (see box p168) promises rooftop terraces from which to enjoy the view of cathedral.

London is blessed with no less than four UNESCO World Heritage Sites: the Tower of London, the cluster of historic buildings around Parliament Square in **Westminster** (pp76-79), soothing **Kew Gardens** (p186) and, above all, the numerous notable attractions in **Greenwich** (pp185-187). Having opened in spring 2010, Discover Greenwich has done a superb job of pulling these disparate sites together. Redevelopment of the Market Square through 2011, reopening

SHORTLIST

Best new
- Discover Greenwich (see box p187)
- 'Enchanted Palace' at Kensington Palace (see box p94)
- Medieval & Renaissance Galleries at the V&A (p85)

Most welcome returns
- Florence Nightingale Museum (p59)
- Jewish Museum (p171)
- Keats House (p171)
- Museum of London (see box p160)

Best views
- London Eye (p63)
- Monument (p161)
- Top deck of a Heritage Routemaster bus (p76)
- View Tube at the Olympic Park (see box p178)

Best free attractions
- British Museum (p119)
- Museum of London (see box p160)
- National Gallery (p76)
- Sir John Soane's Museum (p155)
- Victoria & Albert Museum (p85)
- Wellcome Collection (p124)

Best unsung attractions
- Old Operating Theatre (p65)
- Petrie Museum (p120)

Best late events
- British Museum (p119)
- Tate Britain (p78)
- Victoria & Albert Museum (p85)

Best outdoor
- Swimming in the Hampstead Heath ponds (p170)
- Thames Clipper back from the O2 Arena (p188)

THE BIG BUS SIGHTSEEING TOUR

A hop-on, hop-off bus tour including a free river cruise, walking tours and your choice of recorded commentary or entertaining guides

British Museum

of a repaired Cutty Sark in 2012 and a new wing for the **National Maritime Museum** (p186) by 2013 should keep the district in the headlines.

South Kensington and **Bloomsbury** are the other London essentials. In South Kensington, the V&A's Medieval & Renaissance Galleries have been a big hit, and renewed galleries of 14th- to 17th-century sculpture are due to open here by the end of 2010. A broader refurbishment followed the Cocoon at the Natural History Museum (even the famous whale was briefly inaccessible), and it will be interesting to see the response to the £4 million new Climate Change Gallery at the **Science Museum** (p85), due to open on the second floor in November 2010. In Bloomsbury, half a dozen new rooms have been completed at the world-class **British Museum** (p119).

Smaller scale museums have received a bit of a boost with the Shh… initiative, which promotes 'Small Historic Houses' such as **Handel House** (p107), **Dr Johnson's House** (p149) and the **Benjamin Franklin House**

(p140), while the **Wellcome Collection** (p124) has carved itself a special niche for arresting themed exhibitions: this year look forward to 'High Society', a cultural history of drug use and abuse, and 'Dirt'.

Fans of art are especially well catered for in London. As well as superstars Tate Modern, **Tate Britain** (p78) and the **National Gallery** (p76), visitors can now check out the reborn **Saatchi** (p95) and **Whitechapel** (p180). Watch out too for the grand new Savile Row **Hauser & Wirth** (www.hauserwirth.com) – it's due to open with a Louise Bourgeois show in autumn 2010. Not at all new and the better for it is the creaky old **Courtauld** (p149).

Doing the geography

This book is divided by area. The **South Bank** primarily covers riverside Bankside, home of Tate Modern, and the revamped Southbank Centre. Over the river, **Westminster & St James's** cover the centre of UK politics, while the impressive Victorian museums of **South Kensington,**

the Knightsbridge department stores, and the boutiques and eateries of **Chelsea** lie to the west.

The **West End** includes most of what is now central London. We start north of unlovely Oxford Street, in the elegant, slightly raffish shopping district of **Marylebone**. South, between Marylebone and St James's, is **Mayfair**, as expensive as its reputation but less daunting, with fine mews and pubs. Eastward are **Fitzrovia**, its elegant streets speckled with inviting shops and restaurants; the squares and Georgian terraces of literary **Bloomsbury**, home of academia and the British Museum; and up-and-coming **King's Cross**. Head south for **Covent Garden**, so popular with tourists that locals often forget about the charms of its boutique shopping, and **Soho**, notorious centre of filth and fun.

The **City** comprises the once-walled Square Mile of the original city, now adjoined the focal area for bars and clubs, Shoreditch; **Holborn & Clerkenwell** have wonderful food.

Around these central districts **neighbourhood London** has clusters of fine restaurants, bars and clubs, servicing what are mainly residential zones, but also some of London's must-sees: Greenwich, Kew and Hampton Court Palace.

Making the most of it

Don't be scared of London's public transport: invest in an **Oyster travel smartcard** (p213) and roam cashless through the city by bus, tube (underground trains) and on many of the train services. The excellent London Overground rail – considered part of the underground network when it comes to tickets – has opened a north-south link across the river on the east of town, from New Cross through Shoreditch.

The tube is the easiest mode of transport for newbies, but buses are best to get a handle on the city's topography. Some good sightseeing routes are RV1 (riverside), 7, 8 and 12, but hop on a **Routemaster Heritage Route** (p76) to enjoy a ride on a classic London bus. Crime in central London is low, so walking is a great way to appreciate its many character changes. No one thinks any the less of someone consulting a map – so long as they dive out of the stream of pedestrian traffic while doing so. And, despite our reputation to the contrary, most Londoners are happy to help with directions.

To avoid the worst of the crowds, avoid big attractions at **weekends** and on late-opening nights, and aim to hit exhibitions in the middle of their run. **Last entry** can be up to an hour before closing time (we specify wherever it is more than an hour before), so don't turn up at the last minute and expect to get in. Some sights close at Christmas and Easter – ring ahead to confirm opening hours.

Keats House p9

DON'T MISS: 2011

WHAT'S BEST

Eating & Drinking

The last couple of years have been especially hard for London's restaurateurs, with the crumbling economy ensuring there's been no shortage of restaurant-related casualties. Even so, London has been showing true British 'chin up and carry on' spirit, with lots of restaurant openings, many of them surprisingly high profile. We give **Marcus Wareing at the Berkeley** (p90) the nod slightly ahead of his former mentor, Gordon Ramsay, who reopened Pétrus in spring 2010, but other hotel restaurants we really enjoyed were the Zetter's magnificent **Bistrot Bruno Loubet** (see box p157) and buzzily atmospheric **Dean Street Townhouse & Dining Room** (p132). Ramsay looks set to have a busy year: Boxwood closed at the Berkeley

but is to reopen in dedicated premises elsewhere, and he'll be in charge of the **Savoy Grill** when the hugely renovated classic hotel throws open its doors in summer 2010 (see box p207).

Eats & attractions

Over the last decade, even the museums and galleries have begun to look beyond the shrink-wrapped sandwich to provide visitors with quality food. The **National Dining Rooms** (p79) has long led the field, but Maria Elia's Dining Room in the refurbished **Whitechapel Gallery** (p180) is a gem, and the new **Restaurant at St Paul's** (p165) has given Sir Christopher Wren's cathedral a dining room he would surely have been proud of.

Giaconda Dining Room

Hot zones & Brit cuisine

You can eat well all over London nowadays, but our favourite restaurants still seem to cluster around Soho and Clerkenwell. Towards Covent Garden, we're still loving Paul Merrony's **Giaconda Dining Room** (p142), amid the guitar shops of London's 'Tin Pan Alley', and **Great Queen Street** (p142), but the appearance of **Hix** (see box p131) and **Polpo** (p133) in the heart of Soho confirmed the area's attractions. In Clerkenwell, Anna Hansen – one of the original co-owners of Marylebone's **Providores & Tapa Room** (p103) – has quietly jolted the tired concept of 'fusion food' out of its torpor at **Modern Pantry** (p157), and Exmouth Market is rediscovering that foodie is fun with café-brasserie **Caravan** (p156) opening on the same street as long-term favourite **Moro** (p157). The Michelin judges aren't renowned for their appreciation of high-quality but informal dining,

SHORTLIST

Best new restaurants
- Bistrot Bruno Loubet (see box p157)
- Dean Street Townhouse & Dining Room (p132)
- Hix (see box p131)
- Polpo (p133)

Best new cheaps
- Battersea Pie (p141)
- Comptoir Libanais (p101)
- More (p69)

Best of British
- Albion (p180)
- Great Queen Street (p142)
- St John (p157)
- St Pancras Grand (p125)

Best global scoff
- Hakkasan (p116)
- Modern Pantry (p157)
- Moro (p157)
- Providores & Tapa Room (p103)

Best drop-in nosh
- Hummus Bros (p121)
- Lantana (p116)
- Princi (p135)

Best new drinks
- Bar Pepito (p124)
- Cadogan Arms (p95)
- Mark's Bar (see box p131)
- Terroirs (see box p144)

Best gastropubs
- Cadogan Arms (p95)
- Eagle (p156)

Best traditional pubs
- French House (p132)
- Lamb & Flag (p142)
- Ye Olde Mitre (p158)

Best for cocktails
- Calloon Callay (p165)
- Connaught Bar (p108)

but they sensibly decided British stalwart **St John** (p157), just down the road, should retain its star. This restaurant was the game-changer in modern British cooking in the 1990s and continues to serve brilliantly simple, classic combinations of gutsy, carefully sourced ingredients. A third outpost, this time with bedrooms too, should just have opened in the West End (see box p202).

Indeed, flying the flag for Brit bites has never been more fashionable. **St Pancras Grand** (p125), with chef Billy Reid at the reins, highlights the glory of modern and traditional British cooking. Likewise, Sir Terence Conran's dedication to pure Brit flavour was epitomised in his Boundary Project – **Albion** (p180), the casual caff set on the ground floor, serves unpretentious, nostalgic dishes from kedgeree to welsh rarebit.

Drinking it all in

London's top-end cocktail venues are drawing the capital's drinking scene ever closer to the quality of New York or Sydney, but there are stellar bars for all pockets and occasions: **Mark's Bar** (see box p131) in Soho and **Book Club** (p164) in Shoreditch give a taste of what's on offer, but specialists – 'natural' wines at **Terroirs** (see box p144) near Covent Garden, proper Spanish sherry at **Bar Pepito** (p124) in King's Cross – are also making an impact.

Gastropubs have contributed hugely to the revolution in modern British dining, becoming an enduring feature of the London culinary repertoire, with star openings including the Martin brothers' **Cadogan Arms** (p95) on the King's Road and the **Bull & Last** (p172) in Highgate. Don't neglect the old favourites: **Anchor**

Princi p18

& **Hope** (p66) and, daddy of them all, the **Eagle** (p156) still turn out top nosh in relaxed surroundings.

Ethnic eats

Against the backdrop of all this Britishness, it's pleasing that ethnic eateries continue to flourish. The world's food is well represented by the quality of restaurants, with a more sophisticated take on Chinese cuisine notable: there's a Sichuanese revolution going on, with **Empress of Sichuan** (p132) only the newest recruit. Indian food is still a strong presence, ranging from the haute cuisine of **Cinnamon Club** (p79) to cheap-and-cheerful places like **Chaat** (p180) or **Masala Zone** (p173), but you'll also find home-style Thai from **Rosa's** (p182) on Brick Lane, Korean in Soho at **Bi Bim Bap** (p130), Middle Eastern just off Oxford Street at **Comptoir Libanais** (p101), tapas at **Cambio de Tercio** (p88) in South Kensington, burritos at **Benito's Hat** (p113) in Fitzrovia… next door to the brilliant Spanish-Italian of **Salt Yard** (p117). Everyone says it – but we really believe it's true: the whole world's food can be found without leaving London.

This may be a volatile time for restaurants, but along with the newbies there are plenty of old hands keeping their standards high and their doors open: Richard Corrigan is doing great things at **Corrigan's Mayfair** (p108); **Sheekey's** (p144), **Hakkasan** (p116) and the **Wolseley** (p82) remain favourite treats; and, despite the sad death of far-sighted proprietor Rose Gray in early 2010, the **River Café** (p191) continues to delight with simple and excellent Italian food. Eating well in contemporary London really isn't hard to do.

Neighbourhood watch

The **South Bank**, close to foodie-magnet Borough Market (p70), offers plenty of quality chain options on the riverside – check out Skylon (p70) for a drink with fantastic views – but **Soho**, in the West End just across the river, is probably the best place in London for both cheap and chic bites: canteen-style Busaba Eathai (p130), Hummus Bros (p121) and Princi (p135) do a brisk trade near upmarket neighbours such as Bocca di Lupo (p130), Arbutus (p127) and Dehesa (p132). Also in the West End, **Covent Garden** remains a busy tourist trap, but some very decent options have emerged, from ice-cream at Scoop (p144) to Mexican at Wahaca (p144) or Indian at Masala Zone. Expense-account eats are concentrated in **Mayfair**: top-name chefs here include Claude Bosi at Hibiscus (p108). Further west, **Marylebone** is another foodie enclave, replete with top-notch delis, cafés and – on Sundays – a farmers' market. Superb options here include the formidable L'Autre Pied (p101) and La Fromagerie (p101). Both **South Kensington** and **Chelsea** do expensive, special-occasion destinations, such as Zuma (p90), but the arrival of the likes of Cambio de Tercio and the Cadogan Arms has brought in more affordable fare. The **City** still isn't great for evening eats, though some places now open at weekends. **Clerkenwell** next door is famously a culinary hotspot: from the Modern Pantry to the Clerkenwell Kitchen (p156), via the Eagle, St John and Moro, most London restaurant trends are or have been represented here. **Shoreditch**, just north-east of the City, is still the place for a top night out – and the bars are being joined by interesting restaurants.

St Pancras Grand p17

123 Boutique p23

WHAT'S BEST
Shopping

Londoners are unstoppable shoppers. Yes, they were battered by the recession, but the economic downturn has also underlined their tenacity: unable to resist a bargain, they're still trawling the city's street markets and superluxe department stores and sniffing out the snips in flagship fashion outlets, world-class boutiques and tradition-soaked arcades, on a shopping tour of duty that will surely never end.

In the past couple of years, London's shopkeepers have fallen back on their creative instincts, thinking up increasingly wily ways to tempt in the customers. High-concept pop-up shops, packed with limited edition products, appear and disappear across the capital each month; high-street outlets stock young design talent at budget prices; and department stores are refreshed and renewed. In the City, new shopping behemoth **One New Change** (see box p168) hopes to beguile card-wielders with a roof-top terrace looking out at St Paul's Cathedral, while Europe's biggest mall, **Westfield London** (p192), has been running a great series of events and has a cool multiplex.

Fashionable young things

London's design strength has long been its young upstarts: recent graduates firmly entrenched in the youth scene they design for. Most young Londoners mix vintage with high street, shopping in chain stores full of high-profile design collaborations at rock-bottom prices. Japanese chain **Uniqlo** (p112) has *Dazed & Confused* magazine's creative director Nicola Formacetti on its books,

ART FOR LESS

£49.95
WINSOR & NEWTON
THAMES RADIAL
EASEL
RRP £162

PREMIER PORTFOLIO
BLACK FITTINGS
A1 RRP £76.10 CASS £49.95
A2 RRP £54.65 CASS £32.50
A3 RRP £38.80 CASS £22.50
A4 RRP £28.55 CASS £19.95

£6.95
SEAWHITE A5 CONCERTINA
SKETCHBOOK 70 PAGES
140GSM

£8.95
WINSOR & NEWTON
WINTON OIL 200ML
TITANIUM WHITE
DOUBLE PACK
RRP £22

£10.50
WINSOR & NEWTON HENRY & WILLIAM
COLLECTION INK SET OF 8X14ML
RRP £22

£39.95
DALER ROWNEY
COTSWOLD EASEL
RRP £130.10

£24
LIQUITEX
ACRYLIC
BASICS SET
48 x 22ML
RRP £49.95

£6.95
FABER CASTELL 9000
8B-2H 12 DRAWING
PENCILS
RRP £13.75

£4.35
DALER-ROWNEY
SYSTEM 3 ACRYLIC
250ML POT
ALL COLOURS
RRP £8.75

£4.95
LETRASET
PROMARKER
SET OF 5
RRP £10.45

£3.95
DALER-ROWNEY
OIL PASTEL
SET OF 24 RRP £10.45

£39.95
DALER-ROWNEY
SCREEN
PRINTING KIT
RRP £79.95

system 3
ACRYLIC SCREEN PRINTING SET

STEP BY STEP GUIDE
TO SCREEN PRINTING
on the back of the pack

CASS PROMISE – CREATIVITY AT THE LOWEST PRICES. WE'RE CONFIDENT OUR PRICES CAN'T BE BEATEN

PHTHALO
TURQUOISE
TRANSPARENT
MAGENTA
SCARLET
LAKE
VIRIDIAN

SPEND OVER £30
& GET A FREE BAG

FLAGSHIP STORE: 66-67 COLEBROOKE ROW
ISLINGTON N1 020 7354 2999

ALSO AT: 24 BERWICK ST W1, 220 KENSINGTON HIGH ST W8,
13 CHARING CROSS RD WC2 (NEXT TO THE NATIONAL GALLERY),
AND 58-62 HEATH STREET NW3, HAMPSTEAD STORE OPENING
IN SEPTEMBER 2010. ALL STORES OPEN 7 DAYS WWW.CASSART.CO.UK

CASS ART LONDON

PRICE SUBJECT TO CHANGE AND AVAILABILITY. PRICES VALID AT 01/06/10.

for example, and **Topshop** is a real centre for young talent (see box p102). At the top of Brick Lane, vintage outfitters include Beyond Retro on **Cheshire Street** (p183) and the nearby Thrift Store (p182), while **Camden Market** (p173) rewards careful rummaging.

To find something a little more unusual, get the low-down on sample sales, pop-up shops and one-off shopping events in *Time Out* magazine's weekly Shopping & Style section, or turn off the high street to indulge Londoners' obsession with the boutique. Try A Butcher of Distinction in the **Old Truman Brewery** (p183), b store on **Savile Row** (p112) or Covent Garden's **Koh Samui** (p145). Noteworthy newcomers include perfumier **Le Labo** (p105) and lingerie boudoir **Apartment C** (p103) in Marylebone, and quirkily hip **Jeanette's** (p183) and **123** (p184) in Shoreditch.

When money is no object, Mayfair's hallowed **Dover Street Market** (p110) is London's most revered concept store. It's also worth checking out the well-established department stores: **Selfridges** (p105) and **Liberty** (p136), the latter having been revamped at the hands of fashion consultant Yasmin Sewell, are our favourites. Luxury labels continue to open on **Mount Street** (p112), the historic pink-brick Mayfair road that is fast replacing Sloane Street as the 'in' place to shop: we would have loved to have been a fly on the wall at the gunsmith, antique galleries and traditional butcher when they first clapped eyes on goth-rock designer Rick Owens, the five-floor Lanvin flagship or even the new, budget-friendly **Marc by Marc Jacobs** (p110). Existing luxe residents already included Christian Louboutin and Balenciaga.

DON'T MISS: 2011

SHORTLIST

Best new
- Anthropologie (see box p137)
- Apartment C (p103)
- Bape (p135)
- Caravan (p183)
- Jeanette's (p183)
- 123 Boutique (p184)

Best department stores
- Liberty (p136)
- Selfridges (p105)

Best boutiques
- A Butcher of Distinction in the Old Truman Brewery (p183)
- Jeanette's (p183)
- Koh Samui (p145)

Best shopping streets
- Broadway Market (p182)
- Exmouth Market (p158)
- Lamb's Conduit Street (p122)
- Mount Street (p112)

Best books & music
- Foyles (p136)
- London Review Bookshop (p122)
- Pure Groove (p158)
- Rough Trade East in the Old Truman Brewery (p183)

Best retro clothing
- Brick Lane Thrift Store (p182)
- Rellik (p191)

Cutting-edge concepts
- Dover Street Market (p110)

Best markets
- Borough Market (p70)
- Portobello (p191)

Best sensory experience
- Columbia Road Market (p183)
- Le Labo (p105)

Best of British
- James Smith & Sons (p145)

Get cultural

In a city bursting with history, the steady closure of London's independent bookshops is sad, even incongruous. Still, you can browse the travel literature in the the wonderfully grimy Edwardian conservatory of Daunt Books on **Marylebone High Street** (p105), or the never-ending selection of new titles at **Foyles** (p136), where you can try before you buy in the great café. Persephone Books on **Lamb's Conduit Street** (p122) and the **London Review Bookshop** (p122) are new London classics, while **Cecil Court** (p145) is an irrepressible old stager – long may the landlord's benevolence continue. **Magma** (p158) and the bookstore at the **Photographers' Gallery** (p127) have contemporary art titles.

Don't neglect the museum stores, either: the **London Transport Museum** (p140) and **Southbank Centre** (p73) led the way with strikingly designed gifts, but we're thrilled the renewed **Museum of London** (see box p160) is joining in.

Record and CD shops have also taken a beating, but second-hand vinyl and CDs linger on **Berwick Street** (p135). Indie temple Rough Trade East has settled nicely into the **Old Truman Brewery** (p183), but **HMV** (p117) is the last of Oxford Street's big beasts.

Markets valued

Neighbourhood markets remain the lifeblood of London shopping, but few are still the domain of salt-of-the-earth Cockney costermongers. Instead, you'll find fashion kids showing off their new vintage sunglasses over a soy latte and a bag of heirloom tomatoes. **Borough Market** (p70) is superb for foodies, but canalside **Broadway Market** (p182) is well worth the trek into

Old Spitalfields Market

Hackney. Lush flower market **Columbia Road** (p183) is a lovely Sunday morning outing; try to get there before 11am, then follow Brick Lane down to **Old Spitalfields Market** (p183) and the nearby Sunday (Up)Market, which is great for fashion, crafts and vintage clobber. You'll be an expert in East End street-style by early afternoon.

London's most famous markets are also both going strong: despite ongoing major redevelopment, **Camden**'s markets (p173) remain a major tourist attraction, and – if you can stomach the crowds – **Portobello Road Market** (p191) is terrific for antiques, bric-a-brac and star-spotting. **Alfie's** (p173), also in the vicinity, is more laid-back and full of odd characters.

Neighbourhood watch

With more than 40,000 shops and 80 markets, shopping in London can be exhausting, so limit the territory you cover in each outing, sticking to one or two earmarked areas at a time. **Regent Street** is home to the flagships of many mid-range high-street clothing ranges. For a taste of retail past, **St James's Street** is full of anachronistic specialists, including London's oldest hatter and the royal shoemaker. **Savile Row** has been given a shake-up in recent years by a handful of tailoring upstarts, concept fashion emporium b store and even an Abercrombie & Fitch. **Mayfair** – especially Conduit Street, Bond Streets Old and New, and now Mount Street – remains the domain of major catwalk names such as British big guns Mulberry, Burberry and Vivienne Westwood.

To the north, it's best to hurry across heaving **Oxford Street** with its department stores, budget fashion outlets and language schools and duck instead into pedestrianised Gees Court and St Christopher's Place – pretty, interconnecting alleyways lined with cafés and shops that lead to the bottom of Marylebone. Curving **Marylebone High Street** has excellent fashion, perfumeries, gourmet food shops and chic design stores.

A couple of London's most celebrated streets have recently been lifted out of chain-dominated doldrums. **Carnaby Street** has been salvaged by an influx of quality youth-clothing brands and the Kingly Court centre; the decline of the **King's Road** has halted, with some hip stores taking their cue from the Shop at Bluebird.

Nor should **Covent Garden** be written off as a tourist trap. New flagships have opened up in the piazza, while, to the north-west, cobbled Floral Street and the offshoots from Seven Dials remain fertile boutique-browsing ground. Don't miss sweet little Neal's Yard,

with its wholefood cafés and herbalist. A little further north, **Lamb's Conduit Street** crams in appealing indie shops.

Unless you're looking to work the platinum AmEx among the global designer salons of Sloane Street or marvel at the art nouveau food halls of Harrods, there's little reason to swing by **Knightsbridge**. But do drop in on pretty Ortigia, on a corner of Sloane Square, and the cute shops of Elizabeth Street.

For luxe designer labels without the crush, **Notting Hill** (especially where Westbourne Grove meets Ledbury Road) overflows with feminine boutiques. On the other side of town, **Brick Lane** (mostly around the Old Truman Brewery and on offshoots Cheshire Street and Redchurch Street) has a dynamic collection of offbeat clothing and homeware shops. The boutiques of **Islington** are also worth having a nose around, along Upper Street and, especially, down Camden Passage.

A Butcher of Distinction p23

Dalston Superstore

WHAT'S BEST
Nightlife

When legendary London venues Turnmills and the End closed a few years back, many foretold the death of the city's vital clubbing scene. Not so: the owners simply headed off to different venues where they've continued to do amazing things. People from the End shimmied over to the railway arches of **Cable** (p72), for example, and to venues like **Fire** (p188) in 'Vauxhall Village' – formerly old-school gay turf, now day-and-night partying for everyone. Nor is London yet deprived of superclubs: **Fabric** (p159), still doing a roaring trade in leftfield electronic wiggery, and its young sibling **Matter** (p188), plus the **Ministry of Sound** (p72), keep the big-name DJs in town.

Pioneering **T Bar** (p169) has settled into its not-quite-Shoreditch location near Liverpool Street, but Shoreditch is hardly dying a death without it: the **Last Days of Decadence** (p169) and the **Book Club** (p164) are just two of the many bar-clubs keeping the district alive. Indeed, hybrid 'superpubs' are spreading across the capital. **Star of Bethnal Green** was arguably the first of a new breed of dancefloor-orientated boozers, but **Paradise by Way of Kensal Green** and the **Old Queen's Head** (for all three, see box p171) are now providing solid competition.

If recession has forced promoters out of business, it has also forced them to get more creative. Any space is up for grabs now: witness the excitement about Dalston. Edgier than increasingly gentrified Shoreditch, the upper end of Kingsland Road teems with hip young things searching for the next party. Licensing and/or opening hours for these surreal bars beneath Turkish cafés and video shops are erratic, but established Kingsland Road faves include Visions Video (no.588) and Bar 512 (no.512). **Dalston Superstore** (p184) is considerably less fly-by-night: it's been a massive hit ever since opening.

Take it off!

Burlesque continues to cover the mainstream in kitsch and feathers, with many a regular club night adding a stripper, some twisted magic or a bit of surreal cabaret. The best nights are at the sweet supper club **Volupté** (p159), **RVT** (p189) and the **Bethnal Green Working Men's Club** (p184), with **Bathhouse** (p167) a lively addition to the scene. People are flocking to the West End to the ace basement performance space at the **Leicester Square Theatre** (p138), so we're rather interested to see what waves will be made by the cabaret space that has been planned for new **Hippodrome** casino (see box p140).

Small stage, big music

Clubs weren't the only aspect of London nightlife to see significant downsizing over the last few years, with mid-size gig venues seeming to close every month. Don't be fooled. There's plenty of life on the London music scene. Camden and Shoreditch are thriving with guitar-heavy music bars like **Proud** (p174) and the **Old Blue Last** (p169), and Dalston is again shining bright with a surprisingly broad range of small venues. There's the brilliantly shambolic **Bardens Boudoir** (p184), the cutting-edge **Vortex Jazz Club**

SHORTLIST

Best new venues
- Bathhouse (p167)
- T Bar (p169)

Best indie mash-ups
- Proud (p174)
- Punk (p138)

Best for bands
- Bardens Boudoir (p184)
- Luminaire (p184)
- O2 Empire Shepherd's Bush (p192)

Best for jazz
- Ronnie Scott's (p138)
- Vortex Jazz Club (p185)

Best leftfield dance action
- Cable (p72)
- Fabric (p159)

Rockin' pub-clubs
- Paradise by Way of Kensal Green (see box p171)
- Star of Bethnal Green (see box p171)

For the outer limits
- Café Oto (p184)

Best gay clubbing
- Dalston Superstore (p184)
- Fire/Lightbox (p188)

Best for retro dress-up
- Bathhouse (p167)
- Bethnal Green Working Men's Club (p184)

Best cabaret & drag
- Basement at Leicester Square Theatre (p138)
- Volupté (p159)

Best comedy
- Comedy Store (p136)
- Lowdown at the Albany (p117)
- Soho Theatre (p139)

THE BLUES KITCHEN

LONDON'S BEST BLUES BAR
111-1113 CAMDEN HIGH ST, NW1 7JN

(p185) and the ridiculously all-encompassing **Café Oto** (p184). Oto is one of the few rivals, in our opinion, to the still wonderful **Luminaire** (p174) out in north-west London.

Nor is it all gloom in the larger venues. The **O2** entertainment complex (p188) has pretty much cornered the market for classic rock-pop gigs (from Led Zeppelin to Ultravox), as well as booking pop stars like Britney and, so very nearly, Michael Jackson), and **KOKO** (p174) and the **Scala** (p125) continue to do good work with mid-range bands.

The key point is that London's music scene is defined by rampant diversity. On any night, you'll find death metal, folk whimsy and plangent griots on one or other of the city's many stages.

Gay disco

Despite the influx of straight ravers to some club nights, 'Vauxhall Village' remains the main hub of all things gay and out that want to party hard. **RVT** (p189) is the key venue, a friendly, historic gay boozer that hosts comedy nights, arty performance parties and bear-fondling discos. **Fire** (p188) and its rave-tastic Lightbox room remains the key party place, opening very, very late. The closure of numerous West End venues has also encouraged plenty of polysexual action to up sticks to Shoreditch and Dalston, creating a third gay scene to add to Vauxhall and, of course, Soho. **Dalston Superstore** (p184) is the stand-out venue for the new breed of young, gay Shoreditch hipster.

Just for laughs

Stand-up comedy has gone stadium-sized: Peter Kay and Russell Howard will both be playing sold-out runs at the **O2** enormodome (p188) in 2011. It's not all supernova shows, though: check out the **Comedy Store** (p136), still the one that all the comedians want to play, and the **Soho Theatre** (p139), great for interesting new performers. Line-ups at **Lowdown at the Albany** (p117) remain strong.

While London's nightlife is lively all year, anyone who's come here to see some comedy in late July or August is likely to be disappointed. Most of the city's performers head north to the Edinburgh Festival and consequently many venues are dark. Come in June or October instead: comedians are either trying out fresh shows or touring their Edinburgh triumph.

Matter p26

Making the most of it

Whatever you're doing, check the transport before you go: festivals, repairs and engineering tinkerage throw spanners in the works all year, notably on public holidays, but also many weekends. Regularly updated information can be found at www.tfl.gov.uk. Public transport isn't as daunting as you might think. The tube is self-evident, even to newcomers, but it doesn't run much after midnight (New Year's Eve is the exception). Black cabs are pricey and hard to find at night, but safe. There are also licensed minicabs; on no account take an illegal minicab, even though they're touted outside every club. Far better to research the slow but comprehensive **night bus** system (p214) before leaving your hotel (see www.tfl.gov.uk's Journey Planner). A few minutes working out which bus gets you safe to bed can save hours of blurry-visioned confusion later.

You'll also kick yourself if you came all this way to see an event, only to arrive the one weekend it isn't on – or to find dates have changed. We've done our best to ensure the information in this guide is correct, but things change with little warning: www.timeout.com has the latest details or, if you're already here, buy *Time Out* magazine for weekly listings. Record shops are invaluable for flyers and advice – try the friendly folk at Rough Trade East in the Old Truman Brewery (p183) and Pure Groove (p158) for starters.

If the dates won't quite work out, don't despair. There's something going on here, no matter the day, no matter the hour. So if a useless mate forgets to get tickets, it isn't the end of the world. Even long-in-the-tooth Londoners fall across brand new happenings just by taking the wrong street, and the best way to get a taste of 'real London' – instead of the city every postcard-collecting tourist sees – is to go with the flow. Someone tells you about a party? Check it out. Read about a new band? Get a ticket. Sure, you've some 'essentials' in mind, but if you miss them this time… hell, come back next year.

Paradise by Way of Kensal Green p26

Royal Ballet p33

Arts & Leisure

London isn't just the political hub of Britain – it's the cultural and sporting capital too. Classical music of all types is studied and performed here, ambitious and inventive actors, directors and dancers learn their chops, and films are premièred and shot, but London also has two of the nation's top three football teams, national stadiums for football and rugby, and international centres of tennis and cricket. In the run-up to the 2012 Games there has been a distinct change in priorities, with public funding that had previously been earmarked for the arts redirected to improving sports venues and training, but cannier arts operators have seen the opportunities and funding potential of the Cultural Olympiad, and those with creative ambitions continue to flood into the city.

Classical music & opera

The completion of office block-cum-auditorium **Kings Place** (p125) has been the biggest news in classical music over the last few years. It provides headquarters for the very different Orchestra of the Age of Enlightenment (www.oae.co.uk) and London Sinfonietta (www. londonsinfonietta.org.uk), as well as sculpture galleries and two concert halls with fine acoustics.

Not that London was short of headline venues before Kings Place arrived. At the **Barbican** (p169), the London Symphony Orchestra (http://lso.co.uk) plays 90 concerts a year, while the Royal Festival Hall at the **Southbank Centre** (p73) regularly hosts Esa-Pekka Salonen's Philharmonia Orchestra (www.philharmonia.co.uk) and the

London Philharmonic Orchestra (www.lpo.org.uk), which focuses on Mahler symphonies for the 2010/11 season. In spring 2011, watch out for the London Sinfonietta under the baton of Tom Adès and Chinese piano virtuoso Lang Lang.

There are also two fine opera houses: Covent Garden's **Royal Opera House** (p148) combines assured crowd-pleasers – Mozart, Rossini and Puccini are all included this year – with rarities: the world première of *Anna Nicole* (17 Feb-4 Mar 2011), Mark-Anthony Turnage's opera about Playmate and celebrity widow Anna Nicole Smith. At the **Coliseum** (p148), the English National Opera performs classics (always in English) such as Gounod's *Faust* (18 Sept-16 Oct 2010), a co-production with New York's Metropolitan Opera, and Puccini's *La bohème* (18 Oct 2010-27 Jan 2011), directed by Jonathan Miller. *A Dog's Heart* (20 Nov-4 Dec 2010), an opera – which Simon McBurney, artistic director for the brilliant Complicité theatre group, has based on a Bulgakov satire in which a stray dog becomes a man – should be another highlight.

Much of the city's classical music action happens in superb venues on an intimate scale. The exemplary **Wigmore Hall** (p107), **Cadogan Hall** (p97) and **LSO St Luke's** (p169) are all terrific, atmospheric venues, and a number of London's churches host fine concerts: try **St Martin-in-the-Fields** (p76) and **St John's, Smith Square** (p81).

Dance

The **Royal Ballet** and **English National Ballet** offer the fully elaborated blocks-and-tutus experience. ENB celebrates their 60th anniversary with *The Nutcracker* (10-30 Dec 2010) and *Romeo & Juliet* (5-15 Jan 2011) at

SHORTLIST

Best classical venues
- Cadogan Hall (p97)
- Kings Place (p125)
- Royal Opera House (p148)

Best for dance
- Place (p125)
- Sadler's Wells (p177)

Best for theatre
- BAC (Battersea Arts Centre) (p189)
- Donmar Warehouse (p148)
- National Theatre (p72)
- Royal Court Theatre (p97)

Best cinemas
- BFI Southbank (p72)
- Curzon Soho (p138)

Best festivals
- Breakin' Convention (p43)
- London Film Festival (p37)
- The Proms (p45)

Best bargains
- Prince Charles Cinema (p139)
- Standing tickets at Shakespeare's Globe (p65)
- Standing tickets at the Coliseum (p148)
- £10 Monday at the Royal Court Theatre (p97)

Most innovative work
- London Sinfonietta at Kings Place (p125)
- Royal Court Theatre (p97)
- Simon McBurney at the Coliseum (p148)

Best of the West End
- *Billy Elliot* at the Victoria Palace Theatre (p81)
- *Enron* at the Noël Coward Theatre (p148)
- *Legally Blonde* at the Savoy Theatre (p148)

DON'T MISS: 2011

Legally Blonde at the Savoy

the **Coliseum** (p148), while the Royal Ballet dances a programme largely made up of classics at the **Royal Opera House** (p148), but throws in some more adventurous fare: *Giselle* (11 Jan-19 Feb 2011) and *Swan Lake* (22 Jan-8 Apr 2011) meet Christopher Wheeldon's *Alice's Adventures in Wonderland* (28 Feb-15 Mar 2011).

London offers an unmatched range of performers and dance styles, way beyond the usual choice of classical or contemporary, and – apart from the quieter summer months – there's something worth seeing every night. **Sadler's Wells** (p177) offers a packed programme of top-quality work from native talent and global names. It also hosts must-see festivals: the hip hop of **Breakin' Convention** (p43) is a highlight. Autumn sees **Dance Umbrella** (p36) unfold with cutting-edge work from around the world performed across the city. Keep an eye also

on the **Barbican** (p169) and **Southbank Centre** (see box p68), both of which programme interesting dance-theatre hybrids.

Film

In the death-struggle with increasingly sophisticated home entertainment systems (even mid-brow hotels now often have in-room DVD players), many cinemas are trying to make film-going an event, with luxury seats and auditorium alcohol licences – even the **Westfield London** (p192) Vue multiplex has followed this gentrifying trend. Less pleasing is the growing tendency for mainstream titles to creep on to the playbills of even arthouse cinemas such as the **Curzon Soho** (p138) and Everyman's revamped **Screen on the Green** (p177). This, plus the **Barbican** (p169) temporarily closing two of its three screens and the **ICA** (p83) slimming down its programme in response to the recession, has meant smaller films find it hard to breathe in the capital (see box p83). Cinemas committed to programming foreign and alternative films amount to few more than the redoubtable **BFI Southbank** (p72), which this year launched a terrific London-focused strand called 'Capital Tales'.

Don't fret. As the multiplexes stuff their screens with bloated blockbusters (many presented in the seemingly obligatory 3D or IMAX alternative formats), smaller, less formal venues have begun to pick up the slack – **Cinéphilia West** (p192) is just one example – and major attractions such as **Tate Modern** (p65) and even **St Paul's Cathedral** (p162) include occasional film screenings on their rosters. Keep an eye on *Time Out* magazine or www.timeout.com for all these various venues, and for details of the city's diverse film festivals too.

Theatre & musicals

Despite the recession, London's theatreland is looking healthy and wealthy: economic hard times seem to have sent people to the theatre in search of distraction, rather than chasing them away. Nonetheless, West End producers remain a cautious breed: for the 2010/2011 season you can expect the usual crop of celebrity-led revivals and musicals piggy-backing on nostalgia for popular movies – *Sister Act* (the **Palladium**, p139), *Priscella, Queen of the Desert* (the **Palace Theatre**, p139) and a sassy take on *Legally Blonde* (the **Savoy**, p148) are due to be joined by *Flashdance: the Musical* (the **Shaftesbury**, p148) roughly as this guide hits the shelves.

Acres of press and some brutal reviews greeted *Love Never Dies*

(the **Adelphi**, see box p147), Sir Andrew Lloyd Webber's sequel to his deathlessly popular *Phantom of the Opera* (still playing at Her Majesty's), but we were more impressed by the arrival from Broadway of a revived *Hair* (the **Gielgud**, p138).

The blockbuster musical's dominance of the London stage is certainly under no immediate threat – the 25th anniversary of *Les Misérables* will see two versions playing simultaneously in central London, with the long-runner at the Queen's Theatre joined for a couple of weeks by a **Barbican** (p169) revival – but straight plays have been making a West End comeback. The success of *Jerusalem*, a transfer from the still vital **Royal Court Theatre** (p97), and the timely *Enron* (the **Noël Coward**, p148) showed there is an appetite for drama without a score. Although theatrical subsidies are decreasing, the Royal Court and **National Theatre** (p72) still manage to produce reliably high-quality theatre.

At the younger, cultier end of the scale, watch out for the masters of immersive theatre, **Punchdrunk** (www.punchdrunk.org.uk), whose masked revels send the audience through many-roomed venues in search of the spectacular action – this summer's collaboration with the English National Opera was their most ambitious work to date.

What's on

We've included long-running musicals we think are likely to survive into 2011. However, a new crop will inevitably open through the year, along with seasons at individual venues. *Time Out* magazine and www.timeout.com have the most informed and up-to-date listings.

WHAT'S ON
Calendar

Diwali

The following is our selection of annual events, plus the best one-offs confirmed when this guide went to press. To stay current with what's happening, buy the weekly *Time Out* magazine and check www.timeout.com/london; always confirm dates before making any travel plans. The dates of public holidays are given in **bold**.

September 2010

8 Sept-16 Jan 2011
Eadweard Muybridge
Tate Britain, p78
www.tate.org.uk/britain
Pioneering photographer's work.

11-12 Mayor's Thames Festival
Westminster & Tower Bridges
www.thamesfestival.org
Ends with riverside lantern parade.

14 Sept-2 Oct **Les Misérables**
Barbican, p169
www.barbican.org.uk
Hit musical's 25th anniversary revival.

18 **Tour of Britain**
Central London
www.tourofbritain.co.uk
Last stage of the eight-day cycle race.

18-19 **Open City London**
Various locations
www.openhouselondon.org
Free access to over 600 buildings.

late Sept **Skyride**
Various locations
www.goskyride.com
50,000 cyclists on a traffic-free route.

30 Sept-16 Jan 2011 **Gauguin**
Tate Modern, p65
www.tate.org.uk/modern

25 **Great River Race**
Thames, Richmond to Greenwich
www.greatriverrace.co.uk

26 **Pearly Kings & Queens Harvest Festival**
St Martin-in-the-Fields, p76
www.pearlysociety.co.uk
Cockney Thanksgiving service at 3pm.

26 **Great Gorilla Run**
Mincing Lane, the City
www.greatgorillas.org/london
Fund-raising run through the City,
over 7km, in gorilla suits.

October 2010

Ongoing Les Misérables (see Sept);
Gauguin (see Sept)

5-30 **Dance Umbrella**
Various locations
www.danceumbrella.co.uk
The city's headline dance festival.

13-28 Oct **London Film Festival**
BFI Southbank, p72
www.bfi.org.uk/lff

14-17 **Frieze Art Fair**
Regent's Park, p98
www.friezeartfair.com

late Oct-late Apr 2011 **Veolia
Environmental Wildlife
Photographer of the Year**
Natural History Museum, p85
www.nhm.ac.uk/wildphoto

November 2010

Ongoing Gauguin (see Sept);
Dance Umbrella (see Oct); Veolia
Environmental Wildlife Photographer
of the Year (see Oct)

early Nov **Diwali**
Trafalgar Square, p78
www.london.gov.uk
Celebrated by Hindus, Jains and Sikhs.

4 Nov-6 Mar 2011 **Journey
through the Afterlife: Ancient
Egyptian Book of the Dead**
British Museum, p119
www.britishmuseum.org

5 **Bonfire Night**
Firework displays all over town.

7 **London to Brighton Veteran
Car Run**
Serpentine Road in Hyde Park, p89
www.lbvcr.com

12-21 **London Jazz Festival**
Various locations
www.londonjazzfestival.org.uk

13 **Lord Mayor's Show**
Various locations in the City
www.lordmayorsshow.org
A grand inauguration procession for
the Lord Mayor of the City of London.

14 **Remembrance Sunday
Ceremony**
Cenotaph, Whitehall

mid Nov **State Opening of
Parliament**
Houses of Parliament, p76
www.parliament.uk

20 Nov-4 Dec **A Dog's Heart**
Coliseum, p148
www.eno.org
Opera debut of Simon McBurney, director of ace theatre group Complicité.

Nov-Dec **Christmas Tree & Lights**
Covent Garden & Trafalgar Square
www.london.gov.uk
See box p39.

December 2010

Ongoing Gauguin (see Sept); Veolia
Environmental Wildlife Photographer
of the Year (see Oct); Journey
through the Afterlife (see Nov); A
Dog's Heart (see Nov); Christmas
Tree & Lights (see Nov)

mid Dec **Spitalfields Festival**
Various locations
www.spitalfieldsfestival.org.uk

27 **Christmas Day Bank Holiday**

28 **Boxing Day Bank Holiday**

31 **New Year's Eve Celebrations**
Trafalgar Square & the South Bank
See box p39.

January 2011

Ongoing Gauguin (see Sept); Veolia
Environmental Wildlife Photographer

Festive fun

How to get the best out of Christmas and New Year.

Winter Wonderland

London never used to be much fun at the turn of the year. With no public transport on Christmas Day, the centre of the capital feels eerily deserted – a magical transformation for a city usually teeming with people, but not one that's easy to enjoy unless you've got a designated driver who's happy to forgo the egg nog. And New Year's Eve seemed to involve cramming as many idiots as possible into **Trafalgar Square** (p78), without so much as a drink to keep them warm.

Things have changed. Us Brits might have a reputation for not thinking much of Johnny Foreigner, but we know a good thing when we see it: the explosion of middle European Christmas markets across London is a case in point. Each has its own style – from the traditional market in **Covent Garden** (p140) to the fairground of **Winter Wonderland** (www.hyde parkwinterwonderland.com) – but mulled wine, spiced German cakes and, increasingly, ice rinks are common. For pretty Christmas

lights, skip the commercialised ones on Oxford and Regent Streets and head instead for St Christopher's Place, Marylebone High Street and Covent Garden, while the best window displays are the enchantingly old-fashioned ones at **Fortnum & Mason** (p82) and the annual show-stoppers at **Harvey Nichols** (p92).

More interested in partying than present-buying? The week after Christmas is when the locals go nuts, and the best advice is to do as they do: forget paying inflated prices for a disappointing **New Year's Eve** bash and go out instead on **New Year's Day**. Parties kick off from 5am and attract a cooler crowd, happy in the knowledge they're paying a third of the price for exactly the same DJs as were playing at midnight – check *Time Out* magazine for details. If you do want to join the mob for the trad New Year's Eve bash, head to the South Bank, where a full-on fireworks display is launched from the London Eye and Thames rafts.

Chinese New Year Festival

of the Year (see Oct); Journey
through the Afterlife (see Nov)

3 New Year's Day Holiday

13-31 **London International
Mime Festival**
Various locations
www.mimefest.co.uk

19-23 **London Art Fair**
Business Design Centre, Islington
www.londonartfair.co.uk

February 2011

Ongoing Veolia Environnement
Wildlife Photographer of the Year
(see Oct); Journey through the
Afterlife (see Nov)

early Feb
Chinese New Year Festival
Chinatown & Trafalgar Square
www.londonchinatown.org

mid Feb **Imagine**
Southbank Centre, p73
www.southbankcentre.co.uk
Children's literature festival.

17 Feb-4 Mar **Anna Nicole**
Royal Opera House, p148
www.roh.org.uk
Turnage's opera about the legendary
Playboy pin-up Anna Nicole Smith.

March 2011

Ongoing Veolia Environnement
Wildlife Photographer of the Year
(see Oct); Journey through the
Afterlife (see Nov); Anna Nicole
(see Feb)

8 **Poulters Pancake Day Race**
Guildhall Yard, p161
www.poulters.org.uk
City livery companies race – tossing
pancakes as they go – in full regalia.

early Mar-late Apr
Kew Spring Festival
Royal Botanic Gardens, Kew (p170)
www.kew.org.
World Heritage Site at its very best.

early-late Mar **Word Festival**
Various East End locations
www.londonwordfestival.com
Hip month of literature events taking
over various East End venues.

last 2wks Mar **London Lesbian
& Gay Film Festival**
BFI Southbank, p72
www.llgff.org.uk

26 **Oxford & Cambridge
Boat Race**
On the Thames, Putney to Mortlake
www.theboatrace.org
The 157th outing for Varsity rowers.

Greenwich & Docklands International Festival p45

April 2011

Ongoing Veolia Envirnnement Wildlife Photographer of the Year (see Oct); Kew Spring Festival (see Mar); Lesbian & Gay Film Festival (see Mar)

2 Apr-17 July **The Cult of Beauty: The Aesthetic Movement in Britain, 1860-1900**
Victoria & Albert Museum, p85
www.vam.ac.uk

early Apr-mid May **Spring Loaded**
Place, p125
www.theplace.org.uk
Seven-week dance festival.

17 **London Marathon**
Greenwich Park to the Mall
www.virginlondonmarathon.com

3 days late Apr **London Book Fair**
Earls Court Exhibition Centre
www.londonbookfair.co.uk

22 Good Friday

25 Easter Monday

late Apr **Camden Crawl**
Various locations in Camden
www.thecamdencrawl.com
New musical talent, usually favouring busy indie guitars. See also box p44.

May 2011

Ongoing The Cult of Beauty (see Apr); Spring Loaded (see Apr)

2 Early May Bank Holiday

early May **Breakin' Convention**
Sadler's Wells, p177
www.breakinconvention.com
Jonzi D's terrific three-day festival of contemporary street dance.

late May **Chelsea Flower Show**
Royal Hospital Chelsea, p95
www.rhs.org.uk

30 Spring Bank Holiday

June 2011

Ongoing The Cult of Beauty (see Apr)

early June **Beating Retreat**
Horse Guards Parade, Whitehall
www.army.mod.uk
A pageant of military music and precision marching, beginning at 7pm.

early June **Hampton Court Palace Festival**
www.hamptoncourtfestival.com
Two weeks of adult-oriented rock, world and folk concerts.

early June **Epsom Derby**
Epsom Racecourse
www.epsomderby.co.uk

early June **Royal Ascot**
Ascot Racecourse
www.ascot.co.uk

early June-mid Aug
Opera Holland Park
www.operahollandpark.com

early June **Spitalfields Festival**
Various locations
www.spitalfieldsfestival.org.uk
Classical music, walks and talks.

mid June
Open Garden Squares Weekend
Various locations
www.opensquares.org
Private gardens opened to the public.

mid June **Meltdown**
Southbank Centre, p73
www.southbank.co.uk
A fortnight of music and culture, curated each year by different musicians.

mid June **LIFT (London International Festival of Theatre)**
Various locations
www.liftfest.org.uk

mid June **Wireless Festival**
Hyde Park, p89
www.wirelessfestival.co.uk
Three nights of rock and dance acts in the lovely Royal Park.

Big-hitting microfestivals

The urban festivals that are all the rage in London.

Camden Crawl

The trend can be traced back to the still lively **Camden Crawl** (www.thecamdencrawl.com), which launched back in the early '90s. But it's only been in the last few years that pub crawl-style multi-venue music festivals have become an established feature of the city's musical life, offering Londoners a little slice of festival culture without requiring them to get out of town.

The idea is simple. Festivalgoers are issued with a wristband, which allows access to a number of venues in the same part of town, and are left to chart their own route. Some venues are big, as are some of the acts. Others are tiny pub backrooms, hosting shows by young up-and-comers. A few surprise shows add a little additional spice.

Organised fans plan their evenings with military precision. However, most people end up missing many of the acts they originally wanted to see, usually due to some combination of drunken confusion and full-to-capacity venues, only to stumble across all manner of great new groups by accident. The line-ups capture London's hyperactive listening habits perfectly, veering from maniacal electro-pop to maudlin Americana.

The microfestival trend really took flight in May 2008 with the **Stag & Dagger** festival (www.staganddagger.com), the first of east London's several versions of the Crawl. The concentration of muso pubs and bars around Shoreditch – the likes of the Old Blue Last (p169) and Cargo (83 Rivington Street, 7739 3440, www.cargo-london.com) – perfectly suits the microfestival template, which explains the emergence of the artier but not entirely dissimilar **Concrete & Glass** (www.concreteandglass.co.uk), usually held in the autumn.

Like most of the best of Shoreditch's nightlife, the microfestival has begun a slow migration north into Dalston, where **Land of Kings** (www.landofkings.co.uk) takes over a dozen or so venues in late April. Check *Time Out* magazine or the various event websites for up-to-date programme details.

mid June **Trooping the Colour**
Horse Guards Parade, St James's
www.trooping-the-colour.co.uk
The Queen's official birthday parade.

20 June-3 July **Wimbledon Lawn Tennis Championships**
www.wimbledon.org

late June-early July
City of London Festival
Various locations around the City
www.colf.org
A festival of mostly free music and art, often in historic City venues.

late June-early July **Greenwich & Docklands International Festival**
Various locations
www.festival.org
Four days of outdoor theatricals, usually on an impressively large scale.

late June-late Aug
English Heritage Picnic Concerts
Hampstead Heath, p170
www.picnicconcerts.com
Evening concerts of grown-up pop/rock and light classical at Kenwood House.

July 2011

Ongoing The Cult of Beauty (see Apr); Opera Holland Park (see June); Wimbledon (see June); City of London Festival (see June); Greenwich & Docklands International Festival (see June); English Heritage Picnic Concerts (see June)

early July **Pride London**
Oxford Street to Victoria Embankment
www.pridelondon.org
A huge annual gay and lesbian parade.

early July-late Sept
Watch This Space
National Theatre, p72
www.nationaltheatre.org.uk
Alfresco theatre beside the Thames.

mid July **Lovebox Weekender**
Victoria Park, Hackney
www.lovebox.net
Top-quality weekend music festival.

mid July **Chap Olympiad**
Bedford Square Gardens, Bloomsbury
www.thechap.net
The likes of the Umbrella Jousting are fiercely contested – in Victorian attire.

mid July
Somerset House Summer Series
Somerset House, p155
www.somerset-house.org.uk/music
A dozen concerts in the fountain court.

mid July-mid Sept
The Proms (BBC Sir Henry Wood Promenade Concerts)
Royal Albert Hall, p89
www.bbc.co.uk/proms
London's finest classical music festival.

August 2011

Ongoing Opera Holland Park (see June); English Heritage Picnic Concerts (see June); Watch This Space (see July); the Proms (see July)

early Aug **Underage Festival**
Victoria Park, Hackney
www.underagefestivals.com
A hip and immensely popular music festival for 14- to 18-year-olds.

early Aug
Great British Beer Festival
Earl's Court Exhibition Centre
www.camra.org.uk
A great chance to sample British beer.

early-late Aug
Portobello Film Festival
Various locations in west London
www.portobellofilmfestival.com

27-28 **Notting Hill Carnival**
Various locations in Notting Hill
www.nottinghillcarnival.biz
Europe's biggest street party.

29 Summer Bank Holiday

September 2011

Ongoing Watch This Space (see July); the Proms (see July)

mid Sept **Mayor's Thames Festival**
See above Sept 2010.

mid Sept **Tour of Britain**
See above Sept 2010.

mid Sept **Open City London**
See above Sept 2010.

late Sept **Great River Race**
See above Sept 2010.

late Sept **Skyride**
See above Sept 2010.

late Sept **Great Gorilla Run**
See above Sept 2010.

late Sept-early Nov **Dance Umbrella**
See above Oct 2010.

October 2011

Ongoing Dance Umbrella
(see Sept)

early Oct **Pearly Kings &
Queens Harvest Festival**
See above Sept 2010.

mid Oct-early Nov
London Film Festival

Frieze Art Fair

See above Oct 2010.

mid Oct **Frieze Art Fair**
See above Oct 2010.

from late Oct **Veolia
Environnement Wildlife
Photographer of the Year**
See above Oct 2010.

November 2011

Ongoing Dance Umbrella (see Sept);
London Film Festival (see Oct);
Wildlife Photographer of the Year
(see Oct)

early Nov **Diwali**
See above Nov 2010.

5 **Bonfire Night**

13 **Remembrance Sunday**
See above Nov 2010.

early Nov **London to Brighton
Veteran Car Run**
See above Nov 2010.

early Nov **Lord Mayor's Show**
See above Nov 2010.

mid Nov **London Jazz Festival**
See above Nov 2010.

mid Nov **Opening of Parliament**
See above Nov 2010.

Nov-Dec **Christmas Tree & Lights**
See above Nov 2010.

December 2011

Ongoing Wildlife Photographer of
the Year (see Oct); Christmas Tree
& Lights (see Nov)

mid Dec **Spitalfields Festival**
See above Dec 2010.

26 **Christmas Day Bank Holiday**

27 **Boxing Day Bank Holiday**

31 **New Year's Eve Celebrations**

Itineraries

Looking at London 2012 48

The Wren Route 51

The City by Night 54

Olympic Stadium

Looking at London 2012

The best way to get a sneak preview of the London 2012 Olympic Park is along the banks of the many canals, cuts and rivers that surround it. Given the scale of the site, a bicycle is the best mode of transport round what was until recently neglected industrial wasteland a few miles east of the centre of town. Try to do this itinerary on a weekday, when the cafés, pubs and towpaths are all quieter. The route will work fine beyond the summer 2011 structural completion of the Olympic Park – in fact, more and more cycle paths will be opening as work progresses.

First, a bus. The no.8 takes about half an hour to east London, with well-connected boarding points at Oxford Circus and Liverpool Street station. Hop on (with a pre-bought ticket or charged Oyster card, p213) and get off at St Stephen's Road (stop SM). Walk in the direction

the bus was heading, across Old Ford Road, into the Gun Wharf industrial estate. **Bikeworks** (8980 7998, www.bikeworks.org.uk) is on your left. It opens at 8.30am Monday to Friday, and 10am on Saturday. You can do the described route in a relaxed couple of hours, but hiring the bike for a full day (£18, including helmet, lock and lights, with a £150 credit card deposit) gives you the chance to take plenty of breaks and follow any diversions that appeal.

Bike ready? Helmet on? Good. Turn left out of Gun Wharf on to Old Ford Road and take the immediate left on to Gunmaker's Lane. Turn left off the bridge on to the towpath, then under that bridge heading east.

This is the **Hertford Union Canal**, which connects Regent's Canal to the River Lea. The towpath is an easy ride, apart

VeloPark

from some very steep locks and a few short bone-rattling sections. It does get tight, though, especially at bridges. Remember your towpath etiquette: two tings on the bell to alert pedestrians and bikes coming under a bridge in the opposite direction, and always give way to walkers and joggers.

You'll pass pretty narrowboats all along the route, but there's usually a cluster under a pedestrian bridge with a big red hoop. If you skipped breakfast, cross for Roach Road's Counter Café (07952 696 388); otherwise, keep on a few hundred yards to where the towpath makes a sharp left turn at the Lea Navigation. Here you get a first eyeful of the **Olympic Stadium**'s white girders and spotlight stanchions, elegantly poised over the two waterways.

The towpath heads steeply up over a bridge. Cross the Lea and descend the equally steep far side. Serious students of the developing 2012 Games might want to venture north up the Lea to see what's happening with the Handball Arena, the IBC/MPC (International Broadcast Centre/Main Press

Centre) and dramatic VeloPark, but we're going to head straight south.

All along this section there are fine views of the stadium, growing irresistibly larger on your left as you pedal. To your right, you'll spot the new premises of venerable fish smokery **H Forman & Son**, splendid in its appropriately salmon-pink hue. Keep going through **Old Ford Lock**, one of the prettiest on the Lea, and straight after a cluster of skewed bridges by a clump of new flats, you'll see a signpost tree. Follow the 'Capital Ring' and 'Link to the Greenway 80 yards' pointers up a gentle slope and you're on a ridge alongside the main Olympic Park venues. The only way to get closer to the stadium than this before July 2012 is to book a public tour (0300 2012 001, 9am-5pm weekdays).

The main stadium will demand your attention, but off to the right is the swooping glass roof of Zaha Hadid's **Aquatics Centre**, with a lime-green corrugated iron temporary building facing it. This is the **View Tube** (see box p178), with the fine Container Café serving a short menu of hot snacks, plus cakes and drinks. There are bike stands just beyond the café. The upstairs balcony has superb views and information boards that help you figure out what it is you can see – look out for the **VeloPark** low in the distance.

Return the way you've come, past the row of local art projects, then double back behind the View Tube on a lower path that snakes between construction fences to come out at Pudding Mill Lane DLR station. Go left, away from the stadium, and left again on the next bit of towpath. This takes you to Blaker Road, with more fine stadium views over water.

Head away from the stadium once more, then wheel the bike left along the broad pavement of the busy four-lane High Street (the A118). Take the pedestrian crossing, turn right and remount when you're on the towpath of **Three Mills Wall River**. This is a continuation of the Waterworks River, which runs along the far side of the Olympic Park, where the Olympic Village will be. Some five miles of waterways are being used to transport materials around the site during construction.

Heading south, you'll soon come to the narrowboats of Three Mills Island, with Canary Wharf Tower on the horizon. Head across the grass to your left to admire the pale concrete and jet black hydraulic jacks of **Three Mills Lock**. In the distance is the rust-red, lime-green and grey roof of Bazalgette's impressive Abbey Mills Pumping Station, built back in the 1860s.

Back by the narrowboats, head over the cobbles between the mills that give this little river island its name: the pair of witches' hat structures on the Clock Mill make it the most impressive from the outside. After the cobbles, hop back on the bike and veer left along the

easy path between Bow Creek and the last section of the Lea Navigation. The cluster of Canary Wharf skyscrapers is now large in front of you as you ride past the weeping willow and under a mix of iron railway bridges and concrete, before crossing a stupidly steep white bridge over **Bow Locks**.

Limehouse Cut zooms straight south-west from here towards the marina of Limehouse Basin. Stop and look back over your left shoulder just before it begins its final curve: that spiky white tower is the spire of Hawksmoor's palatial church of St Anne's Limehouse, consecrated in 1730. Turn left into the little park as soon as you can, veering right to pedal gently past the bandstand on to Narrow Street. Another right brings you to the atmospheric **Grapes** pub (76 Narrow Street, E14 8BP, 7987 4396). There are bike stands opposite. Food is served from noon to about 2pm, but the place closes mid-afternoon on weekdays.

Fortified, it's back to the park and across the Cut on the big black pedestrian bridge you previously cycled beneath. Follow the edge of the basin round to the lock gates under the brick bridge, and head north up the **Regent's Canal**. Not long after the Palm Tree pub, the towpath heads steeply up and, from the top, you'll see the start of another canal. It's the Hertford Union again, which will take you back to where you began.

Your bike will need to be checked back in before 6.30pm Monday to Thursday (5.30pm Friday and 5pm Saturday). Once the trusty steed is safely back, hop on the no.8 into town or warm down by walking 15 minutes south on Grove Road to Mile End tube.

To check on the latest progress on all the London 2012 venues, see www.london2012.com.

Here Lived
Sir Christopher Wren
during the building of St Pauls Cathedral

Here also, in 1502, Catherine,
Infanta of Castille & Aragon,
afterwards first Queen
of Henry VIII took shelter
on her first landing in
London

49 Bankside p53

The Wren Route

St Paul's Cathedral is a City landmark with real staying power: in 2010 it was 300 years since Sir Christopher Wren's masterpiece was opened as the centrepiece of the post-Great Fire rebuilding of London. Like some 17th-century Rogers or Foster, Wren and his associates peppered the skyline with spires and towers. Even though many disappeared through demolition or as a result of brutal carpet-bombing during the Blitz, many can still be visited.

Do the route on a weekday – at weekends most churches only open for services – and try to start by about 9am, since this route involves a lot of walking. Opening times and days for the individual churches vary wildly, so don't expect to see inside all of them on any one day.

Jump off the tube at dingy Farringdon station, turn right out of the exit, then immediately left down Farringdon Road until you reach Ludgate Circus. Stand on the west side and admire the view up Ludgate Hill to St Paul's to get an impression of what the cathedral must have looked like when it was first built, rising above the huddle of rooftops and the spires of the lesser Wren churches; the black spire situated to the left of the dome belongs to one of these churches, **St Martin Ludgate**.

Hidden behind you off Fleet Street is **St Bride's** (p155). Its steeple is the tallest of any Wren church and was supposedly the model for the tiered wedding cake. Take the first left off Fleet Street for a closer look. The church was burnt out during the Blitz, so the interior is a reconstruction, albeit a lovely one. Visit the crypt museum to find out about the construction of the church (several generations of wall are exposed, along with various artefacts) and the life and death of Fleet Street – a facsimile of the 30 December 1940 *Evening News* gives a graphic description of the devastation wreaked by one particular wartime raid.

Retrace your steps to Ludgate Circus and climb Ludgate Hill, braving the crowds on the cathedral steps to enter **St Paul's** (p162). You can easily spend a couple of hours here, enough for a climb up to the famous Whispering Gallery to look down within the cathedral, then on up and outside for the giddying views of the City from the Gold Gallery (more than 500 steps from the ground), and finally back down into the crypt beneath. Check out the skull and crossbones on the lintel. In the crypt, Nelson's grand monument is right beneath the central dome, while Wren's tomb is tucked modestly away at the east end in the south aisle.

Leaving the cathedral, turn right and pass through **Temple Bar**, another Wren creation. This gateway once stood at the western end of Fleet Street to mark the boundary between the City of London and Westminster, but it impeded the traffic and was removed by the Victorians. It returned in 2004 to become the entrance to the new Paternoster Square, home to the London Stock Exchange.

Grab a coffee and cross the square to emerge on Newgate Street. Opposite is **Christ Church**, which was almost destroyed during World War II. The ruined nave is now a rose

garden; take a seat and sip your coffee. The surviving tower is a spectacular private home, its ten storeys linked by a lift.

Head east along Angel Street, across Aldersgate Street, to Gresham Street. First you'll see **St Anne & St Agnes**, with a leafy churchyard and regular classical recitals. Further along Gresham Street, catch a glimpse of the tower of **St Alban Wood Street**, like Christ Church now a private house. Continue past **St Lawrence Jewry** – the church of the Corporation of London – to Moorgate, crossing into Lothbury to enter **St Margaret Lothbury** (7606 8330, www. stml.org.uk). This has one of the loveliest interiors of any Wren church, with an impressive wood screen by the great man himself.

Retrace your steps to Moorgate and turn left down Prince's Street to enter Bank tube. Take the Mansion House exit, following the path around to **St Stephen Walbrook** (39 Walbrook, 7606 3998, www.ststephenwalbrook.net), the most grandiose Wren church, a mass of creamy stone with a soaring dome, fabulously bulbous pulpit and incongruous modern altar by Henry Moore.

Turn left out of the church and left again into Cannon Street. Just past Cannon Street station, take another left on to St Swithin's Lane and head downstairs into the brick-vaulted cellar bistro of the Don (the Courtyard, 20 St Swithin's Lane, 7626 2606, www.thedonrestaurant.com), where serious lunches are served to bibulous bankers until 3pm on weekdays.

Turn left back on to Cannon Street, then duck left into Abchurch Lane. **St Mary Abchurch** (7626 0306) is a real gem, with a shallow, painted dome and a beautiful reredos by Grinling Gibbons. It was shattered into 2,000 pieces by a wartime bomb and painstakingly pieced back together.

Back on Cannon Street, head east to reach the top end of London Bridge. Cross the street using the underpass, turning left off King William Street into Monument Street. The **Monument** (p161) is the world's tallest isolated stone column, built to commemorate the Great Fire. It was designed by Wren and his associate Robert Hooke. Brave the 311 steps up to be rewarded with spectacular views over the City and the Thames.

Get back on to Cannon Street and head west to Bow Lane, topped and tailed by churches from Wren's office: at the southern end, **St Mary Aldermary** (7248 4906, www.stmaryaldermary.co.uk) is obscure but beautiful, with flamboyant Gothic vaulting; at the northern end, **St Mary-le-Bow** is famous for its bells, but it's a post-war reconstruction inside.

Retrace your steps down Bow Lane, this time turning right into Queen Victoria Street to reach Peter's Hill and the Millennium Bridge. Cross the river, turning east off the bridge for Shakespeare's Globe (p65). Overshadowed by the theatre, **49 Bankside** is identified by a plaque to be the house from which Wren watched St Paul's rise across the river. This seems unlikely, given the house and cathedral were completed in the same year, but the views are superb. Buy an ice-cream to munch from one of the vans while waiting for the riverbus at Bankside Pier.

Take the Thames Clipper (p214) east to Masthouse Pier, from which it's a ten-minute walk along the river path to Island Gardens. Stock up on fluids from the kiosk, soak up the views of the **Old Royal Naval College** (p185), then cross under the river using the Greenwich Foot Tunnel. Emerging from the tunnel, pass the *Cutty Sark* (still under refurbishment) and turn left into College Approach. The College is one of the most extensive groups of baroque public buildings in England and survives much as Wren planned it. The first building on your left is the wonderful new **Discover Greenwich** (see box p187), which has superb displays, some giving engaging explanations of Wren's work on the hospital. Don't miss the Painted Hall (most of the rich decoration inside is trompe l'oeil), which was built to Wren's designs between 1696 and 1704, and you won't be able to miss the stunning colonnades leading south.

Continue through the college to the eastern gate, turn right into Park Row and enter Greenwich Park. Crowning the hilltop is the Royal Observatory (National Maritime Museum, p186), where crowds wait to stand astride the Prime Meridian Line. Carry on to enter **Flamsteed's House**, the only bit of the complex by Wren. Built for the first Astronomer Royal, it's a dainty contrast to the Royal Naval College, the living quarters cosily domestic. Only the Octagon room hints at Wren's flair.

It's been a long day, so treat yourself to a drink and some food. As you head back to the Cutty Sark, it might be time to explore the other appealing aspect of Discover Greenwich: an attached café, restaurant and bar called the **Old Brewery** (p188). The local Meantime Brewing Company have been developing historically authentic beers to accompany the excellent food here, so that pint of London Porter might be what Wren was drinking as he worked on yet another beautiful building.

ITINERARIES

Oxford Street

The City by Night

Funny things go on in London after dark. Civil servants duck out of Westminster and sneak into secret S&M clubs, and city gents swap their suits for Kanye West sunglasses and dance till sun-up in a hail of drum 'n' bass. The night is when London lets its hair down, and that makes it the best time to catch Londoners without their famous 'reserve'. The following itinerary takes in the best of the bright lights: on foot, by boat and on the tube. Arm yourself with a charged Oyster smartcard (p213) and you're ready to set off.

There's a lot to fit in, so get an early start with a sunset ride on the Thames Clipper (p214) from **Tower Millennium Pier** (close to Tower Hill tube) to the Queen Elizabeth II Pier. You'll get a prime view of three iconic towers – the Tower of London (p162), Tower Bridge (p162) and One Canada

Square, the less-catchy name for Canary Wharf tower – just as the lights come on. Disembark at the former Millennium Dome. Once London's biggest white elephant, it has been reinvented as the surprisingly successful O2 entertainment complex (p189). Depending on your tastes and timing, you might be able to take in an NBA match or the Ultravox comeback tour before you move on.

From the O2, take the steps down to North Greenwich tube and ride the Jubilee Line one stop west to Canary Wharf. Climb through the bowels of the rocketship tower at **One Canada Square** (p179) and change to a Docklands Light Railway (DLR) train (p213) bound for Bank. Surreally empty after dark, the DLR whispers around the knees of some of the tallest buildings in Britain. The bright windows of these banking houses

The City and the South Bank

blast unimaginable amounts of candlepower into the night sky.

Leave Bank station by Exit 4 and sit on the steps of the **Royal Exchange**, one-time home of the London stock exchange and reminiscent of the Parthenon. From this vantage point, you have a view over one of the most valuable intersections in the world. To the right is the fortress wall of the Bank of England (p159) and to the left is Mansion House, the grand pied-à-terre of the Lord Mayor of London. Cross Cornhill to Lombard Street, then bear right on King William Street to reach the river.

As you amble over **London Bridge**, pause to admire one of London's best evening vistas. To the east, the bows of the HMS *Belfast* (p59) strike a military pose in front of the spotlit turrets of Tower Bridge, with the circuit-board towers of Canary Wharf protruding behind. While you're here, it would be a pity not to have a pint in one of London's oldest coaching inns, the George (77

Borough High Street, 7407 2056), a creaky vessel from 1676 with a courtyard that opens up from the east side of Borough High Street.

It's now time to begin one of London's great night-time walks. Returning to London Bridge, pick up the riverside **Thames Path** by Southwark Cathedral. The oldest bits of the cathedral date back more than 800 years, and its retro-choir was the setting for several Protestant martyr trials under Mary Tudor.

Walk west along Montague Street, Clink Street and Bankside to Shakespeare's Globe (p65), which manages to capture some of the turnip-throwing thrill of Elizabethan theatre despite being the brainchild of US movie-actor Sam Wanamaker. A few doors down, Tate Modern (p65) keeps its doors open until 10pm on Friday and Saturday. Stretching north from this powerhouse of modern art, the Millennium Bridge leads the eye inexorably to the dome of St Paul's (p162).

Continue west along the riverfront past the plazas and arcades around the Oxo Tower to emerge amid the brutalist concrete of the **Southbank Centre** (p73). As this is London's premier artistic enclave, you'll almost certainly find something to entertain you: there are plenty of buskers and free events in the Royal Festival Hall, the film programme at the BFI Southbank (p72) is excellent, and there are summer performances in front of the National Theatre (p72). Alternatively, enjoy watching the fairly grown-up skateboarders performing ollies and kickflips in the concrete catacombs under the Queen Elizabeth Hall.

If you'd rather enjoy the views, skip these worthy institutions and take a turn on the space-age Ferris wheel known as the **London Eye** (p63). The wheel only spins until 8pm (9pm in summer), so you'll have to hurry to get here in time, but the top of the arc offers an eagle-eye view over London, from the red beacon atop Canary Wharf in the east to the white chimney stacks of Battersea Power Station to the west to the Houses of Parliament (p76) just opposite.

Take a last breath of Thames air, then duck across Jubilee Gardens and York Road to Waterloo tube. Go three stops northbound on the Northern line to Leicester Square. Emerging from the Underground (p212), scoot quickly east through the awfulness (easier said than done during a movie première) and turn north along Wardour Street to Shaftesbury Avenue, the gateway to London's theatreland. *Les Mis* has been showing in London for 25 years this autumn and doesn't look like it's about to stop, so there's no rush to take in a performance at the Queen's Theatre – instead, walk a block north to **Old Compton Street**

to soak up the carnival atmosphere of London's longest-established gay and lesbian quarter. The pavement cabaret rages through the night on Friday and Saturday – ask for a street seat at Balans (60 Old Compton Street, 7437 5212, www.balans.co.uk) for a prime view of all the beautiful and outrageous people, off to do their beautiful and outrageous things.

Alternatively, hail a rickshaw and demand to be taken to one of Soho's finest eateries. Locals are sceptical of London's rickshaws (and black-cab drivers can't stand them), but rolling through the West End at street-level certainly offers a different vantage point over London. It's only five minutes' pedal to Anthony Demetre's **Arbutus** (p127), a hugely popular restaurant blessed with a counter that can often accommodate diners without bookings.

After night falls, to paraphrase Was Not Was, out come the freaks. And where do they go? Yep, Camden. Digest your dinner on the short walk to Tottenham Court Road tube, then ride the rails north to Camden Town. Although the bovver-boot rebellion of punk has been replaced by a Goth version of Cosplay, this hasn't diminished the spectacle. There are even a few decent bars to relax in. From the station, walk north along Chalk Farm Road beneath the railway arches to enjoy a late drink and arty rock photos at **Proud** (p174). You're perfectly placed to tap into London's exciting live music scene. Tomorrow's headliners at Glastonbury might be found gathering momentum at venues like **Barfly** (p174), conveniently close on Chalk Farm Road. When you finally emerge, engage in a time-hallowed London tradition – trying to hail a black cab to take you back to bed.

London by Area

The South Bank   58

Westminster & St James's   74

South Kensington & Chelsea   84

The West End   98

The City 149

Neighbourhood London 170

Tower Bridge from City Hall

The South Bank

LONDON BY AREA

Tourists have been coming to the South Bank for centuries, but the entertainments here have changed a little. **Shakespeare's Globe** has risen again, but if you're after the prostitutes, gamblers and bear-baiting that traditionally occupied visitors, you'll need a time machine. Instead, enjoy the revitalised **Southbank Centre**, **BFI Southbank** cinema complex and **Hayward** gallery, a cluster of national cultural institutions on which logic has finally been imposed. Or join the multitude strolling along the broad riverside walkway that takes you from Tower Bridge to Westminster Bridge and beyond. This strings together fine views and must-see attractions like **Tate Modern**, the **London Eye** and the Millennium and Hungerford Bridges. **Borough Market** typifies the South Bank's appeal: visitors find it charming, but locals love it too.

Sights & museums

City Hall

Queen's Walk, SE1 2AA (www.london. gov.uk). London Bridge tube/rail. **Open** 8.30am-6pm Mon-Thur; 8.30am-5.30pm Fri. **Admission** free. **Map** p61 F2 ❶
Designed by Foster & Partners, this 45m-tall, eco-friendly rotund glass structure leans squiffily away from the river. Home to London's metropolitan government, it has a huge aerial photo of the city you can walk on in the lower ground floor Visitor Centre and a café.

Design Museum

Shad Thames, SE1 2YD (7403 6933/ www.designmuseum.org). Tower Hill tube or London Bridge tube/rail. **Open** 10am-5.45pm daily. **Admission** £8.50; free-£6.50 reductions. **Map** p61 F2 ❷
The temporary exhibitions in this white 1930s building (previously a banana warehouse) focus on modern and contemporary industrial and fashion design, architecture, graphics

and multimedia developments. The smart Blueprint Café has a fine balcony overlooking the river.

Event highlights John Pawson (22 Sept 2010-27 Feb 2011); '100 Years of Fashion Illustration' (17 Nov 2010-27 Mar 2011).

Fashion & Textile Museum

83 Bermondsey Street, SE1 3XF (7407 8664, www.ftmlondon.org). London Bridge tube/rail. **Open** 11am-6pm Wed-Sun. **Admission** £6.50; free-£3.50 reductions. **Map** p61 F4 ❸

Flamboyant as its founder, fashion designer Zandra Rhodes, this pink and orange museum holds 3,000 of Rhodes' garments, some on permanent display, along with her archive of paper designs, sketchbooks, silk screens and show videos. There are also a shop, a little café and changing exhibitions.

Florence Nightingale Museum

NEW *St Thomas's Hospital, 2 Lambeth Palace Road, SE1 7EW (7620 0374, www.florence-nightingale.co.uk). Westminster tube or Waterloo tube/rail.* **Open** 10am-5pm daily. **Admission** £5.80; free-£4.80 reductions. £16 family. **Map** p60 A3 ❹

The nursing skill and zeal that made Nightingale a Victorian legend are honoured here. Due to reopen for the centenary of her death, the museum is a chronological tour through her family life, the Crimean War and health reforms. Among the period mementoes are her slate and her pet owl, Athena.

Garden Museum

Lambeth Palace Road, SE1 7LB (7401 8865, www.gardenmuseum.org.uk). Lambeth North tube or Waterloo tube/rail. **Open** 10.30am-5pm daily. **Admission** £6; free-£5 reductions. **Map** p60 A4 ❺

The world's first horticulture museum fits neatly into the old church of St Mary's. A new 'belvedere' gallery, constructed of eco-friendly wood sheeting, contains the permanent collection of art, antique tools and horticultural memorabilia. The ground floor has been freed for temporary exhibitions. In the small back garden, a replica 17th-century knot garden was created in honour of John Tradescant, intrepid plant-hunter and gardener to Charles I. Tradescant is buried here.

Event highlights 'Going Dutch: Dutch garden designers' (Oct 2010-Mar 2011).

Golden Hinde

St Mary Overie Dock, Cathedral Street, SE1 9DE (7403 0123, www.golden hinde.org). London Bridge tube/rail. **Open** 10am-5pm daily. **Admission** £6; £4.50 reductions; £18 family. **Map** p61 E2 ❻

This replica of Drake's 16th-century flagship is so meticulous it was able to reprise the privateer's circumnavigatory voyage. On weekends, it swarms with junior pirates, while 'Living History Experiences' allow participants to dress in period clothes, eat Tudor fare and learn the skills of the Elizabethan seafarer; book well in advance.

Hayward

Belvedere Road, SE1 8XX (0871 663 2519, www.hayward.org.uk). Waterloo tube/rail or Embankment tube. **Open** 10am-6pm Mon-Thur, Sat, Sun; 10am-10pm Fri. **Admission** varies. **Map** p60 A2 ❼

This versatile art gallery continues its excellent programme of contemporary exhibitions, often with a strong interactive element. Casual visitors can hang out in the industrial-look café-bar downstairs, or visit free contemporary exhibitions in the inspired Project Space – take the stairs up from the glass foyer extension.

HMS Belfast

Morgan's Lane, Tooley Street, SE1 2JH (7940 6300, http://hmsbelfast.iwm.org. uk). London Bridge tube/rail. **Open** *Mar-Oct* 10am-6pm daily. *Nov-Feb* 10am-5pm daily. **Admission** £10.70; free-£8.60 reductions. **Map** p61 F2 ❽

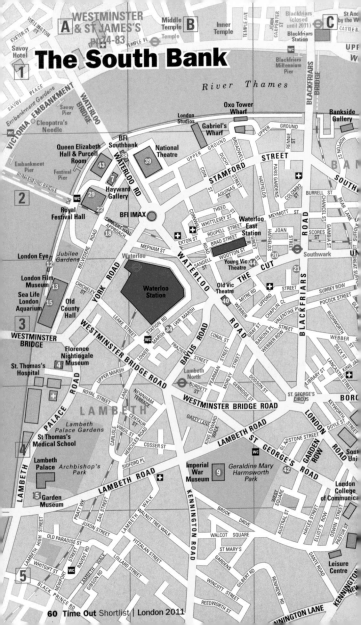

The South Bank

WESTMINSTER & ST JAMES'S **A** pp24-83
Middle Temple **B**
Inner Temple
Blackfriars (closed until 2011) **C**
St An by the W

River Thames

Savoy Hotel

1

VICTORIA EMBANKMENT

Savoy Pier

Embankment Gardens

Cleopatra's Needle

Blackfriars Millennium Pier

WATERLOO BRIDGE

BLACKFRIARS BRIDGE

Embankment

2

HUNGERFORD BRIDGE

Festival Pier

Queen Elizabeth Hall & Purcell Room

BFI Southbank **38**

National Theatre

London Studios

Oxo Tower Wharf

Gabriel's Wharf

Bankside Gallery

BA

SOUTH

43
1
Hayward Gallery

39

UPPER GROUND

STAMFORD STREET

UPPER GROUND

RENNIE ST

BURRELL ST

BEAR LANE

29
22

Royal Festival Hall

BFI IMAX

WATERLOO RD

DUCHY

COIN

AQUINAS ST

HATFIELDS

PARIS GARDENS

COLOMBO

GAMBIA ST

CHANCEL ST

SCORES ST

18

CONCERT HALL APPROACH

THEED

WHITTLESEY ST

MEYMOTT

SANDELL

ROUPELL STREET

BRAD STREET

EXTON ST

Waterloo East Station

JOAN

20

Southwark

London Eye

12

Jubilee Gardens

BELVEDERE ROAD

MEPHAM ST

Waterloo

WOOTTON ST

Young Vic Theatre **14**

THE CUT

SURREY ROW

21

London Film Museum **13**

Sea Life London Aquarium **15**

Old County Hall

WESTMINSTER BRIDGE

YORK ROAD

CHICHELEY ROAD

Waterloo Station

LEAKE STREET

STATION RD

LWR MARSH

MITRE RD

UPFORD

VALENTINE PL

Old Vic Theatre **40**

WEBBER

POCOCK STREET

RUSHWORTH ST

WEBBER

GRAY ST

WEBBER ROW

BARONS PL

SILEX ST

KING JAMES ST

LANCASTER ST

4

Florence Nightingale Museum

St. Thomas's Hospital

WC

UPPER MARSH

ROYAL STREET

NEWNHAM TERRACE

CENTAUR

LWR MARSH

FRAZIER ST

BAYLIS ROAD

CORAL ST

FEARMAN ST

MORLEY ST

GERRIDGE ST

Lambeth North

BURDETT ST

WESTMINSTER BRIDGE ROAD

GODSON ST

ST. GEORGE'S CIRCUS

LIBRARY ST

BORO

KEYWORTH

PALACE ROAD

LAMBETH

Lambeth Palace Gardens

VIRGIL ST

HERCULES RD

CARLISLE

COSSER ST

OAKEY LANE

KING EDWARD ST

LAMBETH ROAD

WESTMINSTER BRIDGE ROAD

LAMBETH ROAD

LONDON ROAD

DOYLE ST

GARDEN ROW

So Uni

4

St Thomas's Medical School

Lambeth Palace

Archbishop's Park

SIDFORD PL

Imperial War Museum

Geraldine Mary Harmsworth Park **9**

42

GLADSTONE STREET

ST GEORGE'S ROAD

WEST SQUARE

AUSTRAL ST

HAYLES STREET

ELLIOT'S ROW

OSWIN STREET

PASTOR ST

London College of Communica

5

Garden Museum

LAMBETH HIGH STREET

OLD PARADISE ST

PRATT ST

SAIL STREET

JUXON STREET

LAMBETH WALK

WALNUT TREE WALK

FITZALAN STREET

KENNINGTON ROAD

BROOK DRIVE

WALCOT SQUARE

ST MARY'S

GARDENS

Leisure Centre

KENNINGTON

5

WHITGIFT ST

WC

BLACK PRINCE RD

NEWPORT ST

RANSEY WALK

GIBSON RD

LOLLARD STREET

JUXON STREET

SAIL STREET

WINCOTT STREET

GILBERT RD

RENFREW RD

REEDWORTH STREET

DANTE ROAD

KENNINGTON NEW

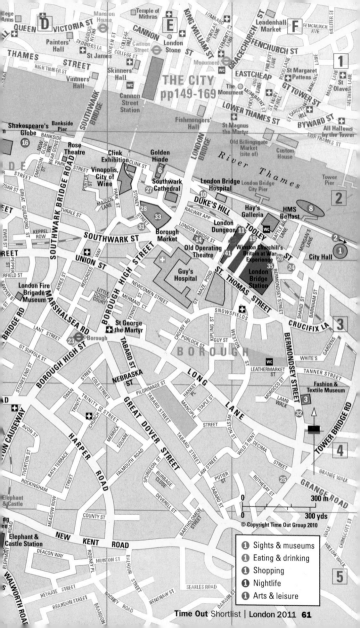

QUEEN **D** VICTORIA ST CANNON **E** KING WILLIAM ST RACECHURCH ST FENCHURCH ST **F**

Painters' Hall
St James
THAMES STREET
Vintners' Hall
Temple of Mithras
Mansion House
CANNON
Cannon Street
London Stone
Skinners' Hall

Leadenhall Market
St Margaret Pattens
St Olave

1

THE CITY
pp149-169

Monument

EASTCHEAP
The Monument

St Mary at Hill
GT TOWER ST

All Hallows by the Tower

Shakespeare's Globe **16**
Bankside Pier

LOWER THAMES ST

St Magnus the Martyr

BYWARD ST

Rose Theatre
Clink Exhibition
Golden Hinde **6**
Southwark Cathedral

Old Billingsgate Market (site of)

Custom House

River Thames

Tower Pier

2

Vinopolis, City of Wine **27**

28

London Bridge Hospital
London Bridge City Pier

HMS Belfast **8**

33
31

SOUTHWARK ST
Borough Market

DUKE'S HILL
10
Hay's Galleria

TOOLEY
Battle Bridge Lane

2

Union St
14
Old Operating Theatre
London Bridge Station
London Dungeon **11**
Winston Churchill's Britain at War Experience **41**
35
24

City Hall **1**

London Fire Brigade Museum
MARSHALSEA RD

ST THOMAS STREET

Guy's Hospital

CRUCIFIX LA

3

BRIDGE RD

St George the Martyr

BOROUGH HIGH ST

23
Borough

SNOWSFIELDS

LEATHERMARKET ST

TANNER STREET

Fashion & Textile Museum **3**

BERMONDSEY STREET

BOROUGH

NEBRASKA ST

LONG LANE

LAMB WALK

32

GREAT DOVER STREET

HARPER ROAD

TOWER BRIDGE RD

4

GRANGE ROAD
GRANGE WALK

25

Elephant & Castle
NEW KENT ROAD
Elephant & Castle Station

0   300 m
0   300 yds

© Copyright Time Out Group 2010

WALWORTH ROAD

5

1 Sights & museums
1 Eating & drinking
1 Shopping
1 Nightlife
1 Arts & leisure

Imperial War Museum

This large light cruiser is the last surviving big gun World War II warship in Europe. Built in 1938, the *Belfast* provided cover for convoys to Russia, and was instrumental in the Normandy Landings. It now makes an unlikely playground for kids, who tear round its guns, bridge and engine room.

Event highlights 'Launch! Shipbuilding Through the Ages' (until 31 Dec 2010).

Imperial War Museum

Lambeth Road, SE1 6HZ (7416 5320, www.iwm.org.uk). Lambeth North tube or Elephant & Castle tube/rail. **Open** 10am-6pm daily. **Admission** free. *Special exhibitions* prices vary. **Map** p60 B4 **9**

Antique guns, tanks, aircraft and artillery are parked up in the main hall of this imposing edifice, which illustrates the history of armed conflict from World War I to the present day. The tone of the museum darkens as you ascend: the third-floor Holocaust Exhibition is not recommended for under-14s; Crimes against Humanity – a minimalist space in which a film exploring contemporary genocide and ethnic violence rolls relentlessly – is unsuitable for under-16s. The ongoing 'Children's War' looks at what life on the Home Front was like for kids.

Event highlights 'The Ministry of Food' (until 3 Jan 2011).

London Bridge Experience

2-4 Tooley Street, SE1 2SY (0800 043 4666, www.thelondonbridgeexperience. com). London Bridge tube/rail. **Open** 10am-6pm daily. **Admission** £19.95; £14.95 reductions. **Map** p61 E2 **10**

Old London Bridge, finished in 1209, was the first Thames crossing made of stone – and London's only Thames bridge until Westminster Bridge was finished in 1750. This kitsch, family-focused exhibition is a costumed tour of the crossing's past, as well as a scary adventure into the haunted foundations: dank, pestilential catacombs peopled by animatronic torture victims.

London Dungeon

28-34 Tooley Street, SE1 2SZ (7403 7221, www.thedungeons.com). London Bridge tube/rail. **Open** *Jan, Feb* 10.30am-5pm daily. *Late Feb, July* 9.30am-6.30pm daily. *Mar, Nov, Dec* 10am-5pm daily. *Apr* 9am-7pm daily. *Late Apr-mid May, June, Sept, Oct* 10am-5.30pm daily. *Late May* 9am-6.30pm daily. *Aug, late Oct* 9.30am-7pm daily. **Admission** £17.95-£23.50; £11.95-£20.50 reductions. **Map** p61 F2 **11**

These railway arches contain a jokey celebration of torture, death and disease. Visitors are led through dry-ice past graves and corpses to experience nasty symptoms in the Great Plague exhibition: an actor-led medley of boils, projectile vomiting and worm-filled skulls. The Great Fire also gets the treatment, and Bloody Mary has joined the Ripper and Sweeney Todd.

London Eye

Jubilee Gardens, SE1 7PB (0870 500 0600, www.londoneye.com). Waterloo tube/rail or Westminster tube. **Open** *Oct-May* 10am-8pm daily. *June-Sept* 10am-9pm daily. **Admission** £17.50; free-£14 reductions. **Map** p60 A3 **12**

It's hard to believe this giant wheel was intended to turn for only five years: it has proved so popular that no one wants it to come down, and pod-by-pod refurbishment is now underway to fit it for another two decades (note the white dummy capsule). A 'flight' takes half an hour, allowing plenty of time to get your snaps of the landmarks. Some people book in advance (taking a gamble with the weather), but you can turn up and queue for a ticket on the day – there can be long waits in summer.

London Film Museum

County Hall, Riverside Building, SE1 7PB (7202 7040, www.londonfilm museum.com). Westminster tube or Waterloo tube/rail. **Open** 10am-5pm Mon-Fri; 10am-6pm Sat, Sun. **Admission** £12; free-£10 reductions. **Map** p60 A3 **13**

LONDON BY AREA

SEE MORE.
BE MORE.
This is NEW YORK CITY
Book Now. Get More.
Book your trip to NYC today with Travelocity on nycgo.com. Get the most out of your stay with special offers on hotels, dining, shopping, museums arts, entertainment and more.
travelocity

The London Film Museum celebrates the silver screen with props from *Star Wars, Superman, The Italian Job* and *Batman*. There's a gallery dedicated to animation, and you can watch interviews with the stars and clips from TV series that made it into film. A new permanent exhibition, 'Charlie Chaplin: The Great Londoner', focuses on the silent film star, who was born nearby.

Old Operating Theatre, Museum & Herb Garret

9A St Thomas's Street, SE1 9RY (7188 2679, www.thegarret.org.uk). London Bridge tube/rail. **Open** 10.30am-5pm daily. **Admission** £5.80; free-£4.80 reductions; £13.75 family. No credit cards. **Map** p61 E2 ㉔
The atmospheric tower that houses this salutary reminder of antique surgical practice used to be part of the chapel of St Thomas's Hospital. Visitors enter by a vertiginous wooden spiral staircase to view an operating theatre dating from 1822 (before the advent of anaesthetics), with tiered viewing seats for students. As fascinatingly gruesome are the operating tools, which look like torture implements.

Sea Life London Aquarium

County Hall, Riverside Building, Westminster Bridge Road, SE1 7PB (0871 663 1678, www.sealife.co.uk). Westminster tube or Waterloo tube/rail. **Open** 10am-6pm Mon-Thur; 10am-7pm Fri-Sun. **Admission** £17.50; free-£16 reductions; £54 family. **Map** p60 A3 ㉕
This is one of Europe's largest aquariums and a huge hit with kids. The inhabitants are grouped by geographical origin, beginning with the Atlantic, where blacktail bream swim alongside the Thames Embankment. The new 'Rainforests of the World' exhibit has introduced poison arrow frogs, crocodiles and piranha. The Ray Lagoon is still popular, though touching the friendly flatfish is no longer allowed (it's bad for their health). Starfish, crabs and anemones can be handled in special open rock pools instead, and the clown fish still draw crowds. There's a mesmerising Seahorse Temple and a tank full of turtles. The centrepieces, though, are the two massive Pacific and Indian Ocean tanks, with menacing sharks quietly circling fallen Easter Island statues and dinosaur bones.

Shakespeare's Globe

21 New Globe Walk, SE1 9DT (7401 9919, www.shakespeares-globe.org). Southwark tube or London Bridge tube/rail. **Open** Exhibition & tours 10am-5pm daily. *Tours* every 15mins. **Admission** £10.50; £6.50-£8.50 reductions; £28 family. **Map** p61 D2 ⑯
The original Globe Theatre, where many of Shakespeare's plays were first staged and which he co-owned, burned down in 1613 during a performance of *Henry VIII*. Nearly 400 years later, it was rebuilt not far from its original site, using construction methods and materials as close to the originals as possible. It's a fully operational theatre, with historically authentic (often very good) performances April to October. In the UnderGlobe is a fine exhibition on the history of the reconstruction and Shakespeare's London. Guided tours, lasting 90mins, run all year.
Event highlights *Henry IV Part I* and *Merry Wives of Windsor* (until 2 Oct 2010).

Tate Modern

Bankside, SE1 9TG (7887 8888, www.tate.org.uk). Southwark tube or London Bridge tube/rail. **Open** 10am-6pm Mon-Thur, Sun; 10am-10pm Fri, Sat. *Tours* hourly, 11am-3pm daily. **Admission** free. *Special exhibitions* prices vary. **Map** p61 D2 ⑰
Thanks to its industrial architecture, this powerhouse of modern art is awe-inspiring even before you enter. It shut down as Bankside Power Station in 1981, then opened as a spectacularly popular museum in 2000. The gallery attracts five million visitors a year to a building intended for half that number, and work has begun on the dramatic

£165m, pyramid-like TM2 extension, due complete in 2012. The cavernous turbine hall houses the Unilever Series of temporary, large-scale installations, while the permanent collection draws from the Tate organisation's magnificent collection of modern art (international works from 1900) to display Matisse, Rothko, Bacon, Twombly and Beuys. The Tate-to-Tate boat service (£4.30 adult) – polka-dot decor by Damien Hirst, bar on board – links with Tate Britain (p78) every 20mins. **Event highlights** Gauguin (30 Sept 2010-16 Jan 2011); The Unilever Series: Ai Weiwei (12 Oct 2010-25 Apr 2011).

Topolski Century

150-152 Hungerford Arches, SE1 8XU (7620 1275, www.topolskicentury.org. uk). Waterloo tube/rail. **Open** 11am-7pm Mon-Sat; noon-6pm Sun.
Admission free. **Map** p60 A2 ⓭
This extensive, recently restored mural depicts the extraordinary jumble of 20th-century events through the roughly painted faces of Bob Dylan, Winston Churchill and many, many others. It's the work of Polish-born expressionist Feliks Topolski, who made his name as a war artist in World War II – he was an eye witness to the horrors of Belsen.

Winston Churchill's Britain at War Experience

64-66 Tooley Street, SE1 2TF (7403 3171, www.britainatwar.co.uk). London Bridge tube/rail. **Open** *Apr-Oct* 10am-5pm daily. *Nov-Mar* 10am-4.30pm daily. **Admission** £12.95; free-£6.50 reductions; £29 family. **Map** p61 F3 ⓳
This old-fashioned exhibition recalls the privations endured by the British during World War II. Visitors descend from street level in an ancient lift to a reconstructed tube station shelter. The experience continues with Blitz-time London: real bombs, rare documents, photos and reconstructed shopfronts. Displays on rationing and food production are fascinating, and the set-piece bombsite quite disturbing.

Eating & drinking

Borough Market (p70) is great for gourmet snackers, while the cluster of chain eateries beside and beneath the Royal Festival Hall, includes **Wagamama** (p120) and, our pick, **Canteen** (below).

Anchor & Hope

36 The Cut, SE1 8LP (7928 9898). Southwark or Waterloo tube/rail. **Open** 5-11pm Mon; noon-11pm Tue-Sat; noon-5pm Sun. **££**. **Gastropub**. **Map** p60 C2 ⓴
The most common complaint about this relaxed gastropub is that it doesn't accept bookings. Still, those who have to wait at the bar get the chance to salivate over the well-sourced, seasonal British menu on the blackboard. Arbroath smokie is a good bet if it's available; other dishes might include cold roast beef and dripping on toast. Sundays have a single 2pm sitting. Weekday lunches are quieter.

Baltic

74 Blackfriars Road, SE1 8HA (7928 1111, www.balticrestaurant.co.uk). Southwark tube. **Open** noon-3pm, 5.30-11.15pm Mon-Sat; noon-10.30pm Sun. **£££**. **Eastern European/cocktail bar**. **Map** p60 C3 ㉑
This stylish spot (in the high-ceiling restaurant, a stunning chandelier is made of hundreds of amber shards) remains London's brightest star to east European food. The menu gives the best of eastern Europe – from Georgian-style lamb with aubergines to Romanian sour cream *mamaliga* (polenta) – a light, modern twist. Great cocktails, many vodkas, eclectic wines and friendly service add to the appeal.

Canteen

Royal Festival Hall, Belvedere Road, SE1 8XX (0845 686 1122, www. canteen.co.uk). Waterloo tube/rail. **Open** 8am-11pm Mon-Fri; 9am-11pm Sat, Sun. **££**. **British**. **Map** p60 A2 ㉒

Sea Life London Aquarium p65

Moving to a new tune

The woman bringing the South Bank's dance up to date.

Dance is more popular than ever in London: **Sadler's Wells** (p177) has seen an amazing 56 per cent rise in audiences over the last six years and a huge range of top-class artists, international and home-grown, across every imaginable style of dance, continues to perform in the city every week. But the view from beyond our borders is that London has slipped away from dance's cutting edge.

Nicky Molloy (above left), new head of dance and performance at **Southbank Centre** (p73), is taking on the task of finding a new identity for dance at the venue. 'I came here and I thought: OK, who else is doing dance, what are they doing and what's missing?' she says. 'I think the obvious thing is that there's a body of international work that's not being programmed in London consistently.'

The work Molloy has in mind is particularly that which pushes beyond dance as pure movement and inhabits the borders between dance, theatre, and visual and performance art. 'Many of the makers who are working now have trained as dancers and choreographers but choose to go quite far from what we would consider to be "bodies moving in space",' says Molloy. 'But they still create work with a knowledge of space, time and all those things that make a choreographic work. They want to reflect on this very complex world, looking at social and political and economic issues, but they realise that dance in its purest form is not enough to really take those ideas on.'

Molloy won't be throwing out everything previously associated with Southbank, like the strong presence of South Asian dance or hip hop shows from B.Supreme and Zoonation, but it will be in with works like Mathilde Monnier and La Ribot's 'Gustavia' (above right), which featured in Molloy's Five Days of May mini-festival. 'I need to be sure that work is really strong,' says Molloy. 'I won't be programming work unless I think it's bloomin' brilliant.'

Canteen is furnished with utilitarian but warm plain oak tables and benches. Dishes range from a bacon sandwich and afternoon jam scones to full roasts. Classic breakfasts (eggs benedict, welsh rarebit) are served all day, joined by the likes of macaroni cheese or sausage and mash from lunchtime. Unpretentious and often busy.

Gladstone Arms

64 Lant Street, SE1 1QN (7407 3962). Borough tube. **Open** noon-11pm Mon-Fri; noon-midnight Sat; noon-10.30pm Sun. **Map** p61 D3 **23**

While the Victorian prime minister still glares from the massive mural on the outer wall, inside is now funky, freaky and candlelit. Gigs (blues, folk, acoustic, five nights a week) take place at one end of a cosy space; opposite, a bar dispenses ales and lagers. Pies provide sustenance, and nice retro touches include an old 'On Air' studio sign.

Magdalen

152 Tooley Street, SE1 2TU (7403 1342, www.magdalenrestaurant.co.uk). London Bridge tube/rail. **Open** noon-2.30pm, 6.30-10.30pm Mon-Fri; 6.30-10.30pm Sat. **£££. British. Map** p61 F3 **24**

Magdalen makes the most of somewhat unprepossessing surroundings. A la carte prices are just about reasonable (£17.50 for flavoursome Middle White belly with veg and good gravy, £16.50 for a beautifully presented fish stew), but portions aren't huge; opt instead for the set lunch, a steal at £15.50 for two courses or £18.50 for three. Poached rhubarb with shortbread and crème anglaise is the best pud. Staff are friendly and efficient.

M Manze

87 Tower Bridge Road, SE1 4TW (7407 2985, www.manze.co.uk). Bus 1, 42, 188. **Open** 11am-2pm Mon; 10.30am-2pm Tue-Thur; 10am-2.15pm Fri; 10am-2.45pm Sat. **£.** No credit cards. **Pie & mash. Map** p61 F4 **25**

The finest remaining purveyor of the dirt-cheap traditional foodstuff of London's working classes. It is not only the oldest pie shop, established in 1902, but the most beautiful, with marble-top tables, tiles and worn wood benches. Expect mashed potato, minced beef pies and liquor (a parsley sauce); braver souls should try the stewed eels.

More

NEW *104 Tooley Street, SE1 2TH (7403 0635, www.moretooleystreet. com). London Bridge tube/rail.* **Open** 8am-11pm Mon-Fri; 10am-11pm Sat; 10am-4pm Sun. **££. Brasserie. Map** p61 F2 **26**

More is a true all-day brasserie. Small, sleek and chic, it swings effortlessly from breakfast muesli and fruit plates to full-on lunches and dinners. Mains consist of classics with added touches, along with more unusual, fusion-style dishes. Jolly staff help to create a feel-good atmosphere.

Rake

14 Winchester Walk, SE1 9AG (7407 0557). London Bridge tube/rail. **Open** noon-11pm Mon-Fri; 10am-11pm Sat. **Pub. Map** p61 E2 **27**

The Veltins lager and Maisels Weiße taps stay in place at this blue-fronted cubicle of a bar, but the likes of Aechte Schlenkerle Rauchbier (a rare smoked variety from Bamberg) and Grisette Fruits des Bois probably won't still be on tap when you arrive. No matter: as the yellow sign says above the bar, there's 'No crap on tap'.

Roast

Floral Hall, Borough Market, Stoney Street, SE1 1TL (7940 1300, www. roast-restaurant.com). London Bridge tube/rail. **Open** 7-9.30am, noon-2.30pm, 5.30-10.30pm Mon-Fri; 8-10.30am, 11.30am-3.30pm, 6-10.30pm Sat; noon-3.30pm Sun. **£££. British. Map** p61 E2 **28**

Perched above the market, Roast celebrates its location with a menu inspired

LONDON BY AREA

by British produce, much of it sourced from stallholders below. Seasonality and freshness are the buzzwords and there's no doubting the quality of the ingredients; enjoy them for less from the bar menu after 3pm.

Skylon
Royal Festival Hall, Belvedere Road, SE1 8XX (7654 7800, www.dandd london.com). Waterloo tube/rail. **Open** noon-1am daily. **£££. Brasserie/ bar**. Map p60 A2 ㉙

There can't be many better transport views in town. Sit near the counter (between two restaurant areas) to watch buses, bridges and boats while supping finely crafted cocktails – the list is mainly twists on 1950s classics, with a focus on tart bellinis. Despite the room's aircraft-hangar proportions, screens and plenty of bronze accents keep the feel intimate. Prices are high, and the food not always impressive.

Tsuru
4 Canvey Street, SE1 8AN (7928 2228, www.tsuru-sushi.co.uk). Southwark tube or London Bridge tube/rail. **Open** 11am-9pm Mon-Fri. **£. Japanese**. Map p61 D2 ㉚

Much of the business is in takeaways for nearby office workers, but this katsu specialist has smart tall wooden stools with matching benches for those who want to eat in. Cold items (spinach with oritashi sauce) are chosen from a chill cabinet of sushi boxes to go, with orders for hot food (curry, teriyaki bento) are taken at the bar. There are sake-tastings and music some nights.

Wine Wharf
Stoney Street, Borough Market, SE1 9AD (7940 8335, www.winewharf. com). London Bridge tube/rail. **Open** noon-11pm Mon-Sat. **Wine bar**. Map p61 E2 ㉛

An extension of the wine-tasting attraction Vinopolis (0870 241 4040, www.vinopolis.co.uk), Wine Wharf inhabits two industrial-chic storeys of a reclaimed Victorian warehouse. The 250-bin list stretches to 1953 d'Yquem and serious champagne but, with nearly half the wines by the glass, you can probably afford to experiment a little.

Shopping

London's own *bouquinistes* sell second-hand books and old prints from trestles by the **BFI** (p72).

Bermondsey Street
London Bridge tube/rail. Map p61 F4 ㉜

Bermondsey Street has become rather cool over the last few years, though you'd hardly believe it on the approach from the north under a grimy railway bridge. Slick shops include bermond-sey167 (no.167), a Brazilian concept store that marries impeccable interior design with highbrow fashion; Amanda Thompson's indulgently feminine Pussy Willow (no.90), posh pet accessory emporium Holly & Lil (no.103); and Cockfighter (no.96), for T-shirts and sweaters. Even the Fashion & Textile Museum (p59) has a little shop to showcase design talent. In a new square, a boutique hotel (p195) and arthouse cinema complete the picture.

Borough Market
Southwark Street, SE1 1TL (7407 1002, www.boroughmarket.org.uk). London Bridge tube/rail. **Open** 11am-5pm Thur; noon-6pm Fri; 8am-5pm Sat. Map p61 E2 ㉝

The foodies' favourite market, which occupies a sprawling site near London Bridge, is a major tourist attraction. Gourmet goodies – rare-breed meats, fruit and veg, cakes and preserves, oils and teas – run the gamut from Flour Power City Bakery's organic loaves to chorizo and rocket rolls from Spanish specialist Brindisa via Neal's Yard Dairy's speciality British cheeses. The market is also open on Thursdays, usually quieter than always-mobbed weekends – Saturday is monstrously busy.

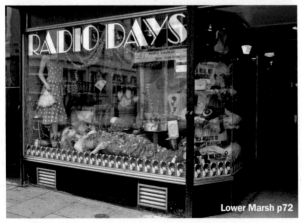

Lower Marsh p72

Lower Marsh

Waterloo tube/rail. **Map** p60 B3 ③④
Lower Marsh Market (7926 2530, www.lower-marsh.co.uk) has been a street market since Victorian times, but has more recently attracted independent shops and cafés: Radio Days (no.87) sells vintage clothes and accessories, Scootercaffè (no. 132) provides mellow vibes and good coffee, and Jane Gibberd (no.20) sells second-hand books.

Nightlife

As well as classical music, theatre and dance, the **Southbank Centre** (opposite) programmes terrific rock, jazz and world music gigs.

Cable

NEW *33A Bermondsey Street, SE1 2EG (7403 7730, www.cable-london.com). London Bridge tube/rail.* **Open** 11pm-6am Fri, Sat; 10pm-5am Sun. **Map** p61 F2 ③⑤
All old-style brickwork and industrial air-con ducts, Cable has two dance arenas, a bar with a spot-and-be-spotted mezzanine, plenty of seats and a great covered smoking area. High-calibre nights include bass-heavy Chew the Fat and Jaded, for tech-house, techno and deep house. Don't hesitate when staff ask to take your thumbprint when you check in your coat: if you lose your ticket, you won't need to wait for the club to clear before claiming it back.

Corsica Studios

Units 4/5, Elephant Road, SE17 1LB (7703 4760, www.corsicastudios.com). Elephant & Castle tube/rail. No credit cards. **Map** p61 D5 ③⑥
This flexible performance space is increasingly used as one of London's more adventurous live music venues and clubs, supplementing the bands and DJs with sundry poets, live painters and wigged-out projectionists. The place is open until midnight or 1am for gigs, and until 6am for some of the club nights.

Ministry of Sound

103 Gaunt Street, SE1 6DP (0870 060 0010, www.ministryofsound.com). Elephant & Castle tube/rail. **Open** 10.30pm-6am Fri; 11pm-7am Sat. **Map** p61 D4 ③⑦
Cool the Ministry ain't (there's little more naff than the VIP rooms here), but home to a killer sound system it is. Trance and epic house night the Gallery has made its home here on Fridays (expect large sets from the likes of Paul Oakenfold), while the Saturday Sessions cover deep techno, fidget house and electro.

Arts & leisure

Free-standing Pit tickets are superb value at the **Globe** (p65), whether for trad Shakespeare or a new play.

BFI Southbank

South Bank, SE1 8XT (7928 3535, 7928 3232 tickets, www.bfi.org.uk). Embankment tube or Waterloo tube/rail. **Map** p60 A2 ③⑧
An esteemed London institution, with an unrivalled programme of retrospective seasons and previews, as well as regular director and actor Q&As. The riverside seating outside the underpowered main café is hugely popular, but the handsome cocktail bar/restaurant alongside the terrific Mediatheque (a free archive-viewing room) is better. Made-for-IMAX kiddie pics and wow-factor documentaries are the usual fare at BFI IMAX (1 Charlie Chaplin Walk, 0870 787 2525), the biggest screen in the country, but there are monster-sized mainstream films too.

National Theatre

South Bank, SE1 9PX (7452 3400, 7452 3000 box office, www.national theatre.org.uk). Embankment or Southwark tube, or Waterloo tube/rail. **Map** p60 B2 ③⑨
This concrete monster is the flagship venue of British theatre. Three auditoriums allow for different kinds of per-

formance: in-the-round, promenade, even classic proscenium arch. Nicholas Hytner's artistic directorship, with landmark successes such as Alan Bennett's *The History Boys*, has shown that the state-subsidised home of British theatre can turn out quality drama at a profit. The Travelex season ensures a widening audience by offering two-thirds of the seats for £10, as does the free outdoor performing arts stage, Watch This Space, in summer. **Event highlights** *Hamlet* (from Sept 2010); Danny Boyle's *Frankenstein*, Peter Hall's *Twelfth Night* (both 2011).

Old Vic
The Cut, SE1 8NB (0844 871 7628, www.oldvictheatre.com). Waterloo tube/rail. **Map** p60 B3 ⑩
The combination of Oscar-winner Kevin Spacey and top producer David Liddiment at this grand, boxy 200-year-old theatre continues to be a commercial success, if not always a critical one. Programming runs from grown-up Christmas pantomimes to the Bridge Project, transatlantic collaborations on serious plays (Chekhov, Shakespeare) directed by Sam Mendes.

Shunt
Joiner Street, SE1 9RL (7378 7776, www.shunt.co.uk). London Bridge tube/rail. **Open** hours vary, Fri, Sat. **Map** p61 E2 ㊶
Run by an artists' collective in the grand, musty arches beneath London Bridge station, Shunt has reopened after station redevelopment threatened to close it for good. Each week a different member decides the programme: expect cabaret, theatre, installations, free jazz or punk-pop, separately or in a variety of combinations. Non-members with photo ID pay at the door, and can then stay until late in the cash bar.

Siobhan Davies Dance Studios
85 St George's Road, SE1 6ER (7091 9650, www.siobhandavies.com).

Elephant & Castle tube/rail. **Map** p60 C4 ㊷
This award-winning venue, designed in consultation with dancers, not only meets their needs but looks amazing. Davies, who founded the company in 1988, often explores spaces outside her theatre, so check with the venue for performance details before setting out.

Southbank Centre
Belvedere Road, SE1 8XX (0871 663 2501 information, 0871 663 2500 tickets, www.southbankcentre.co.uk). Embankment tube or Waterloo tube/rail. **Map** p60 A2 ㊸
In addition to the Hayward (p59), there are three main venues here: the Royal Festival Hall, with nearly 3,000 seats and the Philharmonia and the Orchestra of the Age of Enlightenment as residents; the Queen Elizabeth Hall, which can seat around 900 concert-goers; and the 365-capacity Purcell Room, for regular recitals. A £90m renovation a few years back improved the RFH, externally and acoustically, and since Jude Kelly took over the reins as artistic director the programming has been rich in variety, with music and performance of all types, often presented in appealingly themed festivals. The RFH foyer stage hosts hundreds of free concerts every year, and the riverside terrace is thronged in good weather. See also box p68.

Young Vic
66 The Cut, SE1 8LZ (7922 2922, www.youngvic.org). Southwark tube or Waterloo tube/rail. **Map** p60 B3 ㊹
As the name suggests, the Young Vic has more youthful bravura than its older sister up the road, and draws a younger crowd, who pack out the open-air balcony at its popular restaurant and bar on the weekends. They come to see European classics with a distinctly modern edge, new writing with an international flavour and collaborations with leading companies such as the English National Opera (p148).

LONDON BY AREA

Houses of Parliament p76

Westminster & St James's

LONDON BY AREA

Westminster

More formal than it is inviting, Westminster remains for many the heart of London – if not the heart of Britain. The area is home to the **Houses of Parliament**, the seat of government power for 1,000 years; Britain's very first Parliament met in **Westminster Abbey**, the site also of almost every British coronation. Here too are **Trafalgar Square** and Nelson's Column – tourist photo opportunity by day, host of diverse festivals by night.

Sights & museums

Banqueting House

Whitehall, SW1A 2ER (0844 482 7777, www.hrp.org.uk). Westminster tube or Charing Cross tube/rail. **Open** 10am-5pm Mon-Sat. **Admission** £4.50; free-£3.50 reductions. **Map** p75 C2 ①

This Italianate mansion was built in 1620 and is the sole surviving part of the Tudor and Stuart kings' Whitehall Palace. It features a lavish ceiling by Rubens that glorifies James I, 'the wisest fool in Christendom'. Sometimes closed for corporate dos – phone ahead.

Churchill War Rooms

Clive Steps, King Charles Street, SW1A 2AQ (7930 6961, www.iwm.org.uk). St James's Park or Westminster tube. **Open** 9.30am-6pm daily. **Admission** £12.95; free-£10.40 reductions. **Map** p75 C2 ②

Beneath Whitehall, the cramped and spartan bunker where Winston Churchill planned the Allied victory in World War II remains exactly as it was left on 16 August 1945. There's a tangible sense of wartime hardship, reinforced by wailing sirens and wartime speeches on the free audio guide. Adjoining the War Rooms, the engaging Churchill Museum is devoted to the great man and his famous speeches.

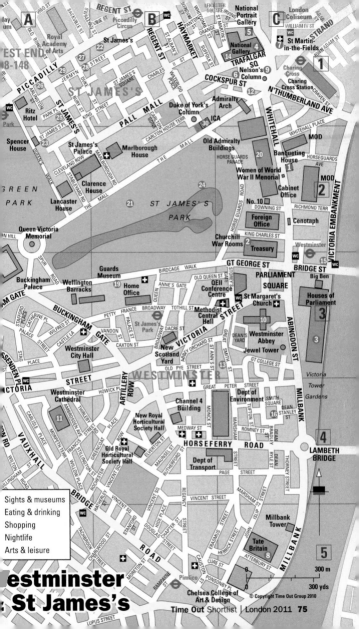

Westminster & St James's

Houses of Parliament

Parliament Square, SW1A 0AA (0870 906 3773 tours, www.parliament.uk). Westminster tube. **Open** phone or check website for details. **Admission** *Visitors' Gallery* free. *Tours* £12; free-£8 reductions. **Map** p75 C3 ❸

Visitors are welcome to observe the debates at the House of Lords and House of Commons – Prime Minister's Question Time at noon on Wednesday is often fiery – but tickets must be arranged in advance through your embassy or MP. The best time to visit is during the summer recess, when tours – taking in ancient Westminster Hall – are organised (book in advance). Most of the original Parliament buildings were destroyed by fire in 1834, with the current neo-Gothic extravaganza completed in 1860.

National Gallery

Trafalgar Square, WC2N 5DN (7747 2885, www.nationalgallery.org.uk). Leicester Square tube or Charing Cross tube/rail. **Open** 10am-6pm Mon-Thur, Sat, Sun; 10am-9pm Fri. *Tours* 11.30am, 2.30pm daily. **Admission** free. *Special exhibitions* prices vary. **Map** p75 C1 ❹

Founded in 1824 to display a collection of just 36 paintings, today the National Gallery is home to more than 2,000 works. There are masterpieces from virtually every European school of art, from austere 13th-century religious paintings to the visceral delights of Van Gogh. Straight ahead on entry, in the North Wing, are 17th-century Dutch, Flemish, Italian and Spanish Old Masters, including Velázquez's *Rokeby Venus*, while the East Wing contains hugely popular French Impressionist and Post-Impressionist paintings by Monet, Renoir and Seurat. You can't see everything in one visit, but free guided tours, audio guides and the Art Start computer system (helping you navigate between your own must-sees) can point you to the highlights.

Event highlights 'Venice: Canaletto and His Rivals' (13 Oct 2010-16 Jan 2011).

National Portrait Gallery

St Martin's Place, WC2H 0HE (7306 0055, www.npg.org.uk). Leicester Square tube or Charing Cross tube/rail. **Open** 10am-6pm Mon-Wed, Sat, Sun; 10am-9pm Thur, Fri. **Admission** free. *Special exhibitions* prices vary. **Map** p75 C1 ❺

Portraits don't have to be stuffy. The NPG has everything from oil paintings of stiff-backed royals to photos of soccer stars and gloriously unflattering political caricatures. The portraits of musicians, scientists, artists, philanthropists and celebrities are arranged in chronological order from the top to the bottom of the building.

Event highlights BP Portrait Awards (June-Sept 2011).

Routemaster buses

Cockspur Street, Stops B & (opposite) S. **Map** p75 C1 ❻

The iconic red double-deckers were withdrawn from service in 2005, but beautifully refurbished Routies run Routes 9 (Stop B) and 15 (Stop S) every 15mins, 9.30am to 6.30pm. No.9 goes west to the Royal Albert Hall, no.15 east via St Paul's to Tower Hill. Unless you're already in possession of an Oyster or Travelcard (p213), you must buy a ticket before boarding.

St Martin-in-the-Fields

Trafalgar Square, WC2N 4JJ (7766 1122, www.smitf.org). Leicester Square tube or Charing Cross tube/rail. **Open** 8am-6pm daily. *Brass Rubbing Centre* 10am-7pm Mon-Wed; 10am-9pm Thur-Sat; 11am-6pm Sun. **Admission** free. *Brass rubbing* £4.50. **Map** p75 C1 ❼

Built in 1726 by James Gibbs, the church has recently benefited from a £36m refurbishment. The bright interior has been fully restored, with Victorian furbelows removed and the addition of a lovely, controversial altar window that shows the Cross, stylised as if rippling on water. The crypt, its café and the London Brass Rubbing Centre have been updated.

LONDON BY AREA

National Portrait Gallery

Rules Supreme

Where the decisions in Britain really get made.

On 1 October 2009, there was a massive change in British constitutional affairs. On that day, London became home to the **UK Supreme Court**. Not that anyone seemed to notice.

The House of Lords had been the final court of appeal for 600 years, but its loss of this historic role was signified by the Justices moving only a short distance across Parliament Square: from the Houses of Parliament to a new home in the Middlesex Guildhall, a neo-Gothic building completed in 1913.

The Supreme Court is open to the public from 10am to 4.30pm Monday to Friday. All you need is a bit of patience to get through the inevitable security gates and you can be present as Justices make and rebut arguments that establish the country's laws.

If the niceties of legal process elude you, there's permanent exhibition downstairs in a former cell area that introduces you to the Justices (with mugshots and mini-CVs), as well as explaining the history of the court. There's even a café and a neat range of branded Supreme Court trinkets.

One balustrade is engraved with choice quotes, selected by those Justices, among which is Ovid's remark: 'Laws were made to prevent the strong from always having their way'. It's terrific being able to watch that process unfold.

■ www.supremecourt.gov.uk

LONDON BY AREA

Event highlights Candlelit evening concerts of Mozart and Vivaldi; lunchtime recitals (Mon, Tue, Fri) are less predictable.

Tate Britain
Millbank, SW1P 4RG (7887 8888, www. tate.org.uk). Pimlico tube. **Open** 10am-5.50pm daily; 10am-10pm 1st Fri of mth. *Tours* 11am, noon, 2pm, 3pm Mon-Fri; noon, 3pm Sat, Sun. **Admission** free. *Special exhibitions* prices vary. **Map** p75 C5 ⑧

Tate Modern (p65) gets all the attention, but the original Tate Gallery has a broader and more inclusive brief. Housed in a stately Portland stone building on the riverside, it's second only to the National (p76) for historical art in London. The collection of British art includes work by Hogarth, Gainsborough, Reynolds, Constable, and Turner (in the Clore Gallery). Modern Brits Stanley Spencer, Lucian Freud and Francis Bacon are well represented, and the Art Now installations showcase up-and-comers. The handy Tate-to-Tate boat service (p65) zips to Tate Modern every 40mins.

Event highlights Eadweard Muybridge (8 Sept 2010-16 Jan 2011); Turner Prize 2010 (5 Oct 2010-2 Jan 2011).

Trafalgar Square
Charing Cross tube/rail. **Map** p75 C1 ⑨

The centrepiece of London, Trafalgar Square was conceived in the 1820s as a homage to Britain's naval power. It has always been a natural gathering-point – semi-pedestrianisation in 2003 made it more so. The focus is Nelson's Column, a Corinthian pillar topped by a statue of naval hero Horatio Nelson, but the contemporary sculpture on the Fourth Plinth brings some fresh colour.

Westminster Abbey
20 Dean's Yard, SW1P 3PA (7222 5152 information, 7654 4900 tours, www.westminster-abbey.org). St James's Park or Westminster tube. **Open** 9.30am-4.30pm Mon, Tue, Thur, Fri; 9.30am-7pm Wed; 9.30am-4.30pm Sat.

Abbey Museum, Chapter House & College Gardens 10am-4pm daily. **Admission** £15; free-£12 reductions; £36 family. *Abbey Museum* free. *Tours* £3. **Map** p75 C3 ⑩

The cultural significance of the Abbey is hard to overstate. Edward the Confessor commissioned it, but it was only consecrated on 28 December 1065, eight days before he died. William the Conqueror had himself crowned here on Christmas Day 1066, followed by every British king and queen since – bar two. Many notables are interred here, with Poets' Corner always a draw. Take a look at the mosaic Cosmati Pavement, unveiled after restoration in spring 2010. The Abbey Museum occupies one of the oldest parts of the Abbey: you'll find effigies of British monarchs, among them Edward II and Henry VII, wearing the robes they donned in life. A café/refectory is due to be added in autumn 2011.

Westminster Cathedral

42 Francis Street, SW1P 1QW (7798 9055, www.westminstercathedral.org.uk). Victoria tube/rail. **Open** 7am-6pm Mon-Fri; 8am-6.30pm Sat; 8am-7pm Sun. *Bell tower* 9.30am-4.30pm daily. **Admission** free; donations appreciated. *Bell tower* £5; £2.50 reductions. **Map** p75 A4 ⑪

With domes, arches and a soaring tower, the architecture of the most important Catholic church in England (built 1895-1903) was heavily influenced by Istanbul's Hagia Sophia mosque. Inside are impressive marble columns and mosaics, and Eric Gill's sculptures of the Stations of the Cross. A lift runs up the 273ft bell tower.

Eating & drinking

Albannach

66 Trafalgar Square, WC2N 5DS (7930 0066, www.albannach.co.uk). Charing Cross tube/rail. **Open** 5pm-1am Wed; 5pm-3am Thur-Sat. **Cocktail bar**. **Map** p75 C1 ⑫

Albannach (as opposed to 'sassanach') specialises in Scotch whiskies and cocktails thereof. Notwithstanding the impressive location facing on to the square, kilted staff, illuminated reindeer and loud office groups can detract from the quality of booze on offer.

Cinnamon Club

Old Westminster Library, 30-32 Great Smith Street, SW1P 3BU (7222 2555, www.cinnamonclub.com). St James's Park or Westminster tube. **Open** 7.30-9.30am, noon-2.30pm, 6-10.45pm Mon-Fri; noon-2.30pm, 6-10.45pm Sat. **££££. Indian**. **Map** p75 C3 ⑬

Aiming to create a complete Indian fine-dining experience, Cinnamon Club provides cocktails, fine wines, tasting menus, breakfasts (Indian, Anglo-Indian, British), private dining-rooms and all attendant flummery in an impressive, wood-lined space. Even the well-priced set meal (£20 for two courses) is invitingly unusual.

National Dining Rooms

Sainsbury Wing, National Gallery, Trafalgar Square, WC2N 5DN (7747 2525, www.thenationaldiningrooms. co.uk). Charing Cross tube/rail. **Open** *Bakery* 10am-5.30pm Mon-Thur, Sun; 10am-8.30pm Fri; 10am-7.30pm Sat. *Restaurant* noon-3.30pm Mon-Thur, Sat, Sun; noon-3.30pm, 5-7.15pm Fri. *Bakery* **£**. *Restaurant* **£££**. **British**. **Map** p75 C1 ⑭

Oliver Peyton's finest restaurant is still in great shape. Cultured, cheeky afternoon teas can be taken, though the real attraction remains the main menu of British staples, immaculately cooked and presented in a nicely relaxed atmosphere. The East Wing's darkly romantic National Café bar-restaurant (7747 5942, www.thenationalcafe.com) opens to 11pm every day but Sunday.

St Stephen's Tavern

10 Bridge St, SW1A 2JR (7925 2286). Westminster tube. **Open** noon-3pm, 5.30-11pm Mon-Fri. **Map** p75 C3 ⑮

LONDON BY AREA

Household Cavalry Museum

Done out with dark woods, etched mirrors and lovely Arts and Crafts-style wallpaper, this is a handsome old pub. The food is reasonably priced and the ales are excellent, but expensive. Brilliantly located opposite Big Ben, it's neither too touristy nor too busy.

Arts & leisure

St John's, Smith Square
Smith Square, SW1P 3HA (7222 1061, www.sjss.org.uk). Westminster tube. **Map** p75 C4 🔞
With its distinctive four towers, this elegant church was completed in 1728. It now hosts orchestral and chamber concerts more or less every night, along with occasional recitals on its magnificent Klais organ. In the crypt, the Footstool restaurant opens for weekday lunches and, for concerts, dinner.

Victoria Palace Theatre
Victoria Street, SW1E 5EA (0844 248 5000, www.victoriapalacetheatre.co.uk). Victoria tube/rail. **Map** p75 A4 🔞
Billy Elliot, scored by Elton John, is set during the 1984 miners' strike. A working-class lad loves ballet – much to the consternation of his salt-of-the-earth dad. Production subject to change.

St James's

Traditional, quiet and terribly exclusive, St James's is where **Buckingham Palace** presides over lovely **St James's Park**. Everything is dignified rather than hurried, whether you're shopping at **Fortnum's** and on **Jermyn Street**, or entertaining in **Dukes** or the **Wolseley**.

Sights & museums

Buckingham Palace & Royal Mews
The Mall, SW1A 1AA (7766 7300 Palace, 7766 7301 Queen's Gallery, 7766 7302 Royal Mews, www.royal collection.org.uk). Green Park tube or Victoria tube/rail. **Open** *State Rooms* mid July-Sept 9.45am-6pm (last entry 3.45pm) daily. *Queen's Gallery* 10am-5.30pm daily. *Royal Mews* Mar-July, Oct 11am-4pm Mon-Thur, Sat, Sun; Aug, Sept 10am-5pm daily. **Admission** *Palace* £16.50; free-£15 reductions; £44 family. *Queen's Gallery* £8.50; free-£7.50 reductions; £21.50 family. *Royal Mews* £7.50; free-£6.75 reductions; £20 family. **Map** p75 A3 🔞
The present home of the British royals is open to the public each year while the family Windsor are away on their summer holidays; you'll be able to see the State Apartments, which are still used to entertain dignitaries and guests of state. At other times of year, visit the Queen's Gallery to see the Queen's personal collection of treasures. Further along Buckingham Palace Road, the Royal Mews is the home of the royal Rolls-Royces, the splendid royal carriages and the horses that pull them.
Event highlights Changing of the Guard (except in rain: 11.30am alternate days, daily Apr-July).

Guards Museum
Wellington Barracks, Birdcage Walk, SW1E 6HQ (7414 3428, www.the guardsmuseum.com). St James's Park tube. **Open** 10am-4pm daily. **Admission** £3; free-£2 reductions. **Map** p75 B3 🔞
This small museum tells the 350-year story of the Foot Guards, using flamboyant uniforms, medals, period paintings and intriguing memorabilia, such as the stuffed body of a Victorian mascot, Jacob the Goose.

Household Cavalry Museum
Horse Guards, Whitehall, SW1A 2AX (7930 3070, www.householdcavalry.co. uk). Westminster tube or Charing Cross tube/rail. **Open** *Mar-Sept* 10am-6pm daily. *Oct-Feb* 10am-5pm daily. **Admission** £6; free-£4 reductions; £15 family. **Map** p75 C2 🔞

The Household Cavalry, the Queen's official guard, get to tell their stories through video diaries at this small but entertaining museum. Separated from the stables by a mere pane of glass, you'll also get a peek – and sniff – of the huge horses that parade outside daily. **Event highlights** Changing of the Guard (except in rain: 11am Mon-Fri; 10am Sat).

St James's Park

St James's Park or Westminster tube. Map p75 B2 ㉑
St James's Park, founded as a deer park, was remodelled on the orders of George IV. The central lake is home to numerous species of wildfowl, including pelicans that are fed at 3pm daily, and the bridge offers a great snap of the palace.

St James's Piccadilly

197 Piccadilly, W1J 9LL (7734 4511/ www.st-james-piccadilly.org). Piccadilly Circus tube. **Open** 8am-6.30pm daily. **Admission** free. Map p75 B1 ㉒
Consecrated in 1684, St James's is the only church Sir Christopher Wren built on an entirely new site. This is a busy church, providing a home for the William Blake Society, and hosting markets in the churchyard: antiques on Tuesday, arts and crafts from Wednesday to Saturday.
Event highlights Free recitals (1.10pm Mon, Wed, Fri).

Eating & drinking

Dukes Hotel

35 St James's Place, SW1A 1NY (7491 4840, www.dukeshotel.co.uk). Green Park tube. **Open** noon-11pm Mon-Sat; noon-10.30pm Sun. **Cocktail bar.** Map p75 A2 ㉓
In 2007, this centenarian hotel transformed its discreet, highly regarded but old-fashioned bar into a swish landmark destination. Dukes' famous dry martinis are flamboyantly made at guests' tables – you should expect to pay plenty for the privilege, but you won't regret it.

Inn The Park

St James's Park, SW1A 2BJ (7451 9999, www.innthepark.com). St James's Park tube. **Open** 8am-9pm Mon-Fri; 9am-9pm Sat, Sun. **££. British café-restaurant.** Map p75 B2 ㉔
Self-service customers fight over tables at the back, while the front terrace overlooking the lake is reserved for the fatter of wallet. The restaurant is open from (build your own) breakfast to dinner, with the accent on in-season, British ingredients. While the quality of the food sometimes disappoints, the location never does.

Sake No Hana

23 St James's Street, SW1A 1HA (7925 8988). Green Park tube. **Open** noon-2.30pm, 6-11pm Mon-Thur; noon-2.30pm, 6-11.30pm Fri, Sat. **££££.** **Japanese.** Map p75 A1 ㉕
The food presentation at Alan Yau's upmarket venture is unmistakably high-end, as is architect Kengo Kuma's cool tatami and cedar design. Sashimi and sushi account for much of the menu, but pricier cooked dishes make menu-perusing more interesting.

Wolseley

160 Piccadilly, W1J 9EB (7499 6996, www.thewolseley.com). Green Park tube. **Open** 7am-midnight Mon-Fri; 8am-midnight Sat, Sun. **££££.** **Brasserie.** Map p75 A1 ㉖
In its gorgeous 1920s room, the Wolseley shimmers with glamour and excitement, and the dining room is filled with a lively social energy and battalions of waiters. No wonder it's a sought-after venue at all times of day: breakfast, brunch, lunch, tea or dinner.

Shopping

Fortnum & Mason

181 Piccadilly, W1A 1ER (7734 8040, www.fortnumandmason.co.uk). Green Park or Piccadilly Circus tube. **Open** 10am-8pm Mon-Sat; noon-6pm Sun. Map p75 A1 ㉗

The revamped Fortnum & Mason (founded in 1707) is stunning: a sweeping spiral staircase soars through the four-storey building, while light floods down from a central glass dome. The iconic eau de nil blue and gold colour scheme with flashes of rose pink is everywhere, both on the store design and on the packaging of the fabulous ground-floor treats, such as chocolates, biscuits, teas and preserves.

Jermyn Street

Green Park or Piccadilly Circus tube.
Map p75 A1 ㉘
If you've got £200 to drop on a shirt, you've come to the right place: Hilditch & Key (no.73), Emma Willis (no.66) and Turnbull & Asser (nos. 71-72) all continue the proud bespoke tradition of this street. You can finish the outfit off with headwear from Bates the Hatter (no.21A), with its wonderful topper-shaped sign and fine old-fashioned interior.

Piccadilly Arcade

Between Piccadilly & Jermyn Street, SW1 (www.piccadilly-arcade.com). Green Park or Piccadilly Circus tube.
Map p75 A1 ㉙
This colonnaded mall of more than a dozen shops opened in 1909. Check out Benson & Clegg tailors, posh mens- and womenswear at Favourbrook, and the stylish men's footwear and rather unusual accessories of Jeffery-West.

Arts & leisure

ICA (Institute of Contemporary Arts)

The Mall, SW1Y 5AH (7930 0493, 7930 3647 box office, www.ica.org.uk). Piccadilly Circus tube or Charing Cross tube/rail. **Open** noon-11pm Wed; noon-1am Thur-Sat; noon-9pm Sun. *Exhibitions* noon-7pm Mon-Wed, Fri-Sun; noon-9pm Thur. **Admission** free.
Map p75 B1 ㉚
This centre for adventurous arts is facing difficult times. See box right.

Cinematic shake-up

How will the ICA's woes affect London film?

Founded in 1947 by a collective of poets, artists and critics, the **ICA** (left) hosts performance art, debates, art-themed clubbing and anything in-between. But for many years, its chief appeal was to film buffs. The ICA had a decided knack for introducing new filmmakers to London audiences, among them Wong Kar-Wai and Takeshi Kitano.

In spring 2010, there was gloomy news for cineastes. Not only did the **Barbican** (p169) confirm it was closing two of its three screens (it's unlikely to reopen their replacement until 2012), but the future of the two cinemas at the ICA hung in the balance. Recessionary debt meant the ICA was facing a top-to-bottom shake-up. Suddenly the city's art-house screens looked very vulnerable.

The litany of the ICA's woes is now well known: the deficit of £600,000; the emergency £1.2m from the Arts Council; the shedding of a third of the staff. But its problems run deeper. Many critics and filmmakers agree that its cinemas failed to retain their unique identity, and the leadership of Ekow Eshun, appointed artistic director in 2005, has been questioned.

Still, supporters of the ICA remain optimistic. They argue that this crisis will provide an opportunity for the centre to redefine itself as an essential part of the city's cultural scene.

LONDON BY AREA

Chelsea Physic Garden p93

South Kensington & Chelsea

LONDON BY AREA

South Kensington

Once known as 'Albertopolis' in honour of the prince who oversaw the inception of its world-class museums, colleges and concert hall, using the profits of the 1851 Great Exhibition, this area is home to the **Natural History Museum**, **Science Museum** and **V&A**; such is the wealth of exhibits in each you'd be foolish to try to 'do' more than one in any single day. The grandiose **Royal Albert Hall** and overblown, splendidly restored **Albert Memorial** also pay homage to the man behind it all, with **Kensington Gardens** a refreshing green backdrop.

Sights & museums

Albert Memorial

Kensington Gardens, SW7 (7495 0916). South Kensington tube. **Tours** 2pm, 3pm 1st Sun of mth. **Admission** *Tours* £5; £4.50 reductions. No credit cards. **Map** p86 B1 ❶

An extraordinary memorial, with an 180ft spire, unveiled 15 years after Prince Albert's death. Created by Sir George Gilbert Scott, it centres on a gilded, seated Albert holding a catalogue of the Great Exhibition.

Brompton Oratory

Thurloe Place, SW7 2RP (7808 0900, www.bromptonoratory.com). South Kensington tube. **Open** 6.30am-8pm daily. **Admission** free; donations appreciated. **Map** p86 C3 ❷

The second biggest Catholic church in the country (after Westminster Cathedral, p79) was completed in 1884, but it feels older – partly because of its baroque Italianate style, partly because much of the decoration pre-dates the structure: Mazzuoli's late 17th-century apostle statues are from Siena cathedral, for example.

Kensington Palace & Gardens

NEW *Kensington Gardens, W8 4PX (0844 482 7777, 0844 482 7799 reservations, www.hrp.org.uk). High Street Kensington or Queensway tube.* **Open** *Nov-Feb* 10am-5pm daily. *Mar-Oct* 10am-6pm daily. **Admission** *Palace* £12.50; free-£11 reductions; £34 family. **Map** p86 A1 ❸

The palace has launched a multimedia show, Enchanted Palace; for details, see box p94. In front of the palace, Kensington Gardens is only delineated from Hyde Park (p89) by the Serpentine and Long Water. Diana's presence is strong: paddle in the ring-shaped Princess Diana Memorial Fountain or make the kids happy by taking them to the pirate-ship climbing frame in the brilliant Diana, Princess of Wales Playground.

Natural History Museum

Cromwell Road, SW7 5BD (7942 5000, www.nhm.ac.uk). South Kensington tube. **Open** 10am-5.50pm daily. **Admission** free. *Tours* free. *Special exhibitions* prices vary. **Map** p86 B3 ❹

The NHM opened in a magnificent, purpose-built, Romanesque palazzo in 1881. Now, the vast entrance hall is taken up by a cast of a diplodocus skeleton, the Blue Zone has a 90ft model of a blue whale, and the Green Zone displays a cross-section through a giant sequoia tree – as well as an amazing array of stuffed birds, among which you can compare the fingernail-sized egg of a hummingbird with an elephant bird egg as big as a football. Some 22 million insect and plant specimens are housed (with the research scientists working on them) in the new, eight-storey, white Cocoon of the Darwin Centre, and a new permanent gallery of the museum's art collection is due to open in late 2010.

Event highlights Veolia Environnement Wildlife Photographer of the Year 2010 (Oct 2010-Apr 2011); 'Animal Sex' (from Feb 2011); 'Dinosaurs' (summer 2011).

Science Museum

Exhibition Road, SW7 2DD (7942 4000, 0870 870 4868 information, www.sciencemuseum.org.uk). South Kensington tube. **Open** 10am-5.45pm daily. **Admission** free. *Special exhibitions* prices vary. **Map** p86 B3 ❺

Only marginally less popular with the kids than its natural historical neighbour, the Science Museum celebrates technology in the service of daily life: from *Puffing Billy*, the world's oldest steam locomotive (built in 1815), via classic cars, to the Apollo 10 command module. In the Wellcome Wing, the Who Am I? gallery (revamped for summer 2010) explores discoveries in genetics, brain science and psychology. Back in the main body of the museum, the third floor is dedicated to flight (stunning new simulators should be here from summer 2010) and the Launchpad gallery features levers, pulleys, explosions and all manner of experiments for kids. A £4m climate science gallery opens in autumn 2010.

Event highlights 'Cosmos & Culture', 'Listening Post' (until 31 Dec 2010).

Serpentine Gallery

Kensington Gardens, W2 3XA (7402 6075, www.serpentinegallery.org). Lancaster Gate or South Kensington tube. **Open** 10am-6pm daily. **Admission** free; donations appreciated. **Map** p86 B1 ❻

This secluded, small and airy gallery mounts rolling, two-monthly exhibitions by up-to-the-minute artists, along with the annual Serpentine Pavilion project (June-Sept), a specially commissioned temporary structure designed by internationally renowned architects.

Victoria & Albert Museum

Cromwell Road, SW7 2RL (7942 2000, www.vam.ac.uk). South Kensington tube. **Open** 10am-5.45pm Mon-Thur, Sat, Sun; 10am-10pm Fri. *Tours* hourly, 10.30am-3.30pm daily. **Admission** free. *Special exhibitions* prices vary. **Map** p86 C3 ❼

LONDON BY AREA

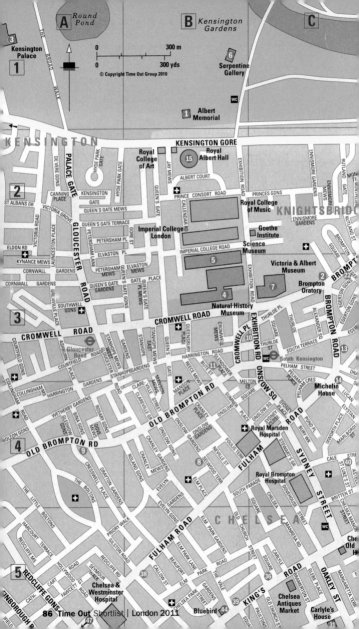

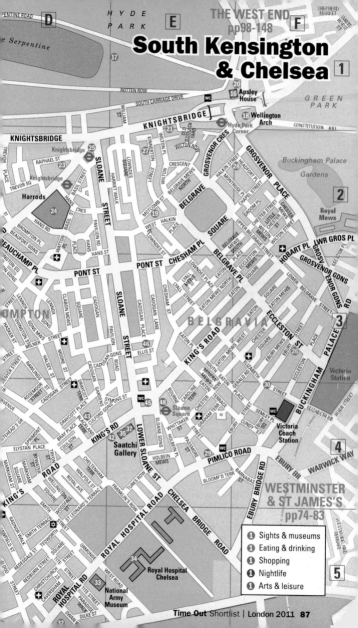

South Kensington & Chelsea

THE WEST END pp98-148

SHEPHERD MARKET

D

E

F

1

HYDE PARK

e Serpentine

SERPENTINE ROAD

17

ROTTEN ROW

SOUTH CARRIAGE DRIVE

WC

20
16 Apsley House

GREEN PARK

CONSTITUTION HILL

WILLIAM

KNIGHTSBRIDGE

21

18 Wellington Arch

Hyde Park Corner

KNIGHTSBRIDGE

25 Knightsbridge

RAPHAEL ST

23

Knightsbridge

TREVOR SQ

KENNINGTON

WILTON PL

WILTON ROW

GROSVENOR CRES

HALKIN STREET

HEADFORT PL

MONTROSE PL

CHAPEL STREET

GROSVENOR PLACE

Buckingham Palace Gardens

2

Royal Mews

TREVOR PLACE

BASIL STREET

SLOANE

LOWNDES SQUARE

CRESCENT

BELGRAVE MEWS NORTH

EATON PL

CHESTER ST

CHESTER MEWS

WILTON ST

CHESTER MEWS

LWR GROS GDNS

Harrods

24

HANS RD

HANS CRES

BASIL ST

STREET

HARRIET WALK

MOTCOMB ST

WEST HALKIN ST

BELGRAVE

UPPER BELGRAVE STREET

WILTON STREET

HOBART PL

GROSVENOR GDNS

BEAUCHAMP PL

BROMPTON GDNS

BEAUFORT GDNS

HANS RD

WALTON

HANS PLACE

PAVILION RD

PONT ST

WEST HALKIN ST

SQUARE

BELGRAVE MEWS SOUTH

ECCLESTON

UPPER BELGRAVE STREET

LOWER BELGRAVE STREET

GROSVENOR GDNS

3

BROMPTON GDNS

PONT ST

CHESHAM PL

BELGRAVE PL

EATON

EATON MEWS NORTH

EATON SQUARE

BELGRAVE MEWS

LOWER BELGRAVE STREET

BUCKINGHAM PALACE

OMPTON

LENNOX GDNS

LENNOX GDNS

CLABON MEWS

CADOGAN

CADOGAN PLACE

CHESHAM STREET

LYALL STREET

CADOGAN LANE

EATON PL

LOWNDES PLACE

LYALL MEWS

EATON MEWS WEST

EATON MEWS SOUTH

EATON

CHESTER ROW

ELIZABETH ST

EBURY MEWS

BELGRAVIA

ECCLESTON ST

ECCLESTON PLACE

Victoria Station

MILNER

HALSEY ST

MOORE ST

DRAYTON GDNS

PAVILION ROAD

SLOANE

STREET

ELLIS ST

46

KING'S ROAD

SOUTH EATON

EATON TERRACE

GERALD ROAD

SEBASTIAN ST

EBURY STREET

ECCLESTON ST

30

STREET

Victoria Station

ROSEMOOR ST

CADOGAN GDNS

CADOGAN

SYMONS ST

WC
45

48

Sloane Square

BOURNE

CAROLINE TERRACE

CHESTER

GRAHAM TERRACE

CUNDY ST

SEMLEY PL

WC

Victoria Coach Station

ELYSTAN PLACE

BRAY PLACE

43

CULFORD GDNS

King's RD

35

42

Saatchi Gallery

COULSON ST

LOWER SLOANE ST

SLOANE GDNS

WHITTAKER ST

HOLBEIN

PASSMORE ST

4

WARWICK WAY

BYWATER ST

CHELTENHAM TERR

WALPOLE ST

FRANKLIN'S ROW

TURK'S ROW

HOLBEIN MEWS

29

PIMLICO ROAD

BLOOMF'D TERR

BARNABAS ST

EBURY BRIDGE RD

EBURY BR

WESTMINSTER & ST JAMES'S pp74-83

KING'S ROAD

RADNOR WALK

SMITH TERRACE

ST LEONARD'S TERRACE

ROYAL HOSPITAL RD

CHELSEA

CHELSEA BRIDGE ROAD

WEST ROAD

34

Royal Hospital Chelsea

ROYAL HOSPITAL RD

33

National Army Museum

ORMONDE

CHRISTCHURCH ST

TITE STREET

DILKE ST

SWAN WALK

❶ Sights & museums
❶ Eating & drinking
❶ Shopping
❶ Nightlife
❶ Arts & leisure

5

The V&A is a superb showcase for applied arts from around the world, and its brilliant FuturePlan programme has revealed some stunning new galleries – notably the wonderful, visually arresting new Medieval and Renaissance Galleries. Among the unmissable highlights of the collection are the seven Raphael Cartoons (painted in 1515 as tapestry designs for the Sistine Chapel), the Great Bed of Ware and the Ardabil carpet, the world's oldest and arguably most splendid floor covering. On the first floor, the new Theatre and Performance Galleries showcase the best of the performing arts, the William & Judith Bollinger Gallery of European jewellery showcases Catherine the Great's diamonds and the Gilbert Collection presents gold snuffboxes and urns.

Event highlights 'Diaghilev & the Ballets Russes' (25 Sept 2010-9 Jan 2011); 'Underground Journeys: Charles Holden's London Transport' (2 Oct 2010-3 Apr 2011); 'The Cult of Beauty: The Aesthetic Movement, 1860-1900' (2 Apr-17 July 2011).

Eating & drinking

Anglesea Arms

15 Selwood Terrace, SW7 3QG (7373 7960, www.capitalpubcompany.com). South Kensington tube. **Open** 11am-11pm Mon-Sat; noon-10.30pm Sun. **Pub. Map** p86 B4 ❽

Nearly 200 years old, the Anglesea was a local for Dickens and DH Lawrence. Aristocratic etchings and 19th-century London photographs adorn the dark, panelled wood walls, adding to the feel of a place lost in time. Real ales are the speciality here, Brakspear Oxford Gold, Hogs Back and Adnams among them. Food, served in a dining area with hearth fire, is traditional English; there's an outdoor terrace for summer.

Cambio de Tercio

163 Old Brompton Road, SW5 0LJ (7244 8970, www.cambiodetercio.co.uk). Gloucester Road or South Kensington tube. **Open** noon-3pm, 7-11.30pm Mon-Sat; noon-3pm, 7-11pm Sun. **Tapas. £££. Map** p86 A4 ❾

Pared down, discreet, smart and decorated not with bulls' heads or hanging hams, but quirky, colourful art, Cambio de Tercio attracts sophisticates and – thanks to the location – Latino ambassadors with their familias. The cooking verges on the extraordinary, with the cured ham and the bread as good as you'd find in Madrid. Waiting staff are knowledgeable and friendly. At no.174, the same owner's Tendido Cero (7370 3685) is a cheaper, but still excellent, version of Cambio.

Madsen

20 Old Brompton Road, SW7 3DL (7225 2772, www.madsenrestaurant.com). South Kensington tube. **Open** noon-10pm Mon; noon-11pm Tue-Thur; noon-midnight Fri, Sat. **££. Scandinavian. Map** p86 C3 ❿

Danes might feel frustrated that this chic, serene and very friendly café-cum-restaurant doesn't catch the excitement surrounding Copenhagen's food scene, but the straightforward home cooking on offer – chicken breast fillet with horseradish cream sauce and roast root vegetables, stegt rødspætte (pan-fried plaice with melted butter and carrots) – is pleasing. Skip the brief, international wine list in favour of the speciality Danish beers.

Oddono's

14 Bute Street, SW7 3EX (7052 0732, www.oddonos.co.uk). South Kensington tube. **Open** 11am-11pm Mon-Thur, Sun; 11am-midnight Fri, Sat. **£. Ice-cream. Map** p86 B3 ⓫

With a minimalist interior and retro seating, this place is all about quality. The focus is on premium ingredients and classic flavours. Even on a grey day, regulars troop in for a fix of vaniglia made from Madagascan vanilla pods. The pistachio is some of the best you'll ever taste, with generous sprinkles of the rich green nut.

Tini

87-89 Walton Street, SW3 2HP (7589 8558, www.tinibar.com). Knightsbridge or South Kensington tube. **Open** 6pm-midnight Mon-Thur; 6pm-1am Fri, Sat; 6pm-12.30am Sun. **Bar. Map** p86 C3 ⑫

Tini is a cocktail lounge hangout for haves and have-yachts, proper posh and a bit ridiculous. Serviced by genteel Gianfrancos in suits and spread under low ceilings, it's laced with traces of pink neon and fancy fleshiness courtesy of Italian-leaning drinks and Pirelli calendars from yesteryear.

Shopping

Caramel Baby & Child

291 Brompton Road, SW3 2DY (7589 7001, www.caramel-shop.co.uk). South Kensington tube. **Open** 10am-6pm Mon-Sat; noon-5pm Sun. **Map** p86 C3 ⑬

Now more than a decade old, Caramel is a great place to head to for tasteful togs for children, from babies to 12-year-olds. The look is relaxed, but the clothes are well finished in modern, muted colour schemes. While the styles have clearly been inspired by the sturdy clothes of the past, they never submit to full-blown nostalgia.

Conran Shop

Michelin House, 81 Fulham Road, SW3 6RD (7589 7401, www.conran.co.uk). South Kensington tube. **Open** 10am-6pm Mon, Tue, Fri; 10am-7pm Wed, Thur; 10am-6.30pm Sat; noon-6pm Sun. **Map** p86 C4 ⑭

Sir Terence Conran's flagship store in this lovely 1909 building showcases furniture and design for every room in the house, and the garden. Portable accessories, gadgets, books, stationery and toiletries make great gifts.

Arts & leisure

Royal Albert Hall

Kensington Gore, SW7 2AP (7589 3203 information, 7589 8212 box office, www.royalalberthall.com). South Kensington tube or bus 9, 10, 52, 452. **Map** p86 B2 ⑮

Another memorial to Queen Victoria's husband, this vast rotunda is best approached for the annual BBC Proms, despite acoustics that do orchestras few favours. Look out for recitals on the great Willis pipe organ and grand ballet extravaganzas at Christmas. **Event highlights** The Proms (mid July-mid Sept 2011).

Knightsbridge

Knightsbridge is about be-seen-in restaurants and designer shops, but that doesn't mean it's particularly stylish. There are terrific people-watching opportunities, though.

Sights & museums

Apsley House

149 Piccadilly, W1J 7NT (7499 5676, www.english-heritage.org.uk). Hyde Park Corner tube. **Open** Nov-Mar 11am-4pm Wed-Sun. Apr-Oct 11am-5pm Wed-Sun. **Admission** £5.70; £4.80 reductions. **Map** p87 E1 ⑯

Called No.1 London because it was the first London building encountered on the road to the City from the village of Kensington, Apsley House was the Duke of Wellington's residence for 35 years. His descendants still live here, but several rooms open to the public and give a superb feel for the man and his era.

Hyde Park

7298 2000, www.royalparks.gov.uk. Hyde Park Corner, Lancaster Gate or Marble Arch tube. **Map** p87 E1 ⑰

At 1.5 miles long and a mile wide, Hyde Park is one of the largest Royal Parks. It was a hotspot for mass demonstrations in the 19th century and remains so today – a march against war in Iraq in 2003 was the largest in British history. The legalisation of public assembly in the park led to the establishment of Speakers' Corner in 1872 (close to

Marble Arch tube), where political and religious ranters – sane and otherwise – still have the floor. Marx, Lenin, Orwell and the Pankhursts have all spoken here. Rowing boats can be hired on the Serpentine.

Wellington Arch

Hyde Park Corner, W1J 7JZ (7930 2726, www.english-heritage.org.uk). Hyde Park Corner tube. **Open** *Apr-Oct* 10am-5pm Wed-Sun. *Nov-Mar* 10am-4pm Wed-Sun. **Admission** £3.50; free-£3 reductions. **Map** p87 F1 ⑱
Built in the 1820s and initially topped by an out-of-proportion equestrian statue of Wellington, since 1912 the 38-ton bronze *Peace Descending on the Quadriga of War* has finished the Arch with a flourish. Three floors of displays cover its history and that of the Blue Plaques scheme; the third gives great winter views from its balcony.

Eating & drinking

Amaya

19 Motcomb Street, 15 Halkin Arcade, SW1X 8JT (7823 1166, www.amaya. biz). Knightsbridge tube. **Open** 12.30-2.15pm, 6.30-11.30pm Mon-Sat; 12.45-2.45pm, 6.30-10.30pm Sun. **£££**.
Indian. **Map** p87 E2 ⑲
Glamorous, stylish and seductive, Amaya is sleekly appointed with sparkly chandeliers, splashes of modern art and a groovy bar. The restaurant's calling card is its sophisticated Indian creations, chosen from a menu that cleverly links dressed-up street food with regal specialities.

Library

Lanesborough, 1 Lanesborough Place, Hyde Park Corner, SW1X 7TA (7259 5599, www.lanesborough.com). Hyde Park Corner tube. **Open** 11am-1am Mon-Sat; noon-10.30pm Sun. **Bar**.
Map p87 F1 ⑳
Surprisingly, those books are real. Whereas bars at other nearby hotels – the Berkeley, say, or the Mandarin

Oriental – draw a younger, more boisterous crowd, the Library remains gentle and mellow long into the night, in part thanks to a tinkling pianist and perpetually low lighting.

Marcus Wareing

NEW *The Berkeley, Wilton Place, SW1X 7RL (7235 1200, www.the-berkeley.co.uk). Hyde Park Corner or Knightsbridge tube.* **Open** noon-2.30pm, 6-10.45pm Mon-Fri; 6-10.45pm Mon-Sat. **££££**. **Haute cuisine**.
Map p87 E2 ㉑
Wareing has jettisoned mentor Gordon Ramsay, but you'd need eagle eyes to notice much difference from when this was Ramsay's Pétrus. The dining room has the same allure, and the carte features much complexity – ballotine of tuna with spicy pineapple, mooli, cardamom and mint – requiring a deft hand to ensure flavours don't go astray. Wareing has just such a hand, and the charms of his restaurant win over most diners. The most significant change is the wine list, which (though still regal) is relatively more affordable.

Racine

239 Brompton Road, SW3 2EP (7584 4477). Knightsbridge or South Kensington tube, or bus 14, 74. **Open** noon-3pm, 6-10.30pm Mon-Fri; noon-3.30pm, 6-10.30pm Sat; noon-3.30pm, 6-10pm Sun. **£££**. **French**. **Map** p86 C3 ㉒
Heavy curtains inside the door allow diners to make a grand entrance into Racine's warm, vibrant 1930s retro atmosphere. The clientele seems to have become less varied in recent times, feeling more male and monied than before, but there's still plenty to enjoy from the menu: try a starter such as garlic and saffron mousse with mussels, or, for dessert, a clafoutis with morello cherries in kirsch.

Zuma

5 Raphael Street, SW7 1DL (7584 1010, www.zumarestaurant.com).

Cadogan Arms p95

Knightsbridge tube. **Open** noon-11pm Mon-Fri, Sun; 12.30-11pm Sat.
££££. Japanese fusion/bar.
Map p87 D2 ㉓
One of London's smartest restaurants, there's more to this 'contemporary izakaya' (Japanese tapas bar, effectively) than its striking wood-and-stone interior. The surprise is that the mix of Japanese and fusion food on the long menu fully justifies the high prices. Zuma's younger sibling Roka/Shochu Lounge (p116) is as good.

Shopping

Harrods
87-135 Brompton Road, SW1X 7XL (7730 1234, www.harrods.com). Knightsbridge tube. **Open** 10am-8pm Mon-Sat; noon-6pm Sun. **Map** p87 D2 ㉔
All the glitz and marble can be a bit much, but in the store that boasts of selling everything, it's hard not to leave with at least one thing you'll like. New additions to the legendary food halls and restaurants include a branch of the Venetian Caffè Florian and the 5J ham and tapás bar, but it's on the fashion floors that Harrods comes into its own, with well-edited collections from the heavyweights. However, the biggest news in 2010 was owner Mohammed Al Fayed selling the place to Qatar Holdings for a reported £1.5bn.

Harvey Nichols
109-125 Knightsbridge, SW1X 7RJ (7235 5000, www.harveynichols.com). Knightsbridge tube. **Open** 10am-8pm Mon-Sat; noon-6pm Sun. **Map** p87 D2 ㉕
The swanky department store feels like it's coasting a little, but you'll still find a worthy clutch of unique brands. In beauty, there's Rodial and New York fave Bliss; for shoes, there are exclusives from the likes of Alejandro Ingelmo and Camilla Skovgaard; in womenswear, check out Derek Lam and Les Chiffoniers. There's a fine food hall on the fifth floor.

Belgravia

Belgravia is characterised by a host of embassies and the fact that everyone living here is very rich. Enjoy strolling through tiny mews, then settle into some plush dining, drinking or shopping.

Eating & drinking

Boisdale of Belgravia
13-15 Eccleston Street, SW1W 9LX (7730 6922, www.boisdale.co.uk). Victoria tube/rail. **Open/food served** noon-1am Mon-Fri; 7pm-1am Sat. **Whisky bar.** Map p87 F3 ㉖
From the labyrinthine bar and restaurant spaces and heated cigar terrace to overstated tartan accents, there's something preposterous about this entire operation. Which we write with utmost affection: there's nowhere quite like this posh, Scottish-themed enterprise, and that includes its sister in the City. Single malts are the tipple of choice.

Nag's Head
53 Kinnerton Street, SW1X 8ED (7235 1135). Hyde Park Corner or Knightsbridge tube. **Open** 11am-11pm Mon-Sat; noon-10.30pm Sun. **Pub.** Map p87 E2 ㉗
It's unusual to see a landlord's name plastered on the front of a pub, but then there aren't many like Kevin Moran left in the trade. The Nag's Head reflects Moran's exuberant eccentricity, both by design (mobiles are banned) and, most strikingly, by accident (the rooms themselves could scarcely be wonkier).

Nahm
Halkin, Halkin Street, SW1X 7DJ (7333 1234, www.halkin.como.bz). Hyde Park Corner tube. **Open** noon-2.30pm, 7-10.45pm Mon-Fri; 7-10.45pm Sat; 7-9.45pm Sun. **££££. Thai.** Map p87 F2 ㉘
Done out in gold and bronze tones, this elegant hotel dining room feels opulent yet unfussy. Tables for two – perfect

for a date – look out over a manicured garden, and the opportunity to share rare dishes of startling flavour combinations from David Thompson's kitchen makes for a memorable meal. Smoky beef stir-fried with oyster sauce, onions and basil was a stand-out.

Shopping

Daylesford Organic

44B Pimlico Road, SW1W 8LJ (7881 8060, www.daylesfordorganic. com). Sloane Square tube. **Open** 8am-8pm Mon-Sat; 10am-4pm Sun. **Map** p87 E4 ㉙
Part of a new wave of chic purveyors of health food, this impressive offshoot of Lady Carole Bamford's Cotswold-based farm shop is set over three floors, and includes a café. Goods include ready-made dishes, and such store-cupboard staples as pulses and pasta.

Elizabeth Street

Sloane Square tube. **Map** p87 F4 ㉚
The location by Victoria Coach Station doesn't inspire confidence, but this is a fine shopping street. You'll find show-stopping jewellery for you at Erickson Beamon (no.38) and stylish accoutrements for your pooch at Mungo & Maud (no.79), as well as fine perfumes at Les Senteurs (no.71) and gorgeous invitations and correspondence cards at Grosvenor Stationery Company (no.47). Tomtom (no.63) sells finest Cuban cigars, while gratification for the stomach is found at French bakery Poilâne (no.46).

Chelsea

It's been more than four decades since *Time* magazine declared that London – by which was meant the **King's Road** – was 'swinging'. These days you're more likely to find suburban swingers wondering where it went than the next Jean Shrimpton, but places like **Shop at Bluebird** have improved the retail

opportunities and the arrival of the **Saatchi Gallery** has put it back on the tourist map. Chelsea proper begins with Sloane Square, spoiled by traffic but redeemed by the edgy **Royal Court Theatre**.

Sights & museums

Carlyle's House

24 Cheyne Row, SW3 5HL (7352 7087, www.nationaltrust.org.uk). Sloane Square tube or bus 11, 19, 22, 49, 211, 239, 319. **Open** *Apr-Oct* 2-5pm Wed-Fri; 11am-5pm Sat, Sun. **Admission** £5.10; £2.60 reductions; £12.80 family. **Map** p86 C5 ㉛
Thomas Carlyle and his wife Jane, both towering intellects, moved to this Queen Anne house in 1834. In 1896, 15 years after Carlyle's death, the house was preserved as a museum, and it's an intriguing snapshot of Victorian life.

Chelsea Physic Garden

66 Royal Hospital Road, SW3 4HS (7352 5646, www.chelseaphysicgarden. co.uk). Sloane Square tube or bus 11, 19, 239. **Open** *Apr-Oct* noon-5pm Wed-Fri; noon-6pm Sun. **Admission** £8; free-£5 reductions. **Map** p87 D5 ㉜
The 165,000sq ft grounds of this gorgeous botanic garden are filled with healing herbs and vegetables, rare trees and dye plants. The garden was founded in 1673 by Sir Hans Sloane with the purpose of cultivating and studying plants for medical purposes.

National Army Museum

Royal Hospital Road, SW3 4HT (7730 0717, www.national-army-museum. ac.uk). Sloane Square tube or bus 11, 137, 239. **Open** 10am-5.30pm daily. **Admission** free. **Map** p87 D5 ㉝
More entertaining than its rather dull exterior suggests, this museum of the history of the British Army kicks off with 'Redcoats', a gallery that starts at Agincourt in 1415 and ends with the American War of Independence. You'll also find some fingertips, frostbitten on

LONDON BY AREA

The enchantment of history

A cool new show takes over at Kensington Palace.

This is what you probably know about **Kensington Palace** (p85): Princess Di lived here before she died in 1997. But did you also know that Mary II died of smallpox here in 1694? That Queen Victoria was born here in 1819 and introduced to her beloved Albert here in 1836? Over a century on, Princess Margaret and Lord Snowdon embraced the Swinging Sixties in the palace, inviting the likes of Peter Sellers and Brit Ekland to their wild parties at the legendary Apartment 1A.

Kensington Palace was a place of glamour, tragedy and love. Now you can immerse yourself in the lives of its princesses thanks to a bold exhibition that merges fashion, art and theatre. Historic Royal Palaces has turned a £12m refurbishment, due for completion in 2012, into an opportunity to stage a dazzlingly creative show.

There's no set path through the exhibition: you wander at your own pace, gleaning information from the knowledgeable palace staff and from 'detectors' (pictured), actors dressed in grey monk-like uniforms who walk the rooms chanting and telling stories. You'll see clothes from the Royal Ceremonial Dress Collection, but there are also new commissions: Vivienne Westwood's 'rebellious dress', for George IV's spirited daughter Charlotte, or Stephen Jones's dream-like installation of hats, inspired by Sir Isaac Newton.

As a child, Queen Victoria had not a moment of privacy – her mother read her journal every night. In her bedroom, designer William Tempest has created 'a dress for dreaming of freedom'. Made from thousands of origami birds that look as if they are about to fly away, it's very moving.

Everest, and Dame Kelly Holmes' gold medals from Athens 2004.

Royal Hospital Chelsea

Royal Hospital Road, SW3 4SR (7881 5200, www.chelsea-pensioners.org.uk). Sloane Square tube or bus 11, 19, 22, 137, 211, 239. **Open** *Apr-Sept* 10am-noon, 2-4pm Mon-Sat; 2-4pm Sun. *Oct-Mar* 10am-noon, 2-4pm Mon-Sat. **Admission** free. **Map** p87 E5 ③④
About 350 scarlet-coated Chelsea Pensioners (retired soldiers) live here, men and – since early 2009 – women. Their quarters, the Royal Hospital, was founded in 1682 by Charles II and the building was designed by Sir Christopher Wren. The museum has more about their life.

Saatchi Gallery

Duke of York's HQ, off King's Road, SW3 4SQ (7823 2363, www.saatchi-gallery.co.uk). Sloane Square tube. **Open** 10am-6pm daily. **Admission** free. **Map** p87 E4 ③⑤
Charles Saatchi's gallery has three floors, providing more than 50,000sq ft of space for temporary exhibitions. Although you might catch the end of 'Newspeak: British Art Now', this erstwhile champion of Brit Art is mainly featuring global art nowadays. Still, some of Saatchi's more famous British acquisitions – among them the brilliant sump-oil installation *20:50* – remain on permanent display.

Eating & drinking

The art deco former garage on the King's Road, **Bluebird** (no.350, 7559 1000, www.danddlondon.com), contains a fine modern European restaurant as well as a shop (p96).

Cadogan Arms

NEW *298 King's Road, SW3 5UG (7352 6500, www.thecadoganarms chelsea.com). Sloane Square tube.* **Open** 11am-11pm daily. **££.** **Gastropub**. **Map** p86 C5 ③⑥

This 19th-century pub was given a rebuild by the Martin brothers, the men behind the Botanist (7 Sloane Square, 7730 0077, www.thebotanistonsloane square.com) up the road. It now has a countrified air, complete with antlers, a stuffed rabbit and fly-fishing paraphernalia, and a smoothly run dining area, but it's a proper boozer with a bar built for drinking. Dishes are expertly cooked and attractively presented; there's also a good cheeseboard.

Gallery Mess

Saatchi Gallery, Duke of York's HQ, King's Road, SW3 4LY (7730 8135). Sloane Square tube. **Open** 9am-9pm daily. **££.** **Brasserie**. **Map** p87 E4 ③⑦
The Saatchi Gallery (above) is home to a fabulous brasserie. You can sit inside surrounded by modern art, but the grounds outside – littered with portable tables until 6pm, if the weather's fair – are an attractive option. There's a simple breakfast menu of pastries, eggs and toast or fry-up until 11.30am, then lunch and dinner take over, with salads, pastas and burgers joined by more ambitious daily specials: perhaps steamed salmon served in a yellow 'curry' broth or saddle of lamb drizzled with yoghurt.

Haché

329-331 Fulham Road, SW10 9QL (7823 3515, www.hacheburgers.com). South Kensington tube. **Open** noon-10.30pm Mon-Fri; noon-11.15 Sat, Sun. **£.** **Burgers**. **Map** p86 B5 ③⑧
Haché is French for 'chopped', but the only Gallic twist on the great American burger here is attention to detail. Rather than underpinning them with skewers, Haché's toasted ciabattas are left ajar so that you can admire the ingredients – they're worth admiring.

Napket

342 King's Road, SW3 5UR (7352 9832, www.napket.com). Sloane Square tube then 11, 19, 22 bus. **Open** 8am-8pm daily. **£.** **Café**. **Map** p86 B5 ③⑨

Looks are everything at this stylish café that goes under the tag-line 'snob food'. The interior is all chic black gloss and space-age perspex, accessorised with iPods on the tables. Food features terrific bread generously filled with high-quality ingredients: try the meal-in-itself club sandwich layered with roast chicken, ham, bacon and emmental. The cakes, though, disappointed.

Tom's Kitchen

27 Cale Street, SW3 3QP (7349 0202, www.tomskitchen.co.uk). South Kensington or Sloane Square tube. **Open** 7-10am, noon-3pm, 6-11pm Mon-Fri; 10am-3pm, 6-11pm Sat, Sun. **££**. **Brasserie**. **Map** p86 C4 ⓬

This is home from home for Chelsea's super-rich, but don't let that put you off. The warm, welcoming room, framed in gleaming white tiles and homespun prints, feels as if it was set up just to make everybody happy. The menu is superb, covering much of what you'd want to eat at any time of day, from the down-home (macaroni cheese) through brasserie classics (moules and steak and chips) to a fine Sunday lunch.

Shopping

Anthropologie

NEW *131-141 King's Road, SW3 5PW (7349 3110, www.anthropologie.eu). Sloane Square tube then bus 11, 19, 22, 319, 211.* **Open** 10am-7pm Mon-Sat; noon-6pm Sun. **Map** p87 D5 ⓭

We were sad to hear of the demise of Antiquarius, a longstanding King's Road landmark, full of dealers in all manner of antiques and collectibles, but it has at least been replaced by some quality. This American shop, which sells deliciously displayed bohemian and vintage-inspired clothes and interior design, now has two shops in London; the other is on Regent Street, see box p137.

Duke of York Square

King's Road, SW3 4LY. **Map** p87 E4 ⓬

West London's first public square for over a century is a former barracks (now home to the Saatchi, p95) transformed into a pedestrian area with fountains and stone benches. Among the high-end high-street clothes shops and terrace cafés, Liz Earle's flagship beauty store (nos.38-39), Myla's luxury lingerie (no.74) and the art books at Taschen (no.12) stand out. There's also a very popular Saturday food market.

John Sandoe

10 Blacklands Terrace, SW3 2SR (7589 9473, www.johnsandoe.com). Sloane Square tube. **Open** 9.30am-5.30pm Mon, Tue, Thur-Sat; 9.30am-7.30pm Wed; noon-6pm Sun. **Map** p87 D4 ⓭

Tucked away on a Chelsea side street, this 50-year-old independent looks just as a bookshop should. The stock is literally packed to the rafters, and of the 25,000 books here, 24,000 are a single copy – so there's serious breadth.

Shop at Bluebird

350 King's Road, SW3 5UU (7351 3873, www.theshopatbluebird.com). Sloane Square tube. **Open** 10am-7pm Mon-Sat; noon-6pm Sun. **Map** p86 B5 ⓬

Part lifestyle boutique and part design gallery, the Shop at Bluebird offers a shifting showcase of clothing for men, women and children (Ossie Clark, Peter Jensen, Marc Jacobs), accessories, books, furniture and gadgets. A recent refurbishment left the shop with a retro feel, all vintage furniture, reupholstered seats and hand-printed fabrics. The menswear range has also had an overhaul, with the addition of various exclusive and sophisticated brands.

Sloane Square

Sloane Square tube. **Map** p87 E4 ⓭

The shaded benches and fountain in the middle of the square provide a lovely counterpoint to the looming façades of Tiffany & Co and the enormous 1930s Peter Jones department store, as well as the grinding traffic. Come summer, the brasserie terraces teem with stereotypical blonde Sloane Rangers sipping rosé; an artier crop of whatever's stylishly edgy will have taken up residence outside the Royal Court Theatre. Nearby, Ortigia's sleek flagship sells divinely packaged smellies.

Arts & leisure

Cadogan Hall

5 Sloane Terrace, SW1X 9DQ (7730 4500, www.cadoganhall.com). Sloane Square tube. **Map** p87 E3 ㊻
Built a century ago as a Christian Science church, this austere building was transformed into a light and airy auditorium. It's hard to imagine how the renovations could have been bettered: the 905-capacity hall is comfortable and the acoustics excellent.

Chelsea Football Club

Stamford Bridge, Fulham Road, SW6 1HS (0871 984 1955, www.chelseafc. com). Fulham Broadway tube. **Map** p86 A5 ㊼
The capital's most recent Premiership winners pipped Manchester United to the title with a stunning 8-0 victory in the very last game of the 2009/2010 season. You're unlikely to get tickets to see any league action here, but you can always check out the museum or seek tickets for European matches or cup ties against lower league opposition.

Royal Court Theatre

Sloane Square, SW1W 8AS (7565 5000, www.royalcourttheatre.com). Sloane Square tube. **Map** p87 E4 ㊽
A hard-hitting theatre in a well-heeled location, the emphasis here has always been on new voices in British theatre – since John Osborne's *Look Back in Anger* in the theatre's inaugural year, 1956, there have been innumerable discoveries made here: not least *Enron*, a successful transfer from here to the Noël Coward (p148) in the West End. All tickets cost £10 on Mondays.

Celeb chef

Heston arrives at the Mandarin Oriental.

Haute cuisine chefs and hotels have been wed for a century, back to the days of Escoffier, celebrity chef at the Savoy. Top chefs have the talent, but rarely the capital for the large, pristine kitchens or brigade of chefs needed to consistently produce first-class results. Luxury hotels have the kitchens, but need 'name' chefs to get them on the map. Collaboration means both get a good deal: the chefs can concentrate on the kitchen without worrying about the rent, while the hotels get a celeb chef to lure in high-rollers.

Heston Blumenthal, the thinking man's chef, has so far resisted the move to a hotel, instead concentrating on his garlanded Fat Duck restaurant in rural Berkshire, the place that brought 'snail porridge' into the mainstream. Yet like many top chefs, Blumenthal's come to realise that celebrity makes him a lot more money than running a restaurant and, with all the television and lab work he's been doing, he's had to get as good as the rest at delegating.

Ashley Palmer-Watts has been Group Executive Chef at the Fat Duck for the last decade, and so is the obvious choice to head up the new restaurant at the Mandarin Oriental hotel. The restaurant is planned for this year, but it's unclear if it will serve signature dishes such as a sorbet which bursts into flame at the click of a waiter's fingers. ■ www.mandarinoriental.com

LONDON BY AREA

Marble Arch

The West End

Marylebone

There is relentless trade on Oxford Street, home to hip **Selfridges**, doughty **John Lewis** and chain flagships for **Uniqlo** and **Topshop**, but few locals esteem the historic thoroughfare. Despite the new Shibuya-style diagonal crossing at Oxford Circus, perhaps an inkling of future improvements, clogged pavements make for unpleasant shopping. Escape the crowds among the pretty boutiques on Marylebone High Street to the north. Among the sights, the **Wallace** is too often overlooked, and **Regent's Park** is one of London's finest green spaces.

Sights & museums

Madame Tussauds

Marylebone Road, NW1 5LR (0870 400 3000, www.madametussauds.com). Baker Street tube. **Open** 9.30am-6pm daily. **Admission** £25.54; £21.46 reductions; £88.78 family. **Map** p99 A1 ①

Founded in Paris in 1770, Madame Tussaud brought her show to London in 1802. There are 300 figures in the collection now, with Angelina, Brad and Keira all receiving the attention their A-list status affords them. Be here before 10am to avoid the queues, or come after 5.30pm and take advantage of the reduced admission charge, or save money by booking online.

Regent's Park

Baker Street or Regent's Park tube. **Map** p99 B1 ②

Regent's Park (open 5am-dusk daily) is one of London's most popular open spaces. Attractions run from the animal noises and odours of London Zoo (p172) to enchanting Open Air Theatre versions of *A Midsummer Night's Dream* that are an integral part of a London summer. Hire a rowing boat on the lake or just walk among the roses.

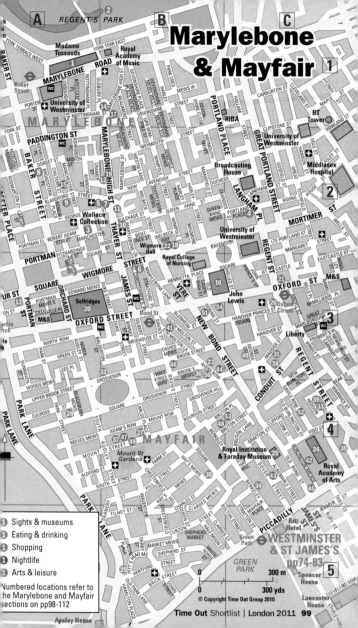

Wallace Collection

Hertford House, Manchester Square,
W1U 3BN (7935 0687, www.wallace
collection.org). Bond Street tube. **Open**
10am-5pm daily. **Admission** free.
Map p99 A2 ❸

This handsome house, built in 1776,
contains an exceptional collection of
18th-century French painting and objets
d'art, as well as a fine array of armour
and weapons. Open to the public since
1900, room after room contains Louis
XIV and XV furnishings and Sèvres
porcelain, while the galleries are hung
with paintings by Titian, Velázquez,
Fragonard and Gainsborough.

Eating & drinking

Artesian

Langham, 1C Portland Place, W1B 1JA
(7636 1000, www.artesian-bar.co.uk).
Oxford Circus tube. **Open** 2pm-1am
daily. **££££**. **Bar**. **Map** p99 C2 ❹

Order any three of the extraordinary
cocktails here, add service, and you
won't get much change from a £50
note. But you'll be drinking them in
style: David Collins has done a fine job
on the decor, the back bar theatrically
lit by huge hanging lamps.

L'Autre Pied

5-7 Blandford Street, W1U 3DB (7486
9696, www.lautrepied.co.uk). Baker
Street tube. **Open** noon-2.45pm, 6-
10.30pm Mon-Sat; noon-3pm, 6.30-
9.30pm Sun. **£££**. **Modern**
European. **Map** p99 A2 ❺

L'Autre Pied offers nuanced cooking in
handsome rooms. Despite the trap-
pings of somewhere that takes food
very seriously, it's an accessible and
relaxing place to eat, and the kitchen
rarely puts a foot wrong, displaying a
light touch and subtle use of herbs.

Comptoir Libanais

NEW *65 Wigmore Street, W1U 1PZ*
(7935 1110, www.lecomptoir.co.uk).
Bond Street tube. **Open** 8am-8pm
daily. **£**. **Lebanese**. **Map** p99 B3 ❻

Part canteen, part deli, Comptoir
Libanais stores cutlery in harissa cans
on its communal bar and is decorated
with kitsch murals. Pick up a wrap
(falafel, say, or chicken kofta) for lunch,
pop by for mint tea and a rosewater
macaron in the afternoon, or linger
over an informal dinner of moussaka
or tagine with organic couscous or rice.
Breads (baked in-house) and sweets are
a key draw. A great pit stop for all ages.

Fairuz

3 Blandford Street, W1U 3DA (7486
8108, 7486 8182, www.fairuz.uk.com).
Baker Street or Bond Street tube. **Open**
noon-11.30pm Mon-Sat; noon-11pm
Sun. **££**. **Middle Eastern**. **Map** p99
B2 ❼

Fairuz is a rough-hewn one-off. A
youngish crowd are attracted by the
relatively low prices at this singularly
rustic and well-regarded Lebanese.
Check out the makloobeh, which is a
terrific stew made of aubergine, rice,
lamb and almonds.

La Fromagerie

2-6 Moxon Street, W1U 4EW (7935
0341, www.lafromagerie.co.uk). Baker
Street or Bond Street tube. **Open** 8am-
7.30pm Mon-Fri; 9am-7pm Sat; 10am-
6pm Sun. **£**. **Café**. **Map** p99 A2 ❽

Famed with foodies for its dedicated
cheese room, Patricia Michelson's high-
end deli also dishes out freshly cooked
café food. Its communal tables are
often packed with devotees.

Galvin Bistrot de Luxe

66 Baker Street, W1U 7DJ (7935 4007,
www.galvinuk.com). Baker Street tube.
Open noon-2.30pm, 6-10.30pm Mon-
Wed; noon-2.30pm, 6-10.45pm Thur-
Sat; noon-3.30pm, 6-9.30pm Sun. **££**.
French. **Map** p99 A2 ❾

Galvin is used for power lunches, but
its lack of stiffness makes it as suitable
for a fun get-together with friends. The
superb chefs might produce the likes
of pithivier of quail and wood pigeon.
Service is occasionally a bit offhand.

LONDON BY AREA

Designs on the high street

Time Out talks to Topshop's freshest design talent.

Quoted in the order pictured above, from left to right.

Gaby Taylor
Designer, Topshop Boutique, 24
Where do you get your ideas?
I love checking out blogs, going to galleries, and I always look to film for ideas. London is a really inspiring place – people here have a great sense of style.

Rachel McCulloch
Junior designer, casualwear, 25
Who do you design for?
I usually have one of my three sisters in mind who are all super-cool but have quite different styles. If I can picture what I'm designing on one of them, I can get more of a vision for the finished garment.

Jess Horton
Design assistant, tops, dresses and skirts, 23
When did you join Topshop?
I started working here about two years ago and have loved every minute. It's so fast-paced you find you're learning so much every day.

Claire Holland
Junior designer, accessories, 24
Who do you design for?
I try to keep in mind what the Topshop girl wants, but introduce 'newness' to make my designs unique.

Kiri Pettersen
Junior designer, jersey tops, 24
Which trends do you love at the moment?
Mermaid hair! I would love a couple of pastel pink streaks at the back of my mane.

Henrietta Emery
Designer, tailoring, 24
Where do you get your ideas?
I love watching old films – *À Bout de Souffle, The Bride Wore Black* – the fashion is always so inspiring.

Golden Eagle

59 Marylebone Lane, W1U 2NY (7935 3228). Bond Street tube. **Open** 11am-11pm Mon-Sat; noon-7pm Sun. **££**. No credit cards. **Pub.** Map p99 B2 ⑩

Every year, we like this pub a bit more. A paint job has brightened it up, but the Golden Eagle remains what it's always been: an unpretentious little boozer (just a clutch of bar stools lined up by the window), not hugely charismatic, but pleasingly untouched by corporate hands.

Golden Hind

73 Marylebone Lane, W1U 2PN (7486 3644). Bond Street tube. **Open** noon-3pm, 6-10pm Mon-Fri; 6-10pm Sat. **£**. **Fish & chips.** Map p99 B2 ⑪

The pastel-hued art deco fryer at this marvellous chip shop is only used to store menus these days (the cooking's done in a back kitchen), but the Golden Hind still oozes local character, entirely in keeping with its Marylebone Lane location. Big portions hit the spot, and the Greek owners and staff really make a fuss over customers.

Providores & Tapa Room

109 Marylebone High Street, W1U 4RX (7935 6175, www.theprovidores. co.uk). Baker Street or Bond Street tube. **Open** noon-2.45pm, 6-10.30pm Mon-Sat; noon-2.45pm, 6-10pm Sun. *Tapa Room* 9-10.30pm Mon-Fri; 10am-3pm, 4-10.30pm Sat; 10am-3pm Sun. **£££**. **Global tapas.** Map p99 B2 ⑫

Chef Peter Gordon dazzles here with such epicurean obscurities as barrel-aged Banyuls vinegar, and produce from his native New Zealand like kumara (a uniquely flavoured sweet potato). The flavours of his complex dishes work in blissful harmony.

Texture

NEW *34 Portman Street, W1H 7BY (7224 0028, www.texture-restaurant. co.uk). Marble Arch tube.* **Open** noon-midnight Tue-Sat. **££££**. **Haute cuisine.** Map p99 A3 ⑬

This period dining room may be grand, but the design is contemporary. Take drinks at the cool-looking bar before slipping into soft leather chairs to peruse the menu and vividly coloured paintings. Chef and co-owner Agnar Sverrisson's dishes come in imaginative sequences, packed with pure and startling flavours. Memorable and fun.

Shopping

Held at St Marylebone Parish Church on Saturdays, **Cabbages & Frocks** market (7794 1636, www.cabbagesandfrocks.co.uk) sells vintage clothing, snacks and independent design. On Sunday mornings visit **Marylebone Farmers' Market**, in Cramer Street carpark at Moxton Street.

Apartment C

NEW *70 Marylebone High Street, W1U 5JL (7935 1854, www.apartment-c.com). Baker Street tube.* **Open** 10am-6pm Mon-Sat; noon-5pm Sun. Map p99 B1 ⑭

A fantasy bachelorette pad, this Marylebone lingerie emporium is a unique concept perfectly rendered. From the boudoir-like fitting rooms and flock of stuffed pigeons to its independent gallery in the basement, it's the city's hippest place to buy smalls.

Cadenhead's Whisky Shop & Tasting Room

26 Chiltern Street, W1U 7QF (7935 6999). Baker Street tube. **Open** 10.30am-6.30pm Mon-Sat. Map p99 A2 ⑮

Cadenhead's is a survivor of a rare breed: the independent whisky bottler. Cadenhead's selects barrels from distilleries all over Scotland and bottles them without filtration or any other intervention. One of a kind.

John Lewis

278-306 Oxford Street, W1A 1EX (7629 7711, www.johnlewis.co.uk). Bond Street or Oxford Circus tube.

LONDON BY AREA

Open 9.30am-8pm Mon-Wed, Fri; 9.30am-9pm Thur; 9.30am-7pm Sat; noon-6pm Sun. **Map** p99 B3 ⑯
Recently renovated – new transparent-sided escalators and a partly glazed roof allow in plenty of natural light – and renowned for solid reliability and the courtesy of its staff, John Lewis also deserves a medal for breadth of stock. The ground-floor cosmetics hall, for example, has glam Crème de la Mer and Eve Lom, but also natural brands like Neal's Yard and Burt's Bees.

Le Labo

NEW *8A Devonshire Street, W1G 6PP (3441 1535, www.lelabofragrances. com). Regent's Park tube.* **Open** 10am-6.30pm Mon-Wed, Fri, Sat; 10am-7pm Thur; noon-5pm Sun. **Map** p99 B1 ⑰
London now has its very own Le Labo perfume boutique: a former estate agent, now kitted out with a slick interior and Japanese mixing den. The brand has a cult following among those who crave designer quality but baulk at anything mass-produced – Le Labo's scents are freshly mixed at point of sale. Perfumes start at £38 a bottle, and we love them all.

Margaret Howell

34 Wigmore Street, W1U 2RS (7009 9009, www.margarethowell.co.uk). Bond Street tube. **Open** 10am-6pm Mon-Wed, Fri, Sat; 10am-7pm Thur. **Map** p99 B2 ⑱
Howell's wonderfully wearable outfits are made in Britain and with an old-fashioned attitude to quality. These principles combine to create the best 'simple' clothes in London. Her pared-down approach means prices seem steep, but these are clothes that will get better with time.

Marylebone High Street

Bond Street or Baker Street tube. **Map** p99 B2 ⑲
With tube stations at its top and bottom, this is one of the most accessible shopping streets in town. Browse the likes of L'Artisan Parfumeur (no.36), elegant lifestyle store Brissi (no.22), inspirational Daunt Books (nos.83-84), the Scandinavian design classics at Skandium (no.86), Kabiri's avant-garde jewellery (no.37) or new concept lingerie store Apartment C (p103). Need a snack? Try 1950s timewarp café Paul Rothe & Son (no.35). For superb, high-fashion artisan shoes, detour to Tracey Neuls (29 Marylebone Lane).

Selfridges

400 Oxford Street, W1A 1AB (0800 123 400, www.selfridges.com). Bond Street or Marble Arch tube. **Open** 9.30am-8pm Mon-Wed, Fri, Sat; 9.30am-9pm Thur; noon-6pm Sun. **Map** p99 A3 ⑳
Selfridges' hyper-energised atmosphere seems recession-proof. The department store remains the first port-of-call for stylish one-stop shopping, and useful floor plans make navigating easy-peasy. On the ground floor, the Wonder Room – 19,000sq ft of luxury brands – goes from strength to strength, and the fashion selections are superb. As well as a slew of events and celeb appearances, there's been a major reworking of the third floor ('3rd Central') and fab new concessions from b store and Alexander Wang. World-class, inventive and contemporary.

Topshop

214 Oxford Street, W1W 8LG (0844 848 7487, www.topshop.com). Oxford Circus tube. **Open** 9am-8pm Mon-Sat; 11.30am-6pm Sun. **Map** p99 C3 ㉑
Topshop's massive, throbbing flagship is a teenage Hades at weekends, but there's nowhere on the high street that's more on-trend. You'll find a boutique of high-fashion designer capsule ranges, vintage clothes, even a Hersheson hairstylist among cheap and well-cut jeans, the Kate Moss range and all manner of other temptations. Topman is catching up with its sister, with a whole new floor having opened last year. See also box p102.

LONDON BY AREA

Royal Institution & Faraday Museum

Arts & leisure

Wigmore Hall

36 Wigmore Street, W1U 2BP (7935 2141, www.wigmore-hall.org.uk). Bond Street tube. **Map** p99 B2 ㉒
Built in 1901 as the display hall for Bechstein Pianos, but now boasting perfect acoustics, art nouveau decor and an excellent basement restaurant, the Wiggy is one of the world's top chamber-music venues. The Monday-lunch recitals and Sunday morning coffee concerts are great value, and pianist Brad Mehldau's involvement in the programming ensures some fine jazz and jazz-classical collaborations.

Mayfair

Mayfair still means money, but these days not necessarily stuffy exclusivity. The tailors of **Savile Row** have loosened their ties a little, and the **Royal Institution** has been given a user-friendly makeover. Even so, there's enough old-world decorum here to satisfy the most fastidious visitor, from elegant shopping arcades to five-star hotels. **Piccadilly Circus** remains its infuriating self.

Sights & museums

Handel House Museum

25 Brook Street (entrance Lancashire Court), W1K 4HB (7399 1953, www. handelhouse.org). Bond Street tube. **Open** 10am-6pm Tue, Wed, Fri, Sat; 10am-8pm Thur; noon-6pm Sun. **Admission** £5; free-£4.50 reductions. **Map** p99 B3 ㉓
George Frideric Handel settled in this Mayfair house aged 37, remaining here until his death in 1759. The house has been beautifully restored with original and recreated furnishings, paintings and a welter of the composer's scores (in the same room as photos of Jimi Hendrix, who lived next door). There are recitals every Thursday.

Royal Academy of Arts

Burlington House, Piccadilly, W1J 0BD (7300 8000, www.royalacademy.org. uk). Green Park or Piccadilly Circus tube. **Open** 10am-6pm Mon-Thur, Sat, Sun; 10am-10pm Fri. **Admission** free. *Special exhibitions* prices vary. **Map** p99 C4 ㉔
Britain's first art school, founded in 1768, moved to the extravagantly Palladian Burlington House a century later. You'll have to pay for blockbuster exhibitions in the Sackler Wing or main galleries ('The Real Van Gogh' was a huge hit this year), but shows in the John Madejski Fine Rooms – drawn from the RA's holdings (which range from Constable to Hockney) – are free. **Event highlights** Summer Exhibition (June-Aug 2011).

Royal Institution & Faraday Museum

21 Albemarle Street, W1S 4BS (7409 2992, www.rigb.org). Green Park tube. **Open** 9am-5pm Mon-Fri. **Admission** free. **Map** p99 C4 ㉕
The Royal Institution has been at the forefront of scientific achievements for more than 200 years. Following a complete rebuild, accessibility is now the key word: a revamp of the Michael Faraday Laboratory (a replica of the electromagnetic pioneer's workspace); a new events programme, with light-hearted Family Fun Days; and the Time & Space restaurant-café.

Eating & drinking

Chisou

4 Princes Street, W1B 2LE (7629 3931, www.chisou.co.uk). Oxford Circus tube. **Open** noon-2.30pm, 6-10.15pm Mon-Sat. **££**. **Japanese**. **Map** p99 C3 ㉖
Chisou looks quiet, but inside it hums with activity. Salted belly pork, and the pure ume cha (rice in a hot broth with pickled plum) are highlights, and there's a serious saké and shochu list. Pop next door for noodles and donburi.

LONDON BY AREA

Connaught Bar

16 Carlos Place, W1K 2AL (7499 7070, www.theconnaught.com). Bond Street tube. **Open** 4pm-1am Mon-Sat. **££££. Cocktail bar**. Map p99 B4 **27**

The Connaught is one of London's most properly old-fashioned luxury hotels (p202) – but this is one hell of a sexy bar, with a sleek, black-and-chrome, cruise-liner style interior, and well-crafted cocktails to match. Across the corridor, the equally impressive Coburg Bar (7499 7070) specialises in more traditional mixed drinks.

Corrigan's Mayfair

28 Upper Grosvenor Street, W1K 7EH (7499 9943, www.corrigansmayfair. com). Marble Arch tube. **Open** noon-3pm, 6-11pm Mon-Fri; 6-10.30pm Sat; noon-4pm, 6-9.30pm Sun. **££££**. **British**. Map p99 A4 **28**

For a fine-dining operation in such a slick setting, Corrigan's is a remarkably relaxed place, with formal yet smiling staff. Dishes from the long menu exceed most expectations: from octopus carpaccio with baby squid to the enigmatic 'chocolate, hazelnut', all beautifully arranged.

Galvin at Windows

Hilton, 22 Park Lane, W1K 1BE (7208 4021, www.galvinatwindows.com). Green Park or Hyde Park Corner tube. **Open** 11am-1am Mon-Wed; 11am-3am Thur, Fri; 3pm-3am Sat; 11am-10.30pm Sun. **Bar**. Map p99 B5 **29**

With the possible exception of Vertigo 42 (p167), there's no more remarkable site for a bar in London: 28 floors up, with an extraordinary panoramic view of the capital, and a sleek interior that mixes art deco glamour with a hint of '70s petrodollar kitsch.

Gaucho Piccadilly

25 Swallow Street, W1B 4QR (7734 4040, www.gauchorestaurants.co.uk). Piccadilly Circus tube. **Open** noon-10.30pm Mon, Sun; noon-11pm Tue-Sat. **£££. Steakhouse**. Map p99 C4 **30**

Steakhouse chic is what the Gaucho chain's flagship restaurant is all about – from its well-stocked Cavas wine shop to a pitch-dark cocktail bar and penchant for cowskin wallpaper. The steaks? Good, sometimes outstanding.

Hibiscus

29 Maddox Street, W1S 2PA (7629 2999, www.hibiscusrestaurant.co.uk). Oxford Circus tube. **Open** noon-2.30pm, 6.30-10pm Tue-Fri; 6-10pm Fri. **£££. Haute cuisine**. Map p99 C3 **31**

Small and intimate, Hibiscus is one of the capital's most exciting places to eat. Chef-patron Claude Bosi is a kitchen magician, playing with texture and flavour in ways that challenge and excite, without making diners feel they're in some weird experiment.

Maze

10-13 Grosvenor Square, W1K 6JP (7107 0000, www.gordonramsay.com). Bond Street tube. **Open** noon-2.30pm, 6-10.30pm daily. **£££. Haute cuisine**. Map p99 B3 **32**

Maze owes its success to recently departed chef Jason Atherton. He earned accolades for his sophisticated tapas, miniature main courses and awe-inspiring desserts. The modern, spacious set-up, with a cocktail bar by the entrance, remains – but how will his successor's food match up?

Momo

25 Heddon Street, W1B 4BH (7434 4040, www.momoresto.com). Piccadilly Circus tube. **Open** noon-2.30pm, 6.30-11.30pm Mon-Sat; 6.30-11.30pm Sun. **£££. North African**. Map p99 C4 **33**

A big reputation, cool Marrakech-style decor, great Maghrebi soundtrack and some of the best North African food in London keep punters pouring in to Momo for an experience to savour.

Nobu Berkeley Street

15 Berkeley Street, W1J 8DY (7290 9222, www.noburestaurants.com). Green Park tube. **Open** noon-2.15pm,

6-11pm Mon-Wed; noon-2.15pm, 6pm-midnight Thur, Fri; 6pm-midnight Sat; 6-9.15pm Sun. *Bar* noon-1am Mon-Wed; noon-2am Thur, Fri; 6pm-2am Sat; 6pm-11pm Sun. £££££. **Japanese fusion**. Map p99 C4 ③④

The upstairs restaurant and sushi bar at this branch of Nobu still buzz with celeb-studded glamour, the cooking is as sublime as the interior is swish.

Only Running Footman

5 Charles Street, W1J 5DF (7499 2988, www.therunningfootman.biz). Green Park tube. **Open** 7.30am-midnight daily. **Pub**. Map p99 B4 ③⑤

Reopening a few years back after a huge refurb, this place looks as if it's been here forever. On the ground floor, jolly chaps prop up the mahogany bar, enjoying three decent ales on draught and an extensive menu: anything from a bacon buttie takeaway to Welsh rarebit with watercress, or £7.50 eggs benedict for breakfast.

La Petite Maison

54 Brooks Mews, W1K 4EG (7495 4774, www.lpmlondon.co.uk). Bond Street tube. **Open** noon-2.15pm, 6-10pm daily. £££. **Mediterranean**. Map p99 B3 ③⑥

Defiantly bucking the recession with ever-full lunch sittings, La Petite Maison hums loudly with the chat of tanned men and glossy-haired women, dressed expensively. But rest assured that the French-Mediterranean food of chef Raphael Duntoye is fabulously uncomplicated in its luxuriousness.

Scott's

20 Mount Street, W1K 2HE (7495 7309, www.caprice-holdings.co.uk). Bond Street or Green Park tube. **Open** noon-10.30pm Mon-Sat; noon-10pm Sun. £££££. **Fish & seafood**. Map p99 B4 ③⑦

Of the celebrity hangouts in the capital, Scott's is the one that most justifies the hype: from the greeting by doorman Sean to the look-at-me contemporary British art on the walls and the glossy Rich List crowd. The food – perhaps tiny boar sausages with chilled rock oysters – gets better and better.

Sketch: The Parlour

9 Conduit Street, W1S 2XJ (0870 777 4488, www.sketch.uk.com). Oxford Circus tube. **Open** 8am-9pm Mon-Fri; 10am-9pm Sat. £££. **Café**. Map p99 C3 ③⑧

Of the three parts of Pierre Gagnaire's legendarily expensive Sketch, which also include Gallery's destination dining and Lecture Room's haute-beyond-haute cuisine, Parlour appeals the most for its tongue-in-cheek sexiness. Saucy nudes illustrate the chairs, and the chandelier appears to be covered with red fishnet tights. The menu includes simple hearty dishes and quirky high-concept creations, such as the club sandwich with red-and-green bread and a layer of stencilled jelly on top.

Tibits

12-14 Heddon Street, W1B 4DA (7758 4110, www.tibits.ch). Oxford Circus tube. **Open** 9am-10.30pm Mon-Wed; 9am-midnight Thur-Sat; 10am-10.30pm Sun. ££. **Vegetarian**. Map p99 C4 ③⑨

It's all California-cool in this groovy vegetarian export from Switzerland. The buffet-cum-pay-per-100g concept left us sceptical at first, but the global offerings have proven to be notches above the usual all-you-can-eat gaff.

Wild Honey

12 St George Street, W1S 2FB (7758 9160, www.wildhoneyrestaurant.co.uk). Bond Street or Oxford Circus tube. **Open** noon-2.30pm, 6-11pm Mon-Sat; noon-3pm, 6-10.30pm Sun. £££. **Modern European**. Map p99 C3 ④⓪

This sister of Arbutus (p127) has both charm and professionalism. The oak-panelled walls could be stifling, but modern artworks banish thoughts of the old world, and a happy buzz predominates. The menu ranges across the best of the UK and Europe.

Shopping

Browns

23-27 South Molton Street, W1K 5RD (7514 0000, www.brownsfashion.com). Bond Street tube. **Open** 10am-6.30pm Mon-Wed, Fri, Sat; 10am-7pm Thur. **Map** p99 B3 ④

Among the 100-odd designers jostling for attention in Joan Burstein's five interconnecting shops (menswear is at no.23) are Chloé and Marc Jacobs. New labels include Felipe Oliveira Baptista, with on-trend oversized blazers and print leggings, as well as exclusives from Balenciaga and James Perse. Browns Focus (nos.38-39, 7514 0063) is younger and more casual; Labels for Less (no.50, 7514 0052) is loaded with last season's leftovers.

Burlington Arcade

Piccadilly, W1 (7630 1411, www.burlington-arcade.co.uk). Green Park tube. **Open** 8am-6.30pm Mon-Wed, Fri; 8am-7pm Thur; 9am-6.30pm Sat; 11am-5pm Sun. **Map** p99 C4 ④

The Royal Arcades in the vicinity of Piccadilly are a throwback to shopping past – Burlington is the largest and, commissioned by Lord Cavendish in 1819, oldest of them. Highlights include collections of classic watches, Luponde Teas, iconic British brands Globe-Trotter and Mackintosh... and the top-hatted beadles who keep order.

Dover Street Market

17-18 Dover Street, W1S 4LT (7518 0680, www.doverstreetmarket.com). Green Park tube. **Open** 11am-6pm Mon-Wed; 11am-7pm Thur-Sat. **Map** p99 C4 ④

Comme des Garçons designer Rei Kawakubo's six-storey space combines the edgy energy of London's indoor markets – concrete floors, Portaloo dressing-rooms – with rarefied labels. Recent additions include the store's own relaxed menswear label, DSM, and Gitman & Co's 1980s-style oxford and gingham check shirts.

Elemis Day Spa

2-3 Lancashire Court, W1S 1EX (7499 4995, www.elemis.com). Bond Street tube. **Open** 9am-9pm Mon-Sat; 10am-6pm Sun. **Map** p99 B3 ④

This leading British spa brand's exotic, unisex retreat is tucked away down a cobbled lane off Bond Street. The elegantly ethnic treatment rooms are a lovely setting in which to relax and enjoy a spot of pampering, from wraps to results-driven facials.

Georgina Goodman

44 Old Bond Street, W1F 4GD (7493 7673, www.georginagoodman.com). Green Park tube. **Open** 10am-6pm Mon-Wed, Fri; 10am-7pm Thur. **Map** p99 C4 ④

Goodman started her business crafting sculptural, made-to-measure footwear from a single piece of untreated vegetan leather, and a couture service is still available at her airy, gallery-like shop. The ready-to-wear range (from £165 for her popular slippers) brings Goodman's individualistic approach to a wider customer base.

Grays Antique Market & Grays in the Mews

58 Davies Street, W1K 5LP; 1-7 Davies Mews, W1K 5AB (7629 7034, www.graysantiques.com). Bond Street tube. **Open** 10.30am-6.30pm Mon-Wed, Fri, Sat; 10.30am-7.30pm Thur; noon-5pm Sun. No credit cards. **Map** p99 B3 ④

More than 200 dealers run stalls in this smart covered market – housed in a Victorian lavatory showroom – selling everything from antiques, art and jewellery to vintage fashion and, with at Biblion (7629 1374, www.biblionmayfair.co.uk), some 20,000 used and antiquarian tomes.

Marc by Marc Jacobs

NEW *24-25 Mount Street, W1K 2RR (7399 1690, www.marcjacobs.com). Bond Street or Green Park tube.* **Open** 11am-7pm Mon-Sat; noon-6pm Sun. **Map** p99 B4 ④

Corrigan's Mayfair p108

Marc by Marc Jacobs boutiques have a staunch cult following. Look out for all manner of branded trinkets and acid-bright gifts at budget prices. A dash of whimsy in deepest Mayfair.

Miller Harris

21 Bruton Street, W1J 6QD (7629 7750, www.millerharris.com). Bond Street or Green Park tube. **Open** 10am-6pm Mon-Sat. **Map** p99 B4 ⑱
Grasse-trained British perfumer Lyn Harris's distinctive, long-lasting scents are made with quality natural extracts and oils, and delightfully packaged.

Mount Street

Bond Street or Green Park tube. **Map** p99 B4 ⑲
Mount Street, with its dignified Victorian terracotta façades and by-appointment art galleries, master butcher Allens (no.117) and cigar shop Sautter (no.106), has taken on a new, cutting-edge persona. At no.12, near the Connaught's cool cocktail bars (p108), Balenciaga has set its super-chic clothes in a glowing sci-fi interior. Here too Britain's first Marc Jacobs (nos.24-25) boutique has been joined by a cheaper, standalone Marc by Marc Jacobs (p110), revered shoe-designer Christian Louboutin (no.17), Parisian perfumer Annick Goutal (no.109) and a five-floor Lanvin (no.128). Further shopping delights (such as Rick Owens) are on South Audley Street.

Paul Smith Sale Shop

23 Avery Row, W1X 9HB (7493 1287, www.paulsmith.co.uk). Bond Street tube. **Open** 10.30am-6.30pm Mon-Wed, Fri, Sat; 10.30am-7pm Thur; 1-5.30pm Sun. **Map** p99 B3 ⑳
Samples and last season's stock can be found at a 30-50% discount. You'll find clothes for men, women and children, as well as a range of accessories.

Postcard Teas

9 Dering Street, W1S 1AG (7629 3654, www.postcardteas.com). Bond Street or *Oxford Circus tube.* **Open** 10.30am-6.30pm Tue-Sat. **Map** p99 B3 ㉑
The range in this exquisite little shop isn't huge, but it is selected with care – usually from single estates. There's a central table for those who want to try a pot. Tea-ware and accessories are also sold, and there are tastings on a Saturday morning.

Savile Row

Oxford Circus or Piccadilly Circus tube. **Map** p99 C4 ㉒
Even Savile Row is moving with the times. US import Abercrombie & Fitch has been ensconced here for a few years now, not far from the cutting-edge and iconoclastic designers (Ute Ploier, Opening Ceremony, Peter Jensen) of b store at no.24A. But be reassured: expensive bespoke tailoring remains the principal activity, with the work-a-day task of shopping for a suit trans-formed into an almost otherworldly experience at such emporiums as Gieves & Hawkes (no.1) or, tailor to Sir Winston Churchill, Henry Poole (no.15).

Timothy Everest

35 Bruton Place, W1J 6NS (7629 6236, www.timothyeverest.co.uk). Bond Street tube. **Open** 10am-6pm Mon-Fri; 11am-5pm Sat. **Map** p99 C4 ㉓
One-time apprentice to the legendary Tommy Nutter, Everest is a star of the current generation of London tailors. He is well known for his relaxed 21st-century definition of style.

Uniqlo

311 Oxford Street, W1C 2HP (7290 7701, www.uniqlo.co.uk). Bond Street or Oxford Circus tube. **Open** 10am-8pm Mon-Wed; 10am-9pm Thur-Sat; noon-6pm Sun. **Map** p99 B3 ㉔
There are two outposts of Uniqlo, Japan's biggest clothes retailer, on Oxford Street alone – but this one is 25,000sq ft and three storeys of flag-ship. Not as cheap as Primark but more stylish, Uniqlo sells simple staples for men and women.

Fitzrovia

West of Tottenham Court Road and north of Oxford Street, Fitzrovia – with its reputation as a gathering point for radicals, writers and boozers, mostly in reverse order – retains enough subtle traces of bohemianism to appeal to the media types that now frequent it. Some of the capital's best hotels and restaurants cluster near Charlotte Street, and these days **Bradley's** or the **Long Bar** are more satisfying places to have a drink than the time-honoured Fitzroy Tavern and Wheatsheaf – unless you're here to pay homage to Dylan Thomas.

Sights & museums

All Saints

7 Margaret Street, W1W 8JG (7636 1788, www.allsaintsmargaretstreet.org. uk). Oxford Circus tube. **Open** 7am-7pm daily. **Admission** free. **Map** p114 B4 **①**
Respite from the tumult of Oxford Street, this 1850s church was designed by William Butterfield, one of the great Gothic Revivalists. Behind the polychromatic brick façade, the shadowy, lavish interior is one of the capital's ecclesiastical triumphs.

BBC Broadcasting House

Portland Place, Upper Regent Street, W1A 1AA (0870 603 0304, www. bbc.co.uk/tours). Oxford Circus tube. **Admission** *Tours* £9.95; £7.50-£8.95 reductions; £15 family. **Map** p114 A4 **②**
There are weekly tours round the BBC headquarters, Britain's first purpose-built broadcast centre, completed in 1932. There are nine tours of various radio studios here each Sunday; booking ahead is essential. Tours are also available at BBC Television Centre (Wood Lane, Shepherd's Bush, W12 7RJ, 0370 603 0304), taking in the news desk, studios and Weather Centre.

BT Tower

60 Cleveland Street, W1. Goodge Street tube. **Map** p114 B3 **③**
The BT Tower (formerly the Post Office Tower) was designed to provide support for radio, TV and telephone aerials. It was opened in 1964 and its crowning glory was a revolving restaurant, closed to the public in 1971 after a bomb attack by the Angry Brigade. The building was Grade II-listed in 2003, but remains accessible only for private functions.

Pollock's Toy Museum

1 Scala Street (entrance Whitfield Street), W1T 2HL (7636 3452, www. pollockstoymuseum.com). Goodge Street tube. **Open** 10am-5pm Mon-Sat. **Admission** £5; free-£4 reductions. **Map** p114 C4 **④**
Housed in a creaky Georgian townhouse, Pollock's is named after one of the last Victorian toy theatre printers. By turns beguiling and creepy, the museum is a nostalgia-fest of old board games, tin trains, porcelain dolls and Robertson's gollies.

Royal Institute of British Architects

66 Portland Place, W1B 1AD (7580 5533, www.architecture.com). Great Portland Street tube. **Map** p114 A3 **⑤**
Temporary exhibitions are held in RIBA's Grade II-listed HQ, which houses a bookshop, café and library, and hosts an excellent lecture series.

Eating & drinking

Benito's Hat

56 Goodge Street, W1T 4NB (7637 3732, www.benitos-hat.com). Goodge Street tube. **Open** 11.30am-10pm Mon-Wed, Sun; 11.30am-11pm Thur-Sat. **£**. **Burritos**. **Map** p114 B4 **⑥**
London's TexMex eateries are ten a peso at the moment, and while there's only one Benito's Hat, the branded interior looks ripe for replication. The production line compiles some of the best

LONDON BY AREA

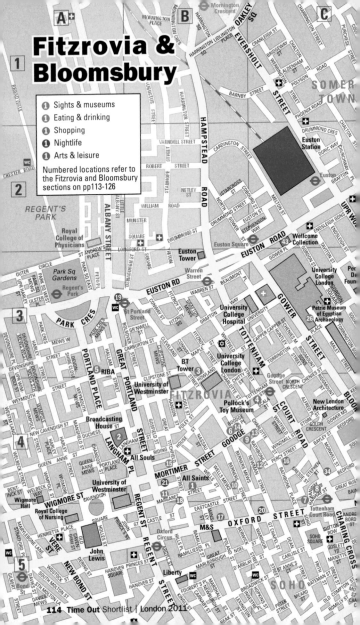

Fitzrovia & Bloomsbury

- ❶ Sights & museums
- ❶ Eating & drinking
- ❶ Shopping
- ❶ Nightlife
- ❶ Arts & leisure

Numbered locations refer to the Fitzrovia and Bloomsbury sections on pp113-126

burritos in town, with the fiery salsa brava made freshly several times daily.

Bradley's Spanish Bar

42-44 Hanway Street, W1T 1UT (7636 0359). Tottenham Court Road tube. **Open** noon-11pm Mon-Sat; 3-10.30pm Sun. **££**. **Pub**. Map p114 C5 **7**

There's a touch of the Barcelona dive bar about this pub and San Miguel on tap, but it ain't really Spanish. Not that the hotchpotch of local workers, shoppers and exchange students who fill the cramped two-floor space care.

Hakkasan

8 Hanway Place, W1T 1HD (7907 1888). Tottenham Court Road tube. **Open** noon-12.30am Mon-Wed; noon-1.30am Thur-Sat; noon-midnight Sun. **££££**. **Chinese**. Map p114 C4 **8**

Alan Yau's no longer running this glam take on the Shanghai teahouse, but its moody, nightclub feel and high-ticket dining still pull a lively, monied crowd. Enjoy the experience for less, by visiting for the lunchtime dim sum.

Lantana

13 Charlotte Place, W1T 1SN (7637 3347, www.lantanacafe.co.uk). Goodge Street tube. **Open** 8am-6pm Mon-Wed; 8am-9pm Thur, Fri; 10am-6pm Sat. **£**. **Café**. Map p114 B4 **9**

The super salads (smoky aubergine or a crunchy sugar snap and red cabbage combo, for example), cakes and sunny breakfasts have drawn a band of regulars to this Antipodean-style eaterie ever since it opened. The espresso machine is the coffee connoisseur's choice – La Marzocco – and the beans come from the excellent Monmouth.

Long Bar

Sanderson, 50 Berners Street, W1T 3NG (7300 5587, www.sanderson london.com). Oxford Circus or Tottenham Court Road tube. **Open** 11am-1am Mon; 11am-1.30am Tue, Wed; 11am-3am Thur-Sat; noon-10.30pm Sun. **Bar**. Map p114 B4 **10**

The Long Bar's early noughties glory days may be a faded memory, but there's still easy glamour for the taking. The bar in question is a long, thin onyx affair, though nabbing one of the eyeball-backed stools is an unlikely prospect. A better bet is the lovely courtyard, where table service, candlelight and watery features make a much nicer setting for cocktails.

Match Bar

37-38 Margaret Street, W1G 0JF (7499 3443, www.matchbar.com). Oxford Circus tube. **Open** 11am-midnight Mon-Sat; 4pm-midnight Sun. **Cocktail bar**. Map p114 B4 **11**

London's Match cocktail bars celebrate the craft of the bartender with a selection of authentic concoctions, such as juleps and fizzes, made from high-end liquor. DJs spin from 7.30pm Thur-Sat.

Newman Arms

23 Rathbone Street, W1T 1NG (7636 1127, www.newmanarms.co.uk). Goodge Street or Tottenham Court Road tube. **Open** noon-12.30am Mon-Fri. **Pub**. Map p114 C4 **12**

The cabin-like Newman Arms has had the decorators in, but is still in touch with its history: a poster for Michael Powell's *Peeping Tom*, filmed here in 1960, faces a black-and-white portrait of former regular George Orwell. In the Famous Pie Room upstairs (you may have to book), pies with a variety of fillings cost around a tenner, and there are good beers on tap downstairs.

Roka & Shochu Lounge

37 Charlotte Street, W1T 1RR (7580 6464, www.rokarestaurant. com). Goodge Street or Tottenham Court Road tube. **Open** noon-3.30pm, 5.30-11.30pm Mon-Fri; 12.30-3.30pm, 5.30-11.30pm Sat; 5.30-10.30pm Sun. **££££**. **Japanese restaurant-bar**. Map p114 C4 **13**

Roka is where to come for restaurant theatre at its best. Smack-bang in the middle of the dining room is the sushi bar and robata grill, putting the chefs centre stage. There's a great saké list, and the brilliant and buzzy basement bar Shochu Lounge (www.shochu lounge.com) – part 21st-century cosmopolitan, part feudal Japan – stays open until midnight.

Salt Yard

54 Goodge Street, W1T 4NA (7637 0657, www.saltyard.co.uk). Goodge Street tube. **Open** noon-11pm Mon-Fri; 5-11pm Sat. **££. Spanish-Italian tapas.** Map p114 B4 ⓮

The artful menu of Iberian and Italian tapas standards served at this dark, calm and classy joint is aimed at diners in search of a slow lunch or lightish dinner. Fine selections of charcuterie and cheese front the frequently changing menu, which features the likes of tuna carpaccio with baby broad beans, and ham croquettes with manchego. One of London's top venues for fuss-free tapas.

Scandinavian Kitchen

61 Great Titchfield Street, W1W 7PP (7580 7161, www.scandikitchen.co.uk). Oxford Street tube. **Open** 8am-7pm Mon-Fri; 10am-6pm Sat; 10am-4pm Sun. **£. Café.** Map p114 B4 ⓯

A lively multicultural crowd of local office workers is kept entertained here by flirty male staff breaking into song (no Abba in our experience) and a self-deprecating sheet of instructions for eating open sandwiches: chicken and green-pepper salad, perhaps, Norwegian smoked salmon, or three types of herring. Soup and hot dogs are also on offer, as well as Gevalia filter coffee. A fun spot for a healthy lunch.

Shopping

Our favourite place for laptop repairs is **Einstein Computer Services** (07957 557065, www. einsteinpcs.co.uk), which operates on a call-out basis only and costs around £20 per hour.

Contemporary Applied Arts

2 Percy Street, W1T 1DD (7436 2344, www.caa.org.uk). Goodge Street or Tottenham Court Road tube. **Open** 10am-6pm Mon-Sat. Map p114 C4 ⓰

This airy gallery, run by the charitable arts organisation, represents more than 300 makers. Work embraces both the functional (jewellery, textiles, tableware) and unique decorative pieces.

HMV

150 Oxford Street, W1D 1DJ (0843 221 0289, www.hmv.co.uk). Oxford Street or Tottenham Court Road tube. **Open** 9am-8.30pm Mon-Wed, Fri, Sat; 9am-9pm Thur; 11.30am-6pm Sun. Map p114 B5 ⓱

With the departure of Zavvi in early 2009, HMV became the last of the mammoth Oxford Street music stores. Plenty of space is given over to DVDs and games, but world, jazz and classical have a whole floor downstairs – and the ground floor has loads of pop, rock and dance music, including some vinyl.

Sniff

1 Great Titchfield Street, W1W 8AU (7299 3560, www.sniff.co.uk). Oxford Circus tube. **Open** 10am-6pm Mon-Wed, Fri, Sat; 10am-7pm Thur. Map p114 B4 ⓲

Sniff aims to be an alternative to the average high-street shoe shop, covering every eventuality from sports to parties. There's a well-balanced mix of brands, established – Ed Hardy, Fornarina, Converse – and up-and-coming – strawberry motif wedges from British designer Miss L Fire.

Nightlife

Lowdown at the Albany

240 Great Portland Street, W1W 5QU (7387 5706, www.lowdownatthealbany. com). Great Portland Street tube. Map p114 A3 ⓳

This rough-around-the-edges basement venue is a simple set-up that

Long Bar p116

hosts stand-up and sketch shows. A good bet for Edinburgh previews.

100 Club
100 Oxford Street, W1D 1LL (7636 0933, www.the100club.co.uk). Oxford Circus or Tottenham Court Road tube. **Map** p114 C5 ❷⓿
Perhaps the most adaptable venue in London, this wide, 350-capacity basement room has provided a home for trad jazz, pub blues, northern soul and punk. These days, it offers jazz, indie acts and ageing rockers such as Nine Below Zero and the Blockheads.

Social
5 Little Portland Street, W1W 7JD (7636 4992, www.thesocial.com). Oxford Circus tube. **Map** p114 B4 ❷❶
A discreet, opaque front hides this day-time diner and DJ bar of supreme quality, a place that still feels, a decade after Heavenly Records opened it, more like a displaced bit of Soho than a resident of boutiquey Marylebone.

Bloomsbury

In bookish circles, Bloomsbury is a name to conjure with: it is the HQ of London University and home to the superb **British Museum**. The name was famously attached to a group of early 20th-century artists and intellectuals (Virginia Woolf and John Maynard Keynes among them), and more recently to the (Soho-based) publishing company that gave us Harry Potter. It is an area that demands an idle browse: perhaps the bookshops of Great Russell Street, Marchmont Street or Woburn Walk, maybe along lovely **Lamb's Conduit Street**.

Sights & museums

British Museum
Great Russell Street, WC1B 3DG (7323 8299, www.britishmuseum.org). Russell Square or Tottenham Court Road tube.

Open 10am-5.30pm Mon-Wed, Sat, Sun; 10am-8.30pm Thur, Fri. *Great Court* 9am-6pm Mon-Wed, Sun; 9am-11pm Thur-Sat. **Admission** free; donations appreciated. *Special exhibitions* vary. **Map** p115 D4 ❷❷
The British Museum is a neoclassical marvel that was built in 1847 – and finished off 153 years later with the magnificent glass-roofed Great Court. This £100m landmark surrounds the domed Reading Room, where Marx, Lenin, Dickens, Darwin, Hardy and Yeats once worked. Star exhibits include ancient Egyptian artefacts – the Rosetta Stone on the ground floor, mummies upstairs – and Greek antiquities that include the stunning marble friezes from the Parthenon. The King's Library is a calm home to a 5,000-piece collection devoted to the formative period of the museum during the Enlightenment (a replica Rosetta Stone is here, if the real one's too crowded). You won't be able to see everything in one day, so buy a guide and pick some showstoppers, or plan several visits. Highlights tours (£8, £5 reductions) focus on specific aspects of the huge collection; free Eye Opener tours offer introductions to particular world cultures.
Event highlights 'Journey through the Afterlife: the Ancient Egyptian Book of the Dead' (4 Nov 2010-6 Mar 2011).

Cartoon Museum
35 Little Russell Street, WC1A 2HH (7580 8155, www.cartoonmuseum.org). Tottenham Court Road tube. **Open** 10.30am-5.30pm Tue-Sat; noon-5.30pm Sun. **Admission** £5.50; free-£4 reductions. **Map** p115 D4 ❷❸
On the ground floor of this former dairy, a brief chronology of British cartoon art is displayed, from Hogarth via Britain's cartooning 'golden age' (1770-1830) to examples of wartime cartoons, ending up with modern satirists such as Ralph Steadman and the *Guardian*'s Steve Bell, alongside fine temporary exhibitions. Upstairs is a celebration of UK comics and graphic novels.

Charles Dickens Museum

48 Doughty Street, WC1N 2LX (7405 2127, www.dickensmuseum.com). Chancery Lane or Russell Square tube. **Open** 10am-5pm daily. **Admission** £6; £3-£4.50 reductions; £15 family. **Map** p115 E3 ㉔

London is scattered with plaques marking addresses where the peripatetic Charles Dickens lived, but this is the only one of them still standing. He lived here from 1837 to 1840, during which time he wrote *Nicholas Nickleby* and *Oliver Twist*. Ring the doorbell to gain access to four floors of Dickensiana, collected over the years from various other of his residences.

Foundling Museum

40 Brunswick Square, WC1N 1AZ (7841 3600, www.foundlingmuseum.org.uk). Russell Square tube. **Open** 10am-5pm Tue-Sat; 11am-5pm Sun. **Admission** £5; free-£4 reductions. **Map** p115 D3 ㉕

Returning to England from America in 1720, Captain Thomas Coram was appalled by the number of abandoned children on the streets and persuaded artist William Hogarth and composer GF Handel to become governors of a new hospital for them. Hogarth decreed the hospital should also be Britain's first public art gallery, and work by Gainsborough and Reynolds is shown upstairs. The most heart-rending display is a tiny case of mementoes that were all mothers were allowed to leave the children they abandoned here.

Petrie Museum of Egyptian Archaeology

University College London, Malet Place, WC1E 6BT (7679 2884, www.petrie.ucl.ac.uk). Goodge Street or Warren Street tube. **Open** 1-5pm Tue-Fri; 10am-1pm Sat. **Admission** free; donations appreciated. **Map** p114 C3 ㉖

Where the Egyptology collection at the the British Museum (p119) is strong on the big stuff, this fabulous hidden museum is dim case after dim case of minutiae. Among the oddities are a 4,000-year-old skeleton of a man ritually buried in a pot. Wind-up torches help you peer into the gloomy corners.

St George's Bloomsbury

Bloomsbury Way, WC1A 2HR (7242 1979, www.stgeorgesbloomsbury.org.uk). Holborn or Tottenham Court Road tube. **Open** 11am-4pm Mon-Fri; 11.30am-5pm Sat; 10.30am-5pm Sun. **Admission** free. **Map** p115 D4 ㉗

Consecrated in 1730, St George's is a grand and typically disturbing work by Nicholas Hawksmoor, with an offset, stepped spire that was inspired by Pliny's account of the Mausoleum at Halicarnassus. Highlights include the mahogany reredos, and 10ft-high sculptures of lions and unicorns clawing at the base of the steeple. There are guided tours and regular concerts.

Eating & drinking

All Star Lanes

Victoria House, Bloomsbury Place, WC1B 4DA (7025 2676, www.allstarlanes.co.uk). Holborn tube. **Open** 5-11.30pm Mon-Wed; 5pm-midnight Thur; noon-2am Fri, Sat; noon-11pm Sun. **Bar & bowling. Map** p115 D4 ㉘

Walk past the lanes and smart, diner-style seating, and you'll find yourself in a comfortable, subdued side bar with chilled glasses, classy red furnishings, an unusual mix of bottled lagers and impressive cocktails. There's an American menu and, at weekends, DJs.

Espresso Room

NEW *31-35 Great Ormond Street, WC1N 3HZ (07932 137380 mobile, www.the espressoroom.com). Holborn tube or bus 19, 38, 55.* **Open** 7am-5pm Mon-Fri. **£**. **Coffee bar. Map** p115 E3 ㉙

We're big fans of this minuscule coffee bar, which serves excellently pulled espressos, faultless flat whites and a few snacks. Carefully selected and roasted beans, top-notch execution – come here for London's best cup of joe.

Hummus Bros

37-63 Southampton Row, WC1B 4DA (7404 7079, www.hbros.co.uk). Holborn tube. **Open** noon-9pm Mon-Fri. **£. Café. Map** p115 D4 ③⓪

The simple and successful formula at this café/takeaway is to serve houmous as a base for a selection of toppings, which you scoop up with excellent pitta bread. The food is nutritious and good value. There's a second branch in Soho (88 Wardour Street, 7734 1311) and a third in the City (128 Cheapside, 7726 8011) – handy for St Paul's (p162), but only open weekday lunchtimes.

Lamb

94 Lamb's Conduit Street, WC1N 3LZ (7405 0713, www.youngs.co.uk). Holborn or Russell Square tube. **Open** 11am-midnight Mon-Sat; noon-10.30pm Sun. **Pub. Map** p115 E3 ③①

Founded in 1729, this Young's pub is the sort of place that makes you misty-eyed for a vanishing era. The Lamb found fame as a theatrical haunt when the A-list included Sir Henry Irving and sundry stars of music hall; they're commemorated in vintage photos, surrounded by well-worn seats, polished wood and vintage knick-knacks.

Museum Tavern

49 Great Russell Street, WC1B 3BA (7242 8987). Holborn or Tottenham Court Road tube. **Open** 11am-11.30pm Mon-Thur; 11am-midnight Fri, Sat; noon-10pm Sun. **££. Pub. Map** p115 D4 ③②

You might be wary when a pub has logoed T-shirts and its own history book, but this Grade II-listed corner pub opposite the British Museum pulls in locals as well as tourists with its fine ales. Past customers have included Sir Arthur Conan Doyle and Karl Marx, who unwound here after hours spent in the old British Library.

Wagamama

4A Streatham Street, WC1A 1JB (7323 9223, www.wagamama.com). Holborn or Tottenham Court Road tube. **Open** noon-11pm Mon-Sat; noon-10pm Sun. **££. Noodle bar. Map** p115 D4 ③③

Since starting life in the basement here in 1992, this chain of shared-table restaurants has become a global phenomenon, with branches as far as Cyprus and Boston. The British Wagamamas all serve the same menu: rice plate meals and Japanese noodles, cooked teppanyaki-style on a flat griddle or simmered in big bowls of spicy soup, and served in double-quick time.

Shopping

Ask

248 Tottenham Court Road, W1T 7QZ (7637 0353, www.askdirect.co.uk). Tottenham Court Road tube. **Open** 10am-7pm Mon-Wed, Fri, Sat; 10am-8pm Thur; noon-6pm Sun. **Map** p114 C4 ③④

Some shops on Tottenham Court Road – London's main street for consumer electronics – feel gloomy and claustrophobic, and hit you with the hard sell. Ask has four capacious, well-organised floors that give you space to browse stock that spans digital cameras, MP3 players, radios, laptops as well as hi-fis and TVs with all the relevant accessories. Prices are competitive.

Ben Pentreath Ltd

17 Rugby Street, WC1N 3QT (7430 2526, www.benpentreath.com). Russell Square tube. **Open** 11am-6pm Tue-Sat. **Map** p115 E3 ③⑤

This tiny homeware store, just off Lamb's Conduit Street (p122), stocks a magical variety of items – crockery, vintage books, masonry fragments, soft furnishings – all in accord with with architect Ben's aesthetic. 'Good things for your home', indeed.

Gosh!

39 Great Russell Street, WC1B 3NZ (7636 1011, www.goshlondon.com). Tottenham Court Road tube. **Open** 10am-6pm Mon-Wed, Sat, Sun; 10am-7pm Thur, Fri. **Map** p115 D4 ③⑥

LONDON BY AREA

Half of the basement room at this comics specialist is given over to comics while the other holds a fine stash of manga. It's graphic novels that take centre stage, though, from early classics like *Krazy Kat* and *Little Nemo* to Alan Moore's *Lost Girls*.

Lamb's Conduit Street

Holborn or Russell Square tube.
Map p115 E3 ⓷⓻

Tucked away among residential back streets, Lamb's Conduit Street is perfect for browsing, whether you fancy quality tailoring from Oliver Spencer (no.62), cult menswear and cute women's knitwear from Folk (no.49), cutting-edge design at Darkroom (no.52) or even a recumbent bicycle at Bikefix (no.48). Refuel at the Lamb (p121) or the Espresso Room (p120), then head off the main drag to Rugby Street for Ben Pentreath (p121) or deco accessories at French's Dairy (no.13).

London Review Bookshop

14 Bury Place, WC1A 2JL (7269 9030, www.lrbshop.co.uk). Holborn tube.
Open 10am-6.30pm Mon-Sat; noon-6pm Sun. **Map** p115 D4 ⓷⓼

An inspiring bookshop, from the stimulating presentation to the quality of the selection. Politics, current affairs and history are well represented on the ground floor, while downstairs, audio books lead on to exciting poetry and philosophy sections. Lovely café too.

Skoob

Unit 66, Brunswick Centre, WC1N 1AE (7278 8760, www.skoob.com). Russell Square tube. **Open** 10.30am-8pm Mon-Sat; 10.30am-6pm Sun.
Map p115 D3 ⓷⓽

A back-to-basics concrete basement that showcases 50,000 titles covering virtually every subject, from philosophy and biography to politics and the occult. You probably won't find quite what you were looking for here – but you're almost certain to come away happily clutching something else.

Nightlife

Bloomsbury Bowling Lanes

Basement, Tavistock Hotel, Bedford Way, WC1H 9EU (7183 1979, www.bloomsburybowling.com). Russell Square tube. **Open** 1pm-2am Mon-Thur; noon-3am Fri, Sat; 1pm-midnight Sun. **Map** p115 D3 ⓸⓪

A hip destination for local students and those wanting a late drink away from Soho, the Lanes also puts on live bands and DJs on Monday, Friday and Saturday, sometimes with a 1950s theme. If you get bored of the bands or the bowling, hole up in a karaoke booth.

King's Cross

North-east of Bloomsbury, the once-insalubrious area of King's Cross is undergoing massive redevelopment around the grand **St Pancras International** station and well-established 'new' **British Library**. The badlands to the north are being transformed (to the tune of £500m) into a mixed-use nucleus called King's Cross Central, with **Kings Place** one sign of things to come.

Sights & museums

St Pancras International

(Pancras Road, 7843 4250, www.stpancras.com; see also p212) welcomes the high-speed Eurostar train from Paris with William Barlow's gorgeous Victorian glass-and-iron train shed. For all the public art, high-end boutiques and eateries (notably **St Pancras Grand**, p125), it's the beauty of the original structure that's the real hit. The neo-Gothic hotel that fronts the station is due to reopen in 2011.

British Library

96 Euston Road, NW1 2DB (7412 7332, www.bl.uk). Euston or King's Cross tube/rail. **Open** 9.30am-6pm Mon,

Bloomsbury Bowling Lanes

Wed-Fri; 9.30am-8pm Tue; 9.30am-5pm Sat; 11am-5pm Sun. **Admission** free; donations appreciated. **Map** p115 D1 ㊵
'One of the ugliest buildings in the world,' opined a Parliamentary committee on the opening of the new British Library in 1997. Don't judge a book by its cover: the interior is a model of cool, spacious functionality, its focal point the King's Library, a six-storey glass-walled tower housing George III's collection in the central atrium. One of the greatest libraries in the world, the BL holds more than 150 million items. In the John Ritblat Gallery, the library's main treasures are displayed: the Magna Carta, original manuscripts from Chaucer and Beatles lyrics. Some great events too.

London Canal Museum

12-13 New Wharf Road, N1 9RT (7713 0836, www.canalmuseum. org.uk). King's Cross tube/rail. **Open** 10am-4.30pm Tue-Sun. **Admission** £3; free-£2 reductions. No credit cards. **Map** p115 E1 ㊷
The museum is housed in a former 19th-century ice warehouse, used by Carlo Gatti for his ice-cream, and includes an interesting exhibit on the history of the ice trade. The part of the collection looking at the history of the waterways and those who worked on them is rather sparse by comparison.

Wellcome Collection

183 Euston Road, NW1 2BE (7611 2222, www.wellcomecollection.org). Euston Square tube or Euston tube/rail. **Open** 10am-6pm Tue, Wed, Fri, Sat; 10am-10pm Thur; 11am-6pm Sun. **Admission** free. **Map** p114 C2 ㊸
Founder Sir Henry Wellcome, a pioneering 19th-century pharmacist and entrepreneur, amassed a vast, grisly and idiosyncratic collection of implements and curios – ivory carvings of pregnant women, used guillotine blades, Napoleon's toothbrush – mostly relating to the medical trade. It's now displayed in this swanky little museum,

along with works of modern art. The temporary exhibitions are usually wonderfully interesting.
Event highlights 'High Society' (11 Nov 2010-27 Feb 2011); 'Dirt' (Mar-Aug 2011).

Eating & drinking

The **Peyton & Byrne** café on the ground floor of the Wellcome (above) is a handy stop, and tea at **Rough Luxe** (p205) is fun.

Camino & Bar Pepito

3 Varnishers Yard, Regents Quarter, N1 9AF (7841 7331, www.camino.uk. com). King's Cross tube/rail. **Open** 8am-3pm, 6.30-11pm Mon-Fri; 9am-4pm, 7-11pm Sat; 11am-4pm Sun. *Bar* noon-midnight Mon-Wed; noon-1am Thur-Sat. **£££. Spanish bar-restaurant**. **Map** p115 D1 ㊹
A big, Spanish-themed bar-restaurant in the heart of the King's Cross construction zone, Camino is a shining beacon of things to come. In the bar you can order good tapas, but it's worth sitting down for a proper meal in the restaurant, where the cooking adheres to the central principle of traditional Spanish food: fine ingredients, simply cooked. Just opposite, a tiny, rustic, Andalusian bodega-style bar (5pm-midnight Wed-Sat) dedicated to Spanish sherry (15 types are on offer) is owned by the same people.

Driver

NEW *2-4 Wharfdale Road, N1 9RY (7278 8827, www.driverlondon.co.uk). King's Cross tube/rail.* **Open** 10am-midnight Mon-Fri; 10am-4am Sat; noon-midnight Sun. *Bar.* **Map** p115 E1 ㊺
Spread over five floors and with décor alternating from urban to intricate, this is a soaring yet svelte Swiss army knife of a venue. You can move from gastrotastic pub-style restaurant to a small roof terrace or the la-di-da lounge and a dining room that, as the night wears on, is transformed into a dancefloor with decks. Most strikingly of all, the

Driver has planted a garden vertically on the outside wall. For the best seats, head to the roof.

Konstam at Prince Albert

2 Acton Street, WC1X 9NA (7833 5040, www.konstam.co.uk). King's Cross tube/rail. **Open** 12.30-3pm, 6.30-10.30pm Mon-Fri; 6.30-10.30pm Sat; 10.30am-4pm Sun. **£££. Eco-restaurant.** Map p115 E2 **46**

The USP at this small, eco-conscious restaurant is that 'over 85% of the produce… is grown or reared within the area covered by the London Underground network'. Which is not to say that owner/chef Oliver Rowe's menu is limited or unimaginative: how about sea bass with almond sauce and purple sprouting broccoli, for example?

St Pancras Grand

Upper Concourse, St Pancras International, Euston Road, NW1 2QP (7870 9900, www.searcys.co.uk/ stpancrasgrand). King's Cross tube/rail. **Open** 11am-11pm daily. **£££. Brasserie.** Map p115 D1 **47**

The revival of British cuisine had hardly been evident at its gateways to the world. Now, London has a station restaurant to be proud of: St Pancras Grand evokes a grand European café with contemporary-brasserie style. The well-sourced food is served simply but with ambition, by first-rate, stripy-aproned staff. The 'longest in Europe' trackside Champagne Bar got all the attention when St Pancras reopened, but the Grand is a far better option.

Nightlife

Big Chill House

257-259 Pentonville Road, N1 9NL (7427 2540, www.bigchill.net). King's Cross tube/rail. **Open** noon-midnight Mon-Wed, Sun; noon-1am Thur; noon-3am Fri, Sat. Map p115 E1 **48**

The Big Chill empire rolls on: the festival that became a record label and a bar most recently opened this three-floor house. There's a great terrace, but the real reasons to attend are the chill vibe and terrific DJs. It costs £5 to enter after 10pm on Friday and Saturday.

Scala

275 Pentonville Road, N1 9NL (7833 2022, www.scala-london.co.uk). King's Cross tube/rail. Map p115 E1 **49**

One of London's best-loved gig venues, this multi-floored monolith is the frequent destination for one-off superparties now that many of London's superclubs have bitten the dust. Built as a cinema shortly after World War I, it is surprisingly capacious and hosts a laudably broad range of indie, electronica, avant hip hop and folk. Its chilly air-conditioning is unrivalled anywhere else in the city – a definite boon should the summer get sultry.

Arts & leisure

Kings Place

90 York Way, N1 9AG (0844 264 0321, www.kingsplace.co.uk). King's Cross tube/rail. Map p115 D1 **50**

Part of a complex of galleries and office space (housing the *Guardian* and *Observer* newspapers), the main 400-seat auditorium opened in late 2008 with a wide-ranging series of concerts. Although Kings Place will be the permanent home of both the London Sinfonietta and the Orchestra of the Age of Enlightenment, there's also jazz, folk, leftfield rock and spoken word – sometimes in the second, smaller room.

Place

17 Duke's Road, WC1H 9PY (7121 1000, www.theplace.org.uk). Euston tube/rail. Map p114 C2 **51**

For genuinely emerging dance, look to the Place. The Robin Howard Dance Theatre has 300 seats raked to a stage 15m by 12m wide – an electrifying space in which to showcase the best new choreographers and dancers. **Event highlights** Resolution! Dance Festival (Jan-Feb 2011).

LONDON BY AREA

British Library p122

Soho

Forever unconventional, packed with restaurants, clubs and bars, Soho remains London at its most game. Shoppers and visitors mingle with the musos, gays, boozers and perverts who have colonised the area since the late 1800s. If you want to drink or eat, you could hardly find a better part of London to do so. Have a wander among the skinny streets that radiate off **Old Compton Street**, Soho's main artery – and see if you can't still find yourself a bit of mischief.

Sights & museums

Leicester Square

Leicester Square tube. **Map** p128 C3 ❶
Leicester Square isn't unpleasant by day, but by night becomes a sinkhole of semi-undressed inebriates out on a big night 'up west'. It was all very different in the 18th century: satirical painter William Hogarth had a studio here, as did artist Sir Joshua Reynolds; both are commemorated in the small central gardens, although it's the Charlie Chaplin statue that gets all the attention. For a long time only the tkts booth (p139) and unlikely neighbours the Prince Charles Cinema (p139) and Notre Dame de France (no.5, 7437 9363, www.notredamechurch.co.uk), with its Jean Cocteau murals, were worthy of attention, but look out for the arrival of two new hotels (see box p202) and a new casino (see box p140).

Photographers' Gallery

NEW *16-18 Ramillies Street, W1A 1AU (0845 262 1618, www.photonet.org.uk). Oxford Circus tube.* **Open** 11am-6pm Tue-Wed, Sat, Sun; 11am-8pm Thur, Fri. **Map** p128 A1 ❷
In late 2008, this excellent photographic gallery moved, with its café and shop, to this transitory space. New six-storey premises will fully open here in due course, probably in 2011.

Ripley's Believe It or Not!

1 Piccadilly Circus, W1J 0DA (3238 0022, www.ripleyslondon.com). Piccadilly Circus tube. **Open** 10am-10.30pm daily. **Admission** £19.95; free-£17.95 reductions; £65 family. **Map** p128 B3 ❸
Over five floors of the Trocadero, this 'odditorium' follows a formula more or less unchanged since Robert Ripley opened his first display in 1933: an assortment of 800 curiosities is displayed, ranging from a two-headed calf to the world's smallest road-safe car.

Soho Square

Tottenham Court Road tube. **Map** p128 C1 ❹
This tree-lined quadrangle was once King's Square – a weather-beaten Charles II stands at the centre, very at home by the mock Tudor gardeners' hut. On sunny days, the grass is covered with smoochy couples and the benches fill up with snacking workers.

Eating & drinking

Since the 1950s, Gerrard and Lisle Streets have been the centre of **Chinatown**, marked by oriental gates, stone lions and pagoda-topped telephone boxes. Old-style diners like **Mr Kong** (21 Lisle Street, 7437 7341) and **Wong Kei** (41-43 Wardour Street, 0871 332 8296) are still here, but we prefer the likes of newbie **Ba Shan** (p130).

Arbutus

63-64 Frith Street, W1D 3JW (7734 4545, www.arbutusrestaurant.co.uk). Tottenham Court Road tube. **Open** noon-2.30pm, 5-11pm Mon-Sat; noon-3.30pm, 5.30-10.30pm Sun. **£££**.
Modern European. **Map** p128 C2 ❺
Providing very fine cooking at very fair prices isn't an easy trick, but this place makes it look easy. Although it's not cheap to eat à la carte, the set lunch and dinner are famously good value. Arbutus also pioneered 250ml carafes for sampling wine from the well-edited list.

Soho &
Covent Garden

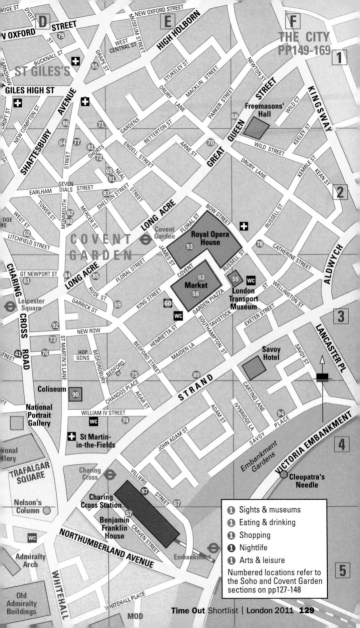

D   OXFORD STREET
NEW OXFORD STREET
E
F   THE CITY
PP149-169   1

ST GILES'S
GILES HIGH ST
HIGH HOLBORN

SHAFTESBURY AVENUE

Freemasons'
Hall   68

GREAT QUEEN STREET

KINGSWAY

SEVEN DIALS

LONG ACRE

COVENT GARDEN

Covent Garden

Royal Opera House   93

ALDWYCH   2

Market   63 58   London Transport Museum   59   WC

WC   60

Leicester Square

Charing Cross Road

STRAND

Savoy Hotel

LANCASTER PL   3

Coliseum   90

National Portrait Gallery

St Martin-in-the-Fields   WC

VICTORIA EMBANKMENT

Embankment Gardens

Cleopatra's Needle   4

TRAFALGAR SQUARE

Nelson's Column

Charing Cross

Charing Cross Station

Benjamin Franklin House   57

87   67

Embankment

Admiralty Arch   WC

Old Admiralty Buildings

NORTHUMBERLAND AVENUE

WHITEHALL

MOD

❶ Sights & museums
❷ Eating & drinking
❸ Shopping
❹ Nightlife
❺ Arts & leisure

Numbered locations refer to the Soho and Covent Garden sections on pp127-148

Baozi Inn

25 Newport Court, WC2H 7JS (7287 6877). Leicester Square tube. **Open** 11.30am-10pm daily. **£.** No credit cards. **Beijing noodles.** Map p129 D3 **6**

The decor, inspired by Beijing hutongs circa 1952, signals kitsch rather than culture, and backless wooden pews are far from conducive to a lingering lunch, yet these Beijing- and Chengdu-style street snacks (including handmade dan dan noodles) are 100% authentic. The baozi themselves – steamed buns filled with pork, radish or egg – are great.

Barrafina

54 Frith Street, W1D 4SL (7813 8016, www.barrafina.co.uk). Leicester Square or Tottenham Court Road tube. **Open** noon-3pm, 5-11pm Mon-Sat; 1-3.30pm, 5.30-10.30pm Sun. **£££. Tapas.** Map p128 C2 **7**

Barrafina is tiny, popular and takes no bookings, but the air is redolent of frying garlic and grilling meat: a fine aroma made more appealing by the dishes waiters carry past as you queue. It's just an open kitchen, stainless-steel bar and tall stools, but what more do you need when the tapas are this good?

Ba Shan

24 Romilly Street, W1D 5AH (7287 3266). Leicester Square tube. **Open** noon-11pm Mon-Thur, Sun; noon-11.30pm Fri, Sat. **££. Sichuanese.** Map p128 C2 **8**

The latest restaurant from the team behind Bar Shu and Baozi Inn (above) looks a treat, with wooden screens and splashes of colour breaking up the sleek, dark décor. The menu, based on xiao chi (small eats), is similar to dim sum, but with many unfamiliar plates. Sichuanese home-style dishes are best.

Bi Bim Bap

NEW *1 Greek Street, W1D 4DJ (7287 3434, www.bibimbapsoho.com). Tottenham Court Road tube.* **Open** noon-3pm, 6-11pm Mon-Sat. **£.** **Korean.** Map p128 C2 **9**

Stick to one of the ten varieties of bibimbap (the classic Korean rice dish, served sizzling in a pot) on offer at this cheap new Korean and you won't go far wrong. Options include mixed mushroom (shiitake, oyster, 'white' and 'black'), seafood, tofu or spicy pork.

Bob Bob Ricard

1 Upper James Street, W1F 9DF (3145 1000, www.bobbobricard.com). Piccadilly Circus tube. **Open** 7am-1am Mon-Fri; 8am-1am Sat, Sun. **£££. Brasserie.** Map p128 B3 **10**

This eccentric new bar-brasserie is a spectacle, from the louche interior (lots of marble and leather, gold chainmail and retro lamp fittings) to the ridiculous, glam pink uniforms of the waiters. 'Classic British favourites', done with variable skill, dominate the menu.

Bocca di Lupo

12 Archer Street, W1D 7BB (7734 2223, www.boccadilupo.com). Piccadilly Circus tube. **Open** 12.30-3pm, 5.30-11pm Mon-Sat. **£££. Italian.** Map p128 B3 **11**

Take an outstanding gastronomic tour of most of Italy's 20 regions with the starter-sized portions of its 'degustation' menu – or larger portions for those who prefer a more traditional Italian meal – served up in an atmosphere of understated luxury at surprisingly reasonable prices.

Busaba Eathai

106-110 Wardour Street, W1F 0TR (7255 8686, www.busaba.com). Oxford Circus or Tottenham Court Road tube. **Open** noon-11pm Mon-Thur; noon-11.30pm Fri, Sat; noon-10pm Sun. **£. Thai.** Map p128 B2 **12**

You usually have to queue at what is the handiest of five branches of this excellent Thai fast-food canteen (the newest is on Panton Street). It combines shared tables and bench seats with a touch of oriental mystique (dark wood, incense) and food that is as good as at many top-price restaurants.

Over at Mark's place

Mark Hix's cool new restaurant and bar.

Mark Hix is part of the small but sparkling constellation of London celebrity chefs who write a bit, cook a bit – and socialise a lot. He used to be head chef at the Ivy and its sibling Caprice Holdings restaurants (among them Scott's, p109, and Sheekey's, p144), and became famous through a cookery column in *The Independent* newspaper. He then opened his own proper restaurant in Farringdon, Hix Oyster & Chop House, to mixed reception: chums in the press loved it; paying customers were disappointed by patchy service and erratic cooking. But Hix's new place (p133) is better – much better.

Mark Hix has two distinguishing traits. The first is his association with YBAs (Young British Artists), which dates back to the Caprice Holdings days; the second is his enthusiasm for British seasonal food. The artistic bent is apparent in both the bohemian clientele and the décor, with the dark, very classic British interior cleverly subverted by artworks which include mobiles by Emin and Hirst.

The British and seasonal mantra has become something of a cliché of late, but Mark Hix does it far better than most, and has been doing it for longer. There's plenty to amuse and interest on the daily changing menu: cod's tongues with girolles; shredded partridge on toast, with piquant elderberries and slivers of water celery; megrim sole, topped with Morecambe Bay shrimps. Desserts include lemon trifle or cider apple and blackberry jelly with vanilla ice-cream.

In the basement, Mark's Bar is groovier than the restaurant, with an A-team of cocktail mixers headed by Nick Strangeway, who displays his characteristic fascination with historic drinks and quality spirits. It may feel like a private club, but (for now at least) it's public. If you're wondering where Cool Britannia went, it's moved here.

Cha Cha Moon

15-21 Ganton Street, W1F 9BN (7297 9800). Oxford Circus tube. **Open** 8am-11pm Mon-Fri; 9am-11.30pm Sat, Sun. **£**. **Hong Kong noodles**. Map p128 A2 ⑬

Like Wagamama before it, Alan Yau's Cha Cha Moon offers fast food of mixed Asian inspiration at low prices, served on long cafeteria-style tables. The main focus is excellent noodle dishes (around £5) from Hong Kong, Shanghai and elsewhere in China.

Dean Street Townhouse & Dining Room

NEW *69-71 Dean Street, W1D 3SE (7434 1775, www.deanstreettownhouse. com). Leicester Square or Piccadilly Circus tube.* **Open** 7am-11.30pm Mon-Thur, 7am-midnight Fri, 8am-midnight Sat, 8am-11.30pm Sun. **£££**. **British**. Map p128 C2 ⑭

One of Soho's most happening restaurants. Dean Street is a hotel (p203) with a dining room and bar that looks ageless and a bit sultry. The dining room by the bar is busy, cramped and loud; the dining room a bit quieter. Comfort food is the key note: mince and tatties, fish and chips, a mixed grill, macaroni cheese, all done with precision in the cooking and wonderful flavours.

Dehesa

25 Ganton Street, W1F 9BP (7494 4170). Oxford Circus tube. **Open** noon-11pm Mon-Sat; noon-5pm Sun. **££**. **Spanish-Italian tapas**. Map p128 A2 ⑮

After running a no-reservations policy for a bit, this informal yet sophisticated spot now takes bookings. Dehesa (black-footed Ibérico pig) appears in nutty-flavoured ham and other charcuterie, but local sourcing comes to the fore in tapas such as confit Old Spot pork belly with cannellini beans.

Dog & Duck

18 Bateman Street, W1D 3AJ (7494 0697). Tottenham Court Road tube.

Open 10am-11.30pm Mon-Sat; noon-10.30pm Sun. **Pub**. Map p128 C2 ⑯

This cosy corner pub has changed little since Orwell hung out here in the 1940s. Today's regulars take their tipples seriously; there are even ale tasting sessions on Monday evenings.

Empress of Sichuan

NEW *6-7 Lisle Street, WC2H 7BG (7734 8128). Leicester Square tube.* **Open** noon-11pm Mon-Thur; noon-11.30pm Fri, Sat; noon-11.30pm Sun. **£££**. **Sichuanese**. Map p128 C3 ⑰

The menu, prefaced by a page stating the chef's credentials, is lengthy, often expensive and intersperses Sichuan with other dishes, but the likes of 'bear's paw tofu' – a classic Sichuan dish, here served as thin slices of pan-fried beancurd with slivers of velvety pork in a pleasingly slithery sauce – are excellent. Service was pleasant, but not very attentive or clued up about explaining the dishes.

Fernandez & Wells

73 Beak Street, W1F 9SR (7287 8124, www.fernandezandwells.com). Oxford Circus or Piccadilly Circus tube. **Open** 7.30am-6pm Mon-Fri; 9am-6pm Sat; 10am-6pm Sun. **£**. **Café**. Map p128 B2 ⑱

If only there were more coffee bars like this in central London: one of their cheese toasties on sourdough bread or pastries make a fine breakfast. At lunch, seats are at a premium but worth the wait. The same people run a Spanish deli around the corner in Lexington Street; their new St Anne's Court café (no.16A) is a short walk away.

French House

49 Dean Street, W1D 5BG (7437 2799, www.frenchhousesoho.com). Leicester Square or Piccadilly Circus tube. **Open** 4-11.30pm Mon-Thur; 4pm-midnight Fri; 5pm-midnight Sat. **Pub**. Map p128 C2 ⑲

Titanic post-war drinkers, the Bacons and the Behans, frequented this small but significant boozer, with the venue's French heritage having enticed De Gaulle to run a Resistance operation from upstairs. Little has changed: beer is served in half pints and bottles of Breton cider are plonked on the famed back alcove table.

Hix & Mark's Bar

[NEW] *66-70 Brewer Street, W1F 9UP (7292 3518, www.hixsoho.co.uk). Piccadilly Circus tube.* **Open** *Restaurant* noon-3pm, 5-11.30pm Mon-Sat; noon-3pm, 5-10.30pm Sun. *Bar* noon-midnight daily. **£££. British/ cocktail bar.** Map p128 B3 ⑳
See box p131.

Imli

167-169 Wardour Street, W1F 8WR (7287 4243, www.imli.co.uk). Tottenham Court Road tube. **Open** noon-11pm Mon-Sat; noon-10pm Sun. **£. Indian tapas.** Map p128 B2 ㉑
Indian tapas is the hook here, but Imli is no passing fad. Cut-price relative of Mayfair's classy Tamarind (20 Queen Street, 7629 3561), this restaurant has plenty of culinary zip. Three dishes amount to a filling two-course meal.

LAB

12 Old Compton Street, W1D 4TQ (7437 7820, www.lab-townhouse.com). Leicester Square or Tottenham Court Road tube. **Open** 4pm-midnight Mon-Sat; 4-10.30pm Sun. **Cocktail bar.** Map p128 C2 ㉒
LAB's two-floor space is invariably packed with Sohoites eager to be fuelled by London's freshest mixologists. Straight out of LAB school (LAB is the London Academy of Bartending), graduates are aided by colleagues of considerable global experience.

Maison Bertaux

28 Greek Street, W1D 5DQ (7437 6007). Leicester Square tube. **Open** 8.30am-11pm Mon-Sat; 8.30am-7.30pm Sun. **£. No credit cards. Café.** Map p128 C2 ㉓

Oozing arty, bohemian charm, this café dates back to 1871 when Soho was London's little piece of the Continent. Battered bentwood tables and chairs add to the feeling of being in a pâtisserie in rural France. The provisions (cream cakes, greasy pastries, pots of tea) really aren't the point.

Milk & Honey

61 Poland Street, W1F 7NU (7292 9949, www.mlkhny.com). Oxford Circus tube. **Open** (non-members) 6-11pm Mon-Fri; 7-11pm Sat. **Cocktail bar.** Map p128 B2 ㉔
You could walk past the inconspicuous door of this semi-mythical, dimly lit speakeasy every day and never know it was here. It's members-only most of the time, but mere mortals can prebook a table until 11pm. What the place lacks in atmosphere in the early evening, it more than makes up for with outstanding cocktails.

Nordic Bakery

14 Golden Square, W1F 9JG (3230 1077, www.nordicbakery.com). Oxford Circus or Piccadilly Circus tube. **Open** 8am-8pm Mon-Fri; 9am-7pm Sat; 11am-6pm Sun. **£. Café.** Map p128 B3 ㉕
A haven of über-stylish Scandinavian cool warmed up with baskets, tea towels, denim aprons and a nature-inspired wall rug. Their fresh-out-of-the-oven cinnamon buns – thick, fluffy and oozing spicy sweetness – are the real deal.

Polpo

[NEW] *41 Beak Street, W1F 9SB (7734 4479, www.polpo.co.uk). Piccadilly Circus tube.* **Open** noon-3pm, 5.30-11pm Mon-Sat; noon-4pm Sun. **££. Italian/wine bar.** Map p128 A2 ㉖
In an 18th-century townhouse that was once home to Canaletto, this is a charming *bacaro* (Venetian-style wine bar). The room has a fashionably distressed look, the wines (served in rustic jugs of 250ml or 500ml) are selected from four good importers, and the food is a procession of small dishes, all of them

Liberty p136

packed with flavour. Some choices are classic Venetian (such as the cicheti bar snack); others are more adventurous.

Princi

135 Wardour Street, W1F 0UF (7478 8888). Leicester Square or Tottenham Court Road tube. **Open** *7am-midnight Mon-Sat; 9am-11pm Sun.* **£. Bakery-café.** Map p128 B1 ㉗

Alan Yau teamed up with an Italian bakery for his latest venture. At the vast, L-shaped granite counter, choose from a broad range of savoury dishes and numerous cakes, tiramisus and pastries. The big slices of pizza have a springy base, the margherita pungent with fresh thyme; caprese salad comes with creamy balls of buffalo mozzarella and big slices of beef tomato. Princi can get hectic, but it's a solid option.

Two Floors

3 Kingly Street, W1B 5PD (7439 1007, www.barworks.co.uk). Oxford Circus or Piccadilly Circus tube. **Open** *noon-11.30pm Mon-Thur; noon-midnight Fri, Sat.* **Bar.** Map p128 A3 ㉘

Sparse, laid-back and bohemian, Two Floors is understated and quite wonderful. Beers and ales here are mainly bottled. There are lunchtime ciabattas too, though even the laziest daytime rendezvous might spark into a raging evening session along the new bar hub of Kingly Street.

Yauatcha

15 Broadwick Street, W1F 0DL (7494 8888). Piccadilly Circus or Tottenham Court Road tube. **Open** *11am-11.30pm Mon-Thur; 11am-11.45pm Fri, Sat; noon-10.45pm Sun.* **£££. Dim sum/ tearoom.** Map p128 B2 ㉙

This groundbreaking dim sum destination is a sultry lounge-like basement den, with glowing fish tanks and starry ceiling lights, where young professionals, Chinese families and suited business people enjoy a succession of freshly prepared, highly impressive, perennial favourites.

Shopping

Albam

23 Beak Street, W1F 9RS (3157 7000, www.albamclothing.com). Oxford Circus tube. **Open** *noon-7pm Mon-Sat; noon-5pm Sun.* Map p128 A3 ㉚

With its refined yet rather manly aesthetic, this menswear label dresses well-heeled gents, fashion editors and regular guys who like no-nonsense style. The focus is on high-quality, classic design with a subtle retro edge.

Anthropologie

NEW *158 Regent Street, W1B 5SW (7529 9800, www.anthropologie.co.uk). Oxford Circus or Piccadilly Circus tube.* **Open** *10am-7pm Mon-Wed, Fri, Sat; 10am-8pm Thur; noon-6pm Sun.* Map p128 A3 ㉛

See box p137.

Bape

NEW *4 Upper James Street, W1F 9DG (7434 2541, http://eu.bape.com). Oxford Circus or Piccadilly Circus tube.* **Open** *11am-7pm Mon-Fri; 11am-6pm Sat; noon-6pm Sun.* Map p128 B3 ㉜

Five hundred people queued eagerly for the opening of this European flagship. Endorsed by Pharrell Williams and distinguished by its pristine white decor, the chic Japanese label's metallic sneaks and camouflage print has discreetly become de rigueur.

Berwick Street

Piccadilly Circus or Tottenham Court Road tube. Map p128 B2 ㉝

The buzzy street market (9am-6pm Mon-Sat), in an area better known for its lurid, neon-lit trades, is one of London's oldest. Dating back to 1778, it's still great for seasonal produce and cheap fabric. The indie record shops that used to be clustered here have taken a pasting over the last few years, but Revival Records (no.30) is full of vinyl beans, and Chris Kerr (no.52), son of legendary 1960s tailor Eddie, is still here crafting brilliant bespoke suits.

LONDON BY AREA

Carnaby Street

Oxford Street tube. **Map** p128 A2 ③④

As famous as the King's Road back when the Sixties Swung, Carnaby Street was until a few years ago more likely to sell you a postcard of the Queen snogging a punk rocker than a fishtail parka. But the noughties have been kind and Carnaby is cool again. Among classy chains (Lush, Muji), Kingly Court (7333 8118, www.carnaby.co.uk) is the real highlight, a three-tiered complex containing a funky mix of chains and independents.

Foyles

113-119 Charing Cross Road, WC2H 0EB (7437 5660, www.foyles.co.uk). Tottenham Court Road tube. **Open** 9.30am-9pm Mon-Sat; noon-6pm Sun. **Map** p128 C2 ③⑤

Probably London's single most impressive independent bookshop, Foyles built its reputation on the sheer volume and breadth of its stock (there are 56 specialist subjects in this flagship store). Its five storeys accommodate other shops too: Ray's Jazz, London's least beardy jazz shop, has moved up to the 3rd floor, giving more room to the first-floor café, which hosts great low-key gigs and readings.

Liberty

Regent Street, W1B 5AH (7734 1234, www.liberty.co.uk). Oxford Circus tube. **Open** 10am-9pm Mon-Sat; noon-6pm Sun. **Map** p128 A2 ③⑥

A creaky, 1920s, mock Tudor department store masterpiece, Liberty has upped its game over the last year with a store-wide revamp – 'renaissance', they called it – that introduced a raft of cool new contemporary labels and a series of inspired events. Shopping here is about more than just spending money; artful window displays, exciting new collections and luxe labels make it an experience to savour. Despite being fashion-forward, Liberty respects its dressmaking heritage with a good haberdashery department.

Playlounge

19 Beak Street, W1F 9RP (7287 7073, www.playlounge.co.uk). Oxford Circus or Piccadilly Circus tube. **Open** 11am-7pm Mon-Sat; noon-5pm Sun. **Map** p128 A3 ③⑦

Compact but full of fun, this groovy little shop has action figures, gadgets, books and comics, e-boy posters, T-shirts and clothes that appeal to kids and adults alike. Those nostalgic for illustrated children's literature shouldn't miss the Dr Seuss PopUps and *Where the Wild Things Are* books.

Nightlife

Borderline

Orange Yard, off Manette Street, W1D 4JB (0844 847 2465, www.mean fiddler.com). Tottenham Court Road tube. **Map** p128 C2 ③⑧

A cramped, sweaty dive bar-slash-juke joint, the Borderline has long been a favoured stop-off for touring American bands of the country and blues type, but you'll also find a variety of indie acts and singer-songwriters down here.

Comedy Camp

Barcode, 3-4 Archer Street, W1D 7AP (7483 2960, www.comedycamp.co.uk). Leicester Square or Piccadilly Circus tube. **Map** p128 B3 ③⑨

This intimate, straight-friendly gay Tuesday night regular is one of the best nights out in town. The audiences are always up for a great evening, and resident host and promoter Simon Happily only books fabulous acts.

Comedy Store

1A Oxendon Street, SW1Y 4EE (0844 847 1728, www.thecomedystore.co.uk). Leicester Square or Piccadilly Circus tube. **Map** p128 C3 ④⓪

The Comedy Store made its name as the home of 'alternative comedy' in the early 1980s. The venue is purpose-built for serious punters, with a gladiatorial semicircle of seats, and still has some of the circuit's best bills.

Regent Street reborn?

Anthropologie revitalises the prime shopping street.

With its bunny-shaped candles, owl-print tea towels and a giant plush narwhal hung over a shabby-chic dining table, **Anthropologie** (p135) has delivered a blow against London cynicism. Battling the city's characteristic gloom into submission, the upbeat US mega-chain opened its first European site on Regent Street in 2009. It was followed in 2010 by another on the King's Road (p96).

'We looked at our London debut as a whole and were excited to find a fabulous building on Regent Street,' explains European MD James Bidwell. Finding the perfect location was one thing, but to breathe new life into an iconic, listed building was quite another. The brand spent months scraping and smashing away at the interior, until they were in a position to rebuild a three-floored mega-store inside the building's shell. It's an ambitious rendering that feels breathtakingly immense, and yet surprisingly intimate.

Shoppers who wander in off the street find themselves in a small anteroom, peppered with trademark craft-edged chic. Move a little further into the store, however, and the space opens into one of the most jaw-dropping new store interiors in the capital. A 200 square metre 'living wall' of plants (fed rather ingeniously from rainwater collected on the roof) spans three floors, leading up from the basement level to a glass atrium that floods the store with natural light.

Anthropologie isn't the only newcomer. Almost all the grand buildings along Regent's Street belong to the Crown Estate, and since 2002 over £750m has been invested in regeneration: Swedish-owned **Gant** and Dutch brand **Sting** are joining the likes of **H&M**, **Apple Store** and **COS**. 'Regent Street is [now] one of the busiest and most innovative shopping destinations in Europe,' says Bidwell. 'We're in great company.'

Hippodrome

NEW *Leicester Square, 10-14 Cranbourn Street, WC2H 7JH (www.hippodrome casino.com). Leicester Square tube.* **Map** p129 D3 ④
See box p140.

Leicester Square Theatre

6 Leicester Place, WC2H 7BX (0844 847 2475, www.leicestersquaretheatre. com). Leicester Square tube. **Map** p128 C3 ④

The main auditorium has a good mix of big-name comedy (Michael McIntyre, Bill Bailey), cabaret (Miranda Sings, Impropera) and straight plays, but we also love the goings-on in the little basement performance space, with its champagne bar. On Friday and Saturday, Just the Tonic delivers top programmes of stand-up.

Madame JoJo's

8-10 Brewer Street, W1F 0SE (7734 3040, www.madamejojos). Leicester Square or Piccadilly Circus tube. **Map** p128 B3 ④

This red and slightly shabby basement space is a beacon for those escaping West End post-work chain pubs. Treasured nights include variety (the London Burlesque Social Club, Kitsch Cabaret, Finger in the Pie Cabaret's talent-spotting showcases) and Keb Darge's long-running Deep Funk.

Pizza Express Jazz Club

10 Dean Street, W1D 3RW (7439 8722, www.pizzaexpress.co.uk). Tottenham Court Road tube. **Map** p128 C1 ④

The upstairs restaurant (7437 9595) is jazz-free, but the 120-capacity basement venue is one of Europe's best modern mainstream jazz venues.

Punk

14 Soho Street, W1D 3DN (7734 4004, www.fabbars.com). Tottenham Court Road tube. **Map** p128 C1 ④

This basement space holds 270 at a squeeze, and the Mapplethorpe-style flower prints and Rock Galpin furniture suit its mix of high-heeled girls and indie mash-ups.

Ronnie Scott's

47 Frith Street, W1D 4HT (7439 0747, www.ronniescotts.co.uk). Leicester Square or Tottenham Court Road tube. **Map** p128 C2 ④

Opened (albeit on a different site) by the British saxophonist Ronnie Scott in 1959, this jazz institution was completely refurbished in 2006. The capacity was expanded to 250, the food got better and the bookings became drearier. Happily, Ronnie's has got back on track, with jazz heavyweights once more dominating in place of the mainstream pop acts who held sway for a while. Lots of fun.

Shadow Lounge

5 Brewer Street, W1F 0RF (7287 7988, www.theshadowlounge.com). Piccadilly Circus tube. **Open** 10pm-3am Mon-Sat. **Map** p128 B3 ④

For professional cocktail waiters, celebrity sightings, suits, cutes and fancy boots, this gay cocktail lounge is your venue. At weekends, expect to queue and pay a hefty cover charge, but it's worth it once you're inside.

Arts & leisure

Curzon Soho

99 Shaftesbury Avenue, W1D 5DY (7292 7686, 0871 703 3988 box office, www.curzoncinemas.com). Leicester Square tube. **Map** p128 C2 ④

All the cinemas in the Curzon group programme a superb range of shorts, rarities, double bills and mini-festivals, but the Curzon Soho is the best – not least because it also has a great ground-floor café and decent basement bar.

Gielgud Theatre

NEW *Shaftesbury Avenue, W1D 6AR (0844 482 5130, 7907 7071 bookings, www.delfontmackintosh.co.uk). Piccadilly Circus tube.* **Map** p128 C3 ④

Hair is a musical about the kind of people you see on the street – if the street you're on is in Manhattan, circa 1967. This version of the 'hippie musical' brings the entire Tony award-winning original Broadway cast to London. Production subject to change.

London Palladium

Argyll Street, W1F 7TF (0844 579 1940, www.sisteractthemusical.com). Oxford Circus tube. **Map** p128 A2 (50)

A musical comedy based on the hit 1992 Whoopi Goldberg movie *Sister Act*, in which a nightclub singer takes refuge from gangsters in a convent. Production subject to change.

Odeon Leicester Square

Leicester Square, WC2H 7LQ (0871 224 4007, www.odeon.co.uk). Leicester Square tube. **Map** p128 C3 (51)

This art deco masterpiece is London's archetypal red-carpet star-studded site for premieres. Catch one of the occasional silent movie screenings with live organ music if you can; otherwise, it will be a comfy viewing of a pricey current blockbuster.

Palace Theatre

Shaftesbury Avenue, W1D 5AY (0871 297 0777, www.priscillathemusical.com). Leicester Square tube. **Map** p128 C2 (52)

Priscilla, Queen of the Desert is brash, trashy and uniquely transporting, thanks to a soundtrack of super-femme anthems ('I Will Survive', 'Finally') and costume design that is on a madly brilliant mission to give the whole of Australia the campest of makeovers. Production subject to change.

Prince Charles Cinema

7 Leicester Place, Leicester Square, WC2H 7BY (0870 811 2559, www.princecharlescinema.com). Leicester Square tube. **Map** p128 C3 (53)

The downstairs screen here offers the best value in town (£4-£9.50) for releases that have ended their first run elsewhere. Upstairs, a new screen shows current releases at higher prices – but at under a tenner, still competitive for the West End. The weekend singalong screenings are very popular.

Prince Edward Theatre

28 Old Compton Street, W1D 4HS (0844 482 5151, www.jerseyboyslondon.com). Leicester Square or Piccadilly Circus tube. **Map** p128 C2 (54)

This is the London home for *Jersey Boys*, the story of Frankie Valli and the Four Seasons. The pace is lively, the sets gritty and the doo-wop standards ('Big Girls Don't Cry', 'Can't Take My Eyes Off You') superbly performed. Production subject to change.

Soho Theatre

21 Dean Street, W1D 3NE (7478 0100, www.sohotheatre.com). Tottenham Court Road tube. **Map** p128 C2 (55)

Its cool blue neon lights, front-of-house café and occasional late-night shows attract a younger, hipper crowd than most theatres. The Soho brings on aspiring writers through regular workshops, and has regular solo comedy shows and drag performances.

tkts

Clocktower Building, Leicester Square, WC2H 7NA (www.officiallondontheatre.co.uk/tkts). Leicester Square tube. **Open** 10am-7pm Mon-Sat; 11am-4pm Sun. **Map** p128 C3 (56)

Anybody can buy tickets here for big shows at much-reduced rates, either on the day or up to a week in advance. It's not uncommon to find the best seats for West End blockbusters sold at half price. Avoid getting ripped off by the touts and come here instead.

Covent Garden

Covent Garden is understandably popular with visitors. A traffic-free oasis in the heart of the city, replete with shops, cafés and bars – as well as the fun **London Transport**

A high-roller hits town

The Hippodrome is set to reopen as a casino.

On the north-east corner of Leicester Square (p127), above an exit from the tube station, is a grand London theatre. At the moment, the only sign of its splendour is high on the roof: a sculpture of a chariot, complete with flamboyantly rearing horses.

The **Hippodrome** (p138) was built by Frank Matcham, master designer of London theatres. From 1900, his Hippodrome hosted circus, variety, dance spectaculars, musicals and gigs. It staged what was probably England's first jazz concert shortly after the end of World War I and from the 1950s, as Talk of the Town, programmed star singers such as Frank Sinatra, Judy Garland, Tom Jones and Dusty Springfield.

The more recent history of this Grade II-listed structure was less distinguished – in the 1980s and '90s it was a tacky Peter Stringfellow nightclub – but a successful season from alt-burlesque circus La Clique in 2008/9 seems to have lodged in the minds of the current developers. Their £15m casino, due to open in mid 2011, will include a 160-seater supper-club for cabaret shows, as well as roulette and blackjack tables, three bars and a signature restaurant. Gordon Ramsay is reported to have been lined up for the latter, although the owners are only talking about 'a renowned Michelin-starred chef'.

Museum – it centres on a restored 19th-century covered market. On the west side of the square, the portico of **St Paul's Covent Garden** hosts escapologists and jugglers. If you're looking for great performances rather than street performances, the **Royal Opera House** is here too.

Sights & museums

Benjamin Franklin House
36 Craven Street, WC2N 5NF (7925 1405, www.benjaminfranklinhouse. org). Charing Cross tube/rail. **Open** pre-booked tours only. *Box office* 10.30am-5pm Wed, Sun. **Admission** £7; free-£5 reductions. **Map** p129 E5 **❺❼**
The house where Franklin lived from 1757 to 1775 can be explored on well-run, pre-booked multimedia 'experiences'. Lasting an intense 45mins, they are led by an actress in character as Franklin's landlady. More straightforward, 20min tours (£3.50) are given by house interns on Mondays.

Covent Garden Piazza
Covent Garden tube. **Map** p129 E3 **❺❽**
Visitors flock to Covent Garden Market for its combination of shopping, outdoor restaurant and café seating, performances by street artists and classical music renditions in the lower courtyard. Most tourists favour the old covered market (7836 9136, www.coventgardenlondon.uk.com), which combines a collection of small and sometimes quirky shops, many of them rather twee, with a range of upmarket gift chain stores. The Apple Market, in the North Hall, has a either arts and crafts (Tue-Sun) or antiques (Mon) stalls set up.

London Transport Museum
The Piazza, WC2E 7BB (7379 6344, www.ltmuseum.co.uk). Covent Garden tube. **Open** 10am-6pm Mon-Thur, Sat, Sun; 11am-6pm Fri. **Admission** £10; free-£8 reductions. **Map** p129 F3 **❺❾**

Tracing the city's transport history from the horse age to the present, this fine museum emerged from redevelopment in 2007 with a much more confident focus on social history and design, illustrated by a superb array of buses, trams and trains. Appropriately, it's now also much easier to get around. The collections are in broadly chronological order, beginning with the Victorian gallery and a replica of Shillibeer's first horse-drawn bus service from 1829.

St Paul's Covent Garden

Bedford Street, WC2E 9ED (7836 5221, www.actorschurch.org). Covent Garden or Leicester Square tube. **Open** 9am-4.30pm Mon-Fri; 9am-12.30pm Sun. **Admission** free; donations appreciated. Map p129 E3 ⑥⓪

Known as the Actors' Church, this magnificently spare building was designed by Inigo Jones for the Earl of Bedford in 1631. Thespians commemorated on its walls range from those lost in obscurity to those destined for immortality. Surely there's no more romantic tribute in London than Vivien Leigh's plaque, simply inscribed with words from Shakespeare's *Antony & Cleopatra*: 'Now boast thee, death, in thy possession lies a lass unparallel'd.'

Eating & drinking

There's a busy **Masala Zone** (48 Floral Street, 7379 0101, www.masalazone.com; see also p173) near the Opera House and market.

Abeno Too

17-18 Great Newport Street, WC2H 7JE (7379 1160, www.abeno.co.uk). Leicester Square tube. **Open** noon-11pm Mon-Sat; noon-10.30pm Sun. **££. Japanese**. Map p129 D3 ⑥①

Okonomiyaki (hearty pancakes with nuggets of vegetables, seafood, pork and other titbits added to a disc of noodles) are cooked to order on hot-plates set into Abeno's tables and counter.

L'Atelier de Joël Robuchon

13-15 West Street, WC2H 9NE (7010 8600, www.joel-robuchon.com). Leicester Square tube. **Open** noon-2.30pm, 5.30-11.30pm Mon-Sat; noon-2.30pm, 5.30-10.30pm Sun. **££££. Modern European**. Map p129 D2 ⑥②

The locations in Joël Robuchon's restaurant empire sound like 007 stopovers – Macau, Hong Kong, Monaco – but Robuchon is no Bond baddie, he's a French superchef. The Japanese-inspired ground-floor L'Atelier is dimly lit, but the open kitchen is an impressively theatrical focal point. A choice of small tasting dishes is the best way to explore the work of this fine chef.

Battersea Pie

NEW *28 Lower Ground Floor, The Market, WC2E 8RA (7240 9566, www.batterseapiestation.co.uk). Covent Garden tube.* **Open** 11am-7pm Mon-Fri; 10am-7pm Sat; 11am-6pm Sun. **£. Pie & mash**. Map p129 E3 ⑥③

With its constant flow of visitors, Covent Garden's many eateries are often tourist traps. Not this one: Battersea Pie provides good-value, proper British food, in pleasant if bustling surrounds. Place your order at the counter, where pie and mash costs a fiver (the changing list might include game, beef and onion, or butternut squash and goat's cheese pies). Served with superb gravies.

Brasserie Max

Covent Garden Hotel, 10 Monmouth Street, WC2H 9LF (7806 1000, www.coventgardenhotel.co.uk). Covent Garden tube. **Open** 7am-11pm Mon-Fri; 8am-11pm Sat; 8am-10.30pm Sun. **£££. Bar/brasserie**. Map p129 D2 ⑥④

Join the crowd of well-to-do creative types for champagne-fuelled powwows and sophisticated banter under the Union Flags that front the stern, stylish Covent Garden Hotel (p202). The well-made cocktails and wines don't come cheap, but with waiters squeezing between punters at the zinc bar there's a buzzy Parisian atmosphere.

Food for Thought

31 Neal Street, WC2H 9PR (7836 9072). Covent Garden tube. **Open** 11.30am-10.30pm Mon-Sat; noon-5pm Sun. £. No credit cards. **Vegetarian café**. Map p129 E2 ⑥⑤

The menu of this very much-loved veggie café changes daily, though you can expect three or four main courses, and a selection of salads and desserts. The laid-back premises are down a steep stairway that, during lunch, usually fills with a patient queue. The ground floor offers the same food to take away.

Giaconda Dining Room

9 Denmark Street, WC2H 8LS (7240 3334, www.giacondadining.com). Tottenham Court Road tube. **Open** noon-2.15pm, 6-9.45pm Mon-Fri. ££. **Modern European**. Map p129 D1 ⑥⑥

A thoroughly likeable restaurant, despite being a little cramped. The food is what most people want to eat most of the time: the owners describe it as French-ish with a bit of Spain and Italy, meaning big-flavoured grills, fish and intriguing assemblages (chicken liver, chorizo, trotters and tripe, for instance).

Gordon's

47 Villiers Street, WC2N 6NE (7930 1408, www.gordonswinebar.com). Embankment tube or Charing Cross tube/rail. **Open** 11am-11pm Mon-Sat; noon-10pm Sun. **Wine bar**. Map p129 E4 ⑥⑦

Gordon's has been serving drinks since 1890, and it looks like it – the place is a specialist in yellowing, candle-lit alcoves. The wine list doesn't bear expert scrutiny and the food is buffet-style, but atmosphere is everything, and this is a great, bustling place.

Great Queen Street

32 Great Queen Street, WC2B 5AA (7242 0622). Covent Garden or Holborn

tube. **Open** noon-2.30pm, 6-10.30pm Mon-Sat; noon-3pm Sun. ££. **British**. Map p129 F1 ⑥⑧

The pub-style room here thrums with bonhomie. Ranging from snacks to shared mains, the menu is designed to tempt and satisfy rather than educate or impress. Booking is essential, and the robust food is worth it. At the Sunday lunch session, diners sit and are served together. The Dive bar downstairs serves snacks as well as drinks.

Lamb & Flag

33 Rose Street, WC2E 9EB (7497 9504). Covent Garden tube. **Open** 11am-11pm Mon-Thur; 11am-11.30pm Fri, Sat; noon-10.30pm Sun. **Pub**. Map p129 E3 ⑥⑨

A pub for over 300 years and a fixture on Rose Street for longer, the unabashedly traditional Lamb & Flag is always a squeeze, but no one minds. The afternoon-only bar upstairs is 'ye olde' to a fault, and sweetly localised by pictures of passed-on regulars.

Lowlander

36 Drury Lane, WC2B 5RR (7379 7446, www.lowlander.com). Covent Garden or Holborn tube. **Open** 10am-11pm Mon-Sat; noon-10.30pm Sun. **Beer bar**. Map p129 E2 ⑦⑩

Brightly logoed and Benelux-themed, the smart Lowlander fills its expansive, long-tabled space easily, thanks to an impressive range of draught (15 options) and bottled beer (100 varieties). The efficient table service adds extra appeal for knackered workers, shoppers and the terminally lazy. Belgian stoemp stew is perfectly made here; mussels come in four sauces.

Rock & Sole Plaice

47 Endell Street, WC2H 9AJ (7836 3785, www.rockandsoleplaice.com). Covent Garden tube. **Open** 11.30am-10.30pm Mon-Sat; noon-9.30pm Sun. ££. **Fish & chips**. Map p129 D1 ⑦①

A chippie since 1874, this busy establishment has walls covered in theatre

Covent Garden Piazza p140

The new face of wine

Terroirs has shaken up the city's wine bars.

'Hints of blackcurrant.' 'Oaky finish.' These phrases you might expect to utter as you swirl wine around your glass, but 'damp cardboard'? 'Sweaty armpits'? Trust the French to come up with a breed of wines that repulse as many drinkers as they enthuse.

Vin naturel ('natural wines') is close, but not quite the right translation) is made with minimal human interference. Restrictions go way beyond those placed by organic farmers on pesticides and artificial fertilisers – vin naturel typically makes the journey from smallholding vines to bottle using the most simplified processes possible while still coming up with something you can call a wine. Notably, the makers try to avoid sulphur (sulphur dioxide is a common preservative across all other wines). This makes vin naturel extremely unpredictable, with huge variations between vintages, but also means you'll encounter real individuality.

The concept has been known in France for decades, but only took root in London when key importers Les Caves de Pyrène opened the hugely popular wine bar Terroirs (right). Even if you don't like the wines, you'll love the bar food: steak served with marrow and snails, pork and pistachio pâté, or maybe just some terrific French cheese.

posters. The ground-floor tables are often all taken (check whether there's space in the basement), and the outside seats are never empty in summer.

Scoop
40 Shorts Gardens, WC2H 9AB (7240 7086, www.scoopgelato.com). Covent Garden tube. **Open** 11am-9pm daily. **£. Ice-cream.** Map p129 D2 ⑦
Long queues are a testament to the quality of the ice-creams, even dairy-free health versions, at this Italian artisan's shop. Flavours include a very superior Piedmont hazelnut type.

J Sheekey
28-34 St Martin's Court, WC2N 4AL (7240 2565, www.j-sheekey.co.uk). Leicester Square tube. **Open** noon-3pm, 5.30pm-midnight Mon-Sat; noon-3.30pm, 6-11pm Sun. **£££. Fish & seafood.** Map p129 D3 ⑦
Sheekey's Oyster Bar opened in 2009, yet another enticement to visit this fine restaurant. Unlike many of London's period pieces (which this certainly is: it was chartered in the mid 19th century), Sheekey's buzzes with fashionable folk. Even if you opt for the main restaurant, your party of four may be crammed on to a table for two, but the accomplished menu will take your mind off it, stretching from modern European to comforting favourites (fish pie, salmon fish cakes).

Terroirs
NEW *5 William IV Street, WC2N 4DW (7036 0660, www.terroirswinebar. com). Charing Cross tube/rail.* **Open** noon-11pm Mon-Sat. **£££. Wine bar.** Map p129 D4 ⑦
See box left.

Wahaca
66 Chandos Place, WC2N 4HG (7240 1883, www.wahaca.co.uk). Covent Garden or Leicester Square tube. **Open** noon-11pm Mon-Sat; noon-10.30pm Sun. **£. Mexican canteen.** Map p129 E3 ⑦

Queues snake into this colourful canteen daily, and Wahaca has a look as cheery as its staff, created from lamps made out of tomatillo cans dotted with bottle tops, wooden crates packed with fruit, and tubs of chilli plants. Choose one of the large plato fuertes (enchiladas, burritos or grilled dishes) if you don't feel like sharing.

Shopping

Cecil Court

www.cecilcourt.co.uk. Leicester Square tube. **Map** p129 D3 🔞
Bookended by Charing Cross Road and St Martin's Lane, picturesque Cecil Court is known for its antiquarian book, map and print dealers. Notable residents include children's specialist Marchpane (no.16), the Italian Bookshop (no.5), Watkins (nos.19 & 21), for occult and New Age titles, and 40-year veteran David Drummond at Pleasures of Past Times (no.11), who specialises in theatre and magic.

Coco de Mer

23 Monmouth Street, WC2H 9DD (7836 8882, www.coco-de-mer.co.uk). Covent Garden tube. **Open** 11am-7pm Mon-Wed, Fri, Sat; 11am-8pm Thur; noon-6pm Sun. **Map** p129 D2 🞷
London's most glamorous erotic emporium sells a variety of tasteful books, toys and lingerie, from glass dildos that double as objets d'art to crotchless culottes and corsets.

Hope & Greenwood

1 Russell Street, WC2B 5JD (7240 3314, www.hopeandgreenwood.co.uk). Covent Garden tube. **Open** 11am-7.30pm Mon-Wed; 11am-8pm Thur, Fri; 10.30am-7.30pm Sat; 11.30am-5.30pm Sun. **Map** p129 F2 🞷
This adorable 1950s-style, letterbox-red cornershop is the perfect place to find the sherbets, chews and chocolates that were once the focus of a proper British childhood. Even the staff look the part: beautifully turned out in a pinny, ready to pop your sweets in a striped paper bag with a smile.

James Smith & Sons

53 New Oxford Street, WC1A 1BL (7836 4731, www.james-smith.co.uk). Holborn or Tottenham Court Road tube. **Open** 9.30am-5.15pm Mon-Fri; 10am-5.15pm Sat. **Map** p129 D1 🞷
For more than 175 years, this charming shop, Victorian fittings still intact, has held its own in the niche market of umbrellas and walking sticks. Forget throwaway brollies that break at the first sign of bad weather and invest in a hickory-crooked City umbrella.

Koh Samui

65-67 Monmouth Street, WC2H 9DG (7240 4280, www.kohsamui.co.uk). Covent Garden tube. **Open** 10am-6.30pm Mon, Fri, Sat; 10.30am-6.30pm Tue, Wed; 10.30am-7pm Thur; noon-5.30pm Sun. **Map** p129 D2 🞨
Vintage pieces sourced from around the world share rail space with a finely tuned selection of heavyweight designers at Koh Samui, resulting in a delightfully eclectic mix of stock, including great independent jewellery designers; prices start at around £50 for a pair of earrings.

Neal's Yard Dairy

17 Shorts Gardens, WC2H 9UP (7240 5700, www.nealsyarddairy.co.uk). Covent Garden tube. **Open** 11am-7pm Mon-Thur; 10am-7pm Fri, Sat. **Map** p129 D2 🞨
Neal's Yard buys from small farms and creameries and matures the cheeses in its own cellars until they're ready to sell. Names such as Stinking Bishop and Lincolnshire Poacher are as evocative as the aromas in the shop.

Poste Mistress

61-63 Monmouth Street, WC2H 9EP (7379 4040, www.office.co.uk). Covent Garden tube. **Open** 10am-7pm Mon-Wed, Fri, Sat; 10am-8pm Thur; 11.30am-6pm Sun. **Map** p129 D2 🞨

The 1970s boudoir decor at this shop makes a suitably glam backdrop for a line-up of high-fashion footwear, plus its own designer-look label. Lulu Guinness bags and other accessories are also sold.

Rokit
42 Shelton Street, WC2H 9HZ (7836 6547, www.rokit.co.uk). Covent Garden tube. **Open** 10am-7pm Mon-Sat; 11am-6pm Sun. **Map** p129 E2 ❸❸

With four locations, Rokit has come a long way since its humble Camden beginnings. This flagship has the most comprehensive selection of second-hand items. You'll find tutus and military wear, cowboy boots and sunglasses, and even classic vintage homeware. Check out the live DJ sets and window performances too.

St Martin's Courtyard
Between St Martin's Lane & Long Acre (www.stmartinscourtyard.co.uk). Covent Garden tube. **Map** p129 D3 ❸❹

Due to have opened in summer 2010, the 25 units of this new development will include Banana Republic, COS and Hoss Intropia, with flagging shoppers sustained by an outpost of Jamie's Italian, as well as Mexican and Indian food (Cantina Laredo, Dishoom).

Stanfords
12-14 Long Acre, WC2E 9LP (7836 1321, www.stanfords.co.uk). Covent Garden or Leicester Square tube. **Open** 9am-7.30pm Mon, Wed, Fri; 9.30am-7.30pm Tue; 9am-8pm Thur; 10am-8pm Sat; noon-6pm Sun. **Map** p129 D3 ❸❺

Three floors of travel guides, literature, maps, language guides, atlases and magazines. The basement houses the full range of British Ordnance Survey maps, and you can plan your next move over Fairtrade coffee in the café.

Unconditional
16 Monmouth Street, WC2H 9DD (7836 6933, www.unconditional. uk.com). Covent Garden tube. **Open**
11am-7pm Mon-Wed, Fri, Sat; 11am-8pm Thur; 12.30-6.30pm Sun. **Map** p129 D1 ❸❻

Adding a bit of hard-edged urban cool to the lovely but somewhat chichi Monmouth Street, Unconditional specialises in menswear and womenswear with a twist, peddling its eponymous London label alongside a small selection of other brands, including Sharon Wauchob, Rick Owens and Zucca.

Nightlife

Heaven
The Arches, Villiers Street, WC2N 6NG (7930 2020, www.heaven-london.com). Embankment tube or Charing Cross tube/rail. **Map** p129 E4 ❸❼

London's most famous gay club is a bit like *Les Misérables* – it's camp, full of history and tourists love it. Popcorn (Mon) has long been a good bet, but it's really all about G-A-Y (Thur-Sat). For years, divas with an album to flog (Madonna, Kylie, Girls Aloud) have turned up to play here at the weekend.

12 Bar Club
22-23 Denmark Place, WC2H 8NL (7240 2622, www.12barclub.com). Tottenham Court Road tube. **Open** 11am-3am Mon-Sat; 6pm-midnight Sun. No credit cards. **Map** p129 D1 ❸❽

This cherished hole-in-the-wall – if smoking were still allowed, this is the kind of place that would be full of it – books a grab-bag of stuff. The size (capacity 100, a stage that barely accommodates a trio) dictates a predominance of singer-songwriters.

Arts & leisure

Adelphi Theatre
NEW *The Strand, WC2E 7NA (0844 412 4651, www.adelphitheatre.co.uk). Covent Garden tube or Charing Cross tube/rail.* **Map** p129 E3 ❸❾

Sir Andrew Lloyd Webber's big sequel to *Phantom* has arrived; see box right. Production subject to change.

Love Never Dies

Lloyd Webber's Phantom returns after 20 years away.

There was a time when only satirists could have imagined Maggie Thatcher-bashing comic Ben Elton and the king of the capitalist-friendly genre of musicals, Andrew Lloyd Webber, getting into bed together. Yet satire has a strange way of coming true – and, a decade after Thatch fell from power, Elton and Lloyd Webber produced their first musical, the football-inspired *Beautiful Game*. Their second collaboration, *Love Never Dies*, is the first sequel to a musical ever staged in the West End.

The *Phantom of the Opera* has been one of Lloyd Webber's great critical and commercial successes, appearing in 124 cities across the world. The original cast recording was the first such to enter the UK charts at number one and is the biggest-selling cast album.

Two decades on, its sequel spirits audiences to Manhattan, ten years after the end of *Phantom*. The deformed denizen of the Paris Opéra has relocated to Coney Island, where he's proprietor of fairground attraction Phantasma. But he's still mooning over soprano Christine Daaé with whom, *Phantom* 'phans' will recall, he enjoyed a mist-wreathed encounter in a candlelit punt. So, using the pseudonym Mr Y, he summons her to be his new star.

When the truth of her new employer's identity dawns on Christine, her husband Raoul – formerly dashing, now a boozy gambler – isn't pleased, especially as it seems she and the Phantom made more than music back in that punt, putting the paternity of Christine's son Gustave in doubt.

For us, Christine comes across as a pallid sap and, despite all the hectic CGI visuals, Bob Crowley's art deco sets are too sparse and sanitised to provide fairground thrills. But will that be enough to prevent this becoming Lloyd Webber's latest megahit?

Coliseum

St Martin's Lane, WC2N 4ES (0871 911 0200, www.eno.org). Leicester Square tube or Charing Cross tube/rail. **Map** p129 D4 **30**

Built as a music hall in 1904, the home of the English National Opera (ENO) is in sparkling condition following a renovation in 2004. The ENO itself is in solid shape under the youthful stewardship of music director Edward Gardner, with occasional duds offset by surprising sell-outs (the extraordinary, flamboyantly staged *Grand Macabre* by Ligeti). All works are in English, and prices are generally cheaper than at the Royal Opera House.

Donmar Warehouse

41 Earlham Street, WC2H 9LX (0844 871 1624, www.donmarwarehouse. com). Covent Garden or Leicester Square tube. **Map** p129 E2 **31**

Artistic director Michael Grandage has kept the Donmar on a fresh, intelligent path, its combination of artistic integrity and an intimate space hard to resist. Perhaps that's why film stars clamour to perform here, among them Nicole Kidman, Gwyneth Paltrow, Gillian Anderson and Ewan McGregor.

Noël Coward Theatre

NEW *St Martin's Lane, WC2N 4AU (0844 482 5140, 7907 7071 box office, www.delfontmackintosh.co.uk). Leicester Square tube.* **Map** p129 D3 **32**

Enron, a surprise hit play about the American hucksters who came to symbolise the banking crisis, is more than a simple tale of hubris: a notable absence of humility, despite deaths caused, livelihoods lost and heroes of the stock market brought low, is reinforced by Rupert Goold's terrific if rather unsubtle production. Production subject to change.

Royal Opera House

Bow Street, WC2E 9DD (7304 4000, www.roh.org). Covent Garden tube. **Map** p129 E2 **33**

The Royal Opera House was founded in 1732 on the profits of his production of John Gay's *Beggar's Opera*; the current building, constructed roughly 150 years ago but extensively remodelled, is the third on the site. Organised tours explore the massive eight-floor building, taking in the main auditorium, the costume workshops and sometimes a rehearsal. The glass-roofed Floral Hall, Crush Bar and Amphitheatre Café Bar are open to the general public. Critics argue the programming can be a little spotty, especially given the famously elevated ticket prices at the top end. Never mind: there are still fine productions, many of them under the baton of Antonio Pappano. This is also home to the Royal Ballet.

Savoy Theatre

NEW *The Strand, WC2R 0ET (7907 7071, www.ambassadortickets.com). Charing Cross tube/rail.* **Map** p129 F4 **34**

A pepped-up, candy-coloured hymn to sisterhood – in which Malibu Barbie Elle Woods takes on the overprivileged preppies at Harvard and wins – *Legally Blonde* is the best legal high in town. Laurence O'Keefe and Nell Benjamin's music and lyrics give the movie an irresistible makeover: highlights are super-smart rhyming dialogues that actually propel the plot, rhythmic, catchy tunelets, and a flawless British cast. Production subject to change.

Shaftesbury Theatre

NEW *210 Shaftesbury Avenue, WC2H 8DP (0844 579 1940, www.shaftesbury theatre.com). Holborn or Tottenham Court Road tube.* **Map** p129 D1 **35**

Flashdance – that blithely uplifting film about a woman who can both dance *and* weld – was a box office smash in 1983, aided no doubt by its era-defining electro-schmaltz soundtrack. With original scribe Tom Hedley writing once more, the musical version – due to open in autumn 2010 – should retain some of the movie's naïve charm. Production subject to change.

Somerset House p155

The City

Holborn to Clerkenwell

The City of London collides with the West End in Holborn and Clerkenwell. Bewigged barristers inhabit the picturesque **Inns of Court**, while City boys pull on trainers to head from their loft apartments to the latest restaurant in one of London's foodiest areas. Although the future of its splendid Victorian wrought-iron structure remains at issue, **Smithfield Market** still has butchers hauling meat around at the crack of dawn – to the consternation of bug-eyed clubbers weaving unsteadily home from superclub **Fabric**.

Sights & museums

Courtauld Gallery

The Strand, WC2R 1LA (7848 2526, www.courtauld.ac.uk/gallery). Temple tube. **Open** 10am-6pm daily. **Admission** £5; free-£4 reductions. Free 10am-2pm Mon. **Map** p150 A4 **1**
In the north wing of Somerset House (p155), the Courtauld's select collection of paintings contains several works of world importance. Although there are outstanding works from earlier periods (don't miss Lucas Cranach's wonderful *Adam & Eve*), the collection's strongest suit is its holdings of Impressionist and post-Impressionist paintings, such as Manet's astonishing *A Bar at the Folies-Bergère* and numerous works by Cézanne. Hidden downstairs, the sweet gallery café is too often overlooked.

Dr Johnson's House

17 Gough Square, off Fleet Street, EC4A 3DE (7353 3745, www.dr johnsonshouse.org). Chancery Lane or Temple tube, or Blackfriars rail. **Open** *May-Sept* 11am-5.30pm Mon-Sat. *Oct-Apr* 11am-5pm Mon-Sat. **Admission** £4.50; free-£3.50 reductions; £10 family. No credit cards. **Map** p150 B4 **2**

The City

1 Sights & museums
1 Eating & drinking
1 Shopping
1 Nightlife
1 Arts & leisure

River Thames

300 m
300 yds

© Copyright Time Out Group 2010

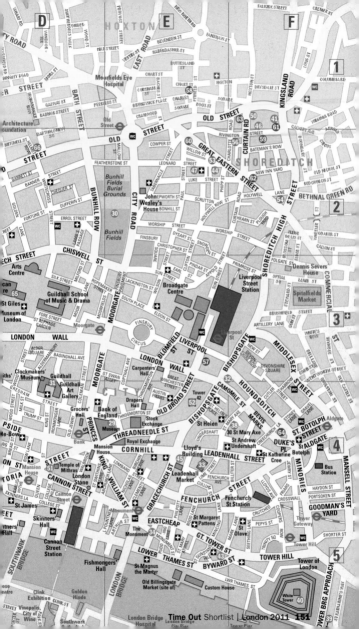

Famed as the author of one of the first, surely the most significant and beyond doubt the wittiest dictionary of the English language, Dr Samuel Johnson (1709-84) also wrote poems, a novel and one of the earliest travelogues. You can tour the stately Georgian townhouse off Fleet Street where Johnson came up with his inspired definitions – 'to make dictionaries is dull work,' was his definition of the word 'dull'.

Fleet Street
Chancery Lane or Temple tube.
Map p150 B4 ❸
The first printing press on this legendary street of newspapers was installed behind St Bride's Church (p155) in 1500 by William Caxton's assistant, Wynkyn de Worde, but it wasn't until 1702 that London's first daily newspaper, the *Daily Courant*, rolled off the presses. By the end of World War II, half a dozen newspaper offices were churning out scoops and scandals between the Strand and Farringdon Road, gradually all moving away once Rupert Murdoch had won his bitter war with the print unions in the 1980s; the last of the news agencies, Reuters, followed suit in 2005. Interesting relics of the industry include the Portland-stone Reuters building (no.85), the Egyptian-influenced Daily Telegraph building (no.135) and the sleek, black, art deco Daily Express building (nos.121-128).

Hunterian Museum
Royal College of Surgeons, 35-43 Lincoln's Inn Fields, WC2A 3PE (7869 6560, www.rcseng.ac.uk/museums). Holborn tube. **Open** 10am-5pm Tue-Sat. **Admission** free. **Map** p150 A4 ❹
John Hunter (1728-93) was a pioneering surgeon and anatomist, and physician to King George III. His huge collection of medical specimens can be viewed in this two-floor museum. The sparkling glass cabinets belie the goriness of many of the exhibits – these include various bodily mutations, the brain of 19th-century mathematician Charles Babbage, and Churchill's dentures.

Museum & Library of the Order of St John
St John's Gate, St John's Lane, EC1M 4DA (7324 4005, www.sja.org.uk/ museum). Farringdon tube/rail. **Open** 10am-5pm Mon-Fri; 10am-4pm Sat. *Tours* 11am, 2.30pm Tue, Fri, Sat. **Admission** free; suggested donation £5, £4 reductions. **Map** p150 C2 ❺
A collection of artefacts (illuminated manuscripts, armour, Islamic items) related to the Order of Hospitaller Knights, from Jerusalem, Malta and the Ottoman Empire, is on display here. A separate collection relates specifically to the evolution of the modern ambulance service. The museum is due to reopen this year after major refurbishments; phone or check the website for for up-to-date details.

St Bartholomew-the-Great
West Smithfield, EC1A 9DS (7606 5171, www.greatstbarts.com). Barbican tube, or Farringdon tube/rail. **Open** 8.30am-5pm Mon-Fri (until 4pm Nov-Feb); 10.30am-4pm Sat; 2.30-6.30pm Sun. **Admission** £4; £3 reductions; £10 family. **Map** p150 C3 ❻
This atmospheric medieval church was chopped about during Henry VIII's reign: the interior is now firmly Elizabethan, although it also contains donated works of modern art and an ancient font. You may recognise the main hall from the movies *Shakespeare in Love* and *Four Weddings & a Funeral*. Just around the corner, the Museum of St Bartholomew's Hospital (7601 8152, www.bartsandthelondon. nhs.uk/museums), in the hospital's North Wing, explains the history of medicine, taking you back to the days when surgery and carpentry were kindred occupations.
Event highlights Guided tour of the church and the Great Hall's Hogarth paintings (2pm Fri, £5; book ahead on 7837 0546).

Bistrot Bruno Loubet p156

Clerkenwell Kitchen p156

St Bride's Church

Fleet Street, EC4Y 8AU (7427 0133, www.stbrides.com). Temple tube, or Blackfriars rail. **Open** 8.30am-5.30pm Mon-Fri; 11am-3pm Sat; 11am-noon, 6.30-7.30pm Sun. Times vary Mon-Sat, so phone ahead. **Admission** free. **Map** p150 B4 **7**

St Bride's, 'the journalists' church', contains a shrine to hacks killed in action. The interior was rebuilt after being bombed out in the Blitz. Down in the crypt, a quietly excellent museum displays fragments of the churches that have existed on this site since the sixth century and tells the story of the newspapers on Fleet Street. According to local legend, the spire was the inspiration for the classic tiered wedding cake.

Sir John Soane's Museum

13 Lincoln's Inn Fields, WC2A 3BP (7405 2107, www.soane.org). Holborn tube. **Open** 10am-5pm Tue-Sat; 10am-5pm, 6-9pm 1st Tue of mth. *Tours* 11am Sat. **Admission** free; donations appreciated. *Tours* free-£5. **Map** p150 A3 **8**

Architect Sir John Soane (1753-1837) was an obsessive collector of art, furniture and architectural ornamentation, partly for enjoyment and partly for research. He turned his house into a museum to which 'amateurs and students' should have access. Much of the museum's appeal derives from the domestic setting, but the real wow is the Monument Court. At its lowest level is a 3,000-year-old sarcophagus of alabaster so fine that it's almost translucent, as well as the cell of Soane's fictional monk Don Giovanni. **Event highlights** Monthly candlelit tours – always book in advance.

Somerset House & the Embankment Galleries

The Strand, WC2R 1LA (7845 4600, www.somersethouse.org.uk). Temple tube or Charing Cross tube/rail. **Open** 10am-6pm daily. *Tours* phone for details. **Admission** *Courtyard & terrace* free.

Embankment Galleries £8; free-£6 reductions. **Map** p150 A5 **9**

Architect Sir William Chambers spent the last 20 years of his life from 1775 working on this neo-classical edifice overlooking the Thames. Effectively the first purpose-built office block in the world, it was built to accommodate learned societies such as the Royal Academy, and also the Inland Revenue. The Inland Revenue is still here, but the rest of the building is open to the public. It houses the wonderful Courtauld (p149) and has a beautiful courtyard with choreographed fountains, a terraced café and classy restaurant, as well as some interesting temporary exhibitions.

Temple Church & Middle Temple

Fleet Street, EC4Y 7BB (7353 8559, www.templechurch.com). Temple tube. **Open** 2-4pm Tue-Fri; phone or check website for details. **Admission** free. **Map** p150 B4 **10**

The quadrangles of Middle Temple (7427 4800, www.middletemple.org.uk) and Inner Temple (7797 8250, www.innertemple.org.uk) have been lodgings for training lawyers since medieval times, with Temple Church – the private chapel of the mystical Knights Templar, its structure inspired by Jerusalem's Church of the Holy Sepulchre – serving the religious requirements of both. Its rounded apse contains the worn gravestones of several Crusader knights. Tours of Inner Temple can be arranged (min five people, £10 each; 7797 8241). **Event highlights** Organ recitals in Temple Church (Wed lunchtimes).

Eating & drinking

Predecessor to the superlative Hix (p133), the **Hix Oyster & Chop House** (36-37 Greenhill Rents, EC1M 6BN, 7017 1930, www.hix oysterandchophouse.co.uk) is also a fine establishment.

Bistrot Bruno Loubet

NEW Zetter, St John's Square, 86-88 Clerkenwell Road, EC1M 5RJ (7324 4455, www.thezetter.com). Farringdon tube/rail. **Open** 7.30-10.30am, noon-2.30pm, 6-10.30pm Mon-Fri, 7.30am-3pm, 6-10.30pm Sat; 7.30am-3pm, 6-10pm Sun. £££. **Modern European**. Map p150 C2 ⑪

The menu at this new bistro is thoughtfully constructed to satisfy novelty seekers, but won't scare off the conservative palate – slow-cooked hare is on the menu, but so is a confit lamb shoulder with white beans that's pepped up with North African preserved lemon and harissa. Playful French desserts are another strength, and the staff are charming, all smiles and very efficient. See also box opposite.

Caravan

NEW 11-13 Exmouth Market, EC1R 4QD, www.caravan exmouth.co.uk). Farringdon tube/rail or bus 19, 38. **Open** 8.30-11.30am, noon-11pm Mon-Fri; 10am-4pm, 5-11pm Sat; 10am-4pm, 5-10pm Sun. ££. **Brasserie**. Map p150 B1 ⑫

This all-day café is a newcomer that feels as if it's been open for ever. The staff know the menu well, and are friendly without being overwrought with chumminess. The all-day menu of small and large plates displays the sort of polygastronomy you'd find in New Zealand and Australia, but the weekend brunch menu comprises fry-ups, eggs on sourdough and fruity porridge. The cakes are good and the Probat roaster prepares coffee beans daily.

Clerkenwell Kitchen

27-31 Clerkenwell Close, EC1R 0AT (7101 9959, www.theclerkenwellkitchen. co.uk). Angel tube or Farringdon tube/rail. **Open** 8am-5pm Mon-Wed, Fri; 8am-11pm Thur. ££. **Eco-restaurant**. Map p150 B2 ⑬

Tucked away in an office development for creatives, Clerkenwell Kitchen has a ready supply of enthusiasts who pop in for coffees, sandwiches, lunch meetings and quiet moments with the Wi-Fi. High-quality, fairly priced meals made with seasonal produce are served from noon: restaurant-calibre food in a stylishly informal café setting. Enjoy with a glass of wine or Meantime beer.

Le Comptoir Gascon

61-63 Charterhouse Street, EC1M 6HJ (7608 0851, www.comptoirgascon.com). Farringdon tube/rail. **Open** noon-2pm, 7-10pm Tue, Wed; noon-2pm, 7-10.30pm Thur, Fri; 10.30am-2.30pm, 7-10pm Sat. ££. **French**. Map p150 C3 ⑭

Comptoir is the modern rustic cousin (dainty velour chairs, exposed pipes, open brickwork, pottery dishes) of the more famous and highfalutin Club Gascon (57 West Smithfield, 7796 0600, www.clubgascon.com), but it exudes as much class and confidence as its forebear in the presentation of delectable regional specialities of Gascony. The posh café vibe is enhanced by capable and amiable French staff.

Eagle

159 Farringdon Road, EC1R 3AL (7837 1353). Farringdon tube/rail. **Open** noon-11pm Mon-Sat; noon-5pm Sun. ££. **Gastropub**. Map p150 B2 ⑮

Widely credited with being the first gastropub (it opened in 1991), this is still recognisably a pub that serves quality food: noisy, often crowded, with no-frills service and dominated by a giant open range where T-shirted cooks toss earthy grills in theatrical bursts of flame. The Med-influenced menu has stayed true to 'big flavours'.

Jerusalem Tavern

55 Britton Street, EC1M 5UQ (7490 4281, www.stpetersbrewery.co.uk). Farringdon tube/rail. **Open** 11am-11pm Mon-Fri. **Pub**. Map p150 C3 ⑯

Tilting, creaking and uneven, the tatty Jerusalem serves sought-after ales from Suffolk's St Peter's brewery. A rag-tag and loyal crowd muses over the *Evening Standard* crossword and, in winter, a cosy fireplace encourages the desire for warm sustenance. Haddock and salmon fish cakes fit the bill nicely.

Modern Pantry

47-48 St John's Square, EC1V 4JJ (7250 0833, www.themodernpantry. co.uk). Farringdon tube/rail. **Open** *Café* 8am-11pm Mon-Fri; 9am-11pm Sat; 10am-10pm Sun. *Restaurant* noon-3pm, 6-10.30pm Tue-Fri; 6-10.30pm Sat. **££. International**. Map p150 C2 ⑰
A culinary three-parter in a pair of Georgian townhouses that feels savvy and of the moment. Both pantry (take-away) and café are at street level; upstairs are adjoining, informal dining rooms. Service is spot on and the menu fuses all kinds of ingredients. Weekend brunch is special – but busy.

Moro

34-36 Exmouth Market, EC1R 4QE (7833 8336, www.moro.co.uk). Farringdon tube/rail or bus 19, 38, 341. **Open** 12.30-10.30pm Mon-Sat. **£££. Spanish-North African**. Map p150 B2 ⑱
Moro has an enduring popularity that seems unassailable. It's fully booked night after night, so phone at least 48 hours ahead if you want to sample the secret of its success: high-quality cooking and a convivial dining space on Exmouth Market (p158). The inventive menu is Moorish – Spanish accents to essentially North African food.

St John

26 St John Street, EC1M 4AY (7251 0848/4998, www.stjohnrestaurant. com). Barbican tube or Farringdon tube/rail. **Open** noon-3pm, 6-11pm Mon-Fri; 6-11pm Sat; 1-3pm Sun. **£££. British**. Map p150 C2 ⑲
The leading light of the modern British cooking revival, St John is an austere-looking place, opened in the shell of a smokehouse by chef-patron Fergus Henderson in 1995. Its spirit hasn't changed: the focus is on seasonal and unusual British ingredients, simply

A superchef returns

Loubet is back – and his food's better than ever.

Bruno Loubet was one of the city's most celebrated chefs during the early 1990s. Bistrot Bruno in Soho was a triumph of modern French cooking, served in a convivial setting for a fair price. But over the next decade he kept upgrading to increasingly fussy and expensive restaurants, with a frequency that most reserve for upgrading mobile phones. He eventually had enough, moving to Brisbane, Australia, for a better family life. That was in 2002.

London has moved on a lot in the past decade, but Loubet has returned to open a restaurant, **Bistrot Bruno Loubet** (opposite), that produces some dishes that are paragons of their type. The slow-cooked hare (lièvre royale), for example, is matched by a dense, dark, reduced sauce of a type common in Escoffier's day, yet updated and lightened by the slightly comical topping of a single, onion-filled raviolo.

Loubet's classical training in haute cuisine and his interest in French *cuisine de terroir* have clearly kept the Bordeaux-born chef grounded, despite his enthusiasm for North African and Asian flavours. On our first visit in the third week after opening, he was visible in the open kitchen, working calmly and smoothly despite an almost full house. Luring Loubet to the Zetter (p208) to buck the place up was a stroke of brilliance.

cooked and presented. Less expensive is the short menu at the boisterous no-reservations bar. See also box p202.

Seven Stars

53 Carey Street, WC2A 2JB (7242 8521). Chancery Lane or Holborn tube. **Open** 11am-11pm Mon-Fri; noon-11pm Sat; noon-10.30pm Sun. **££. Gastropub.** Map p150 A4 ⑳

Roxy Beaujolais' flagship pub is a fantastic social hub for London characters, from eccentric lawyers to burlesque babes. If you can squeeze into the small interior, you'll get a slice of low-rent, bohemian London. One of the few City pubs where £6 for a large burgundy doesn't mean you're being ripped off.

Three Kings of Clerkenwell

7 Clerkenwell Close, EC1R 0DY (7253 0483). Farringdon tube/rail. **Open** noon-11pm Mon-Sat. No credit cards. **Pub.** Map p150 B2 ㉑

Rhino heads, Egyptian felines and Dennis Bergkamp provide the decorative backdrop against which a regular bunch of discerning bohos glug Old Speckled Hen, London Pride, Scrumpy Jack cider or Beck's Vier, and tap the well-worn tables to the Cramps and other gems from an excellent jukebox.

Vinoteca

7 St John Street, EC1M 4AA (7253 8786, www.vinoteca.co.uk). Farringdon tube/rail. **Open** noon-11pm Mon-Sat; noon-5pm Sat. **Wine bar.** Map p150 C3 ㉒

Inspired by the Italian enoteca (a blend of off-licence and wine bar, with bar snacks thrown in), Vinoteca is far more of a gastropub in spirit. But even if you want no more than a plate of bread and olive oil, come here for the impressive 200-bottle wine list, of which a range of 19 are available by the glass.

Ye Old Mitre

1 Ely Court, at the side of 8 Hatton Gardens, EC1N 6SJ (7405 4751).

Chancery Lane tube or Farringdon tube/rail. **Open** 11am-11pm Mon-Fri. **Pub.** Map p150 B3 ㉓

The secluded location requires you to slink down an alleyway just off Hatton Garden, where you'll be transported to a parallel pub universe where the clientele are disconcertingly friendly and the staff (in pristine black and white uniforms) briskly efficient. A Monday-to-Friday joint, it's a pint-sized pub that's earned its top-notch reputation.

Shopping

Exmouth Market

Angel tube or Farringdon tube/rail, or bus 19, 38. Map p150 B1 ㉔

A terrific collection of eateries and shops are scattered along this short pedestrianised street. Brill (no.27) is a small CD shop-cum-café with an excellently curated selection, and ec one (no.41) a showcase of jewellery from more than 50 designers. Marco Araldi and Keng Wai Lee's colourful bags and accessories are made on the premises at Bagman & Robin (no.47). Space EC1 (no.25) is good for knowingly kitsch gifts, and there are great books at Clerkenwell Tales (no.30). Chic eats at Moro (p157) or Caravan (p156) are balanced by beer and foosball in cheery Café Kick (no.43; Bar Kick is on p164).

Magma

117-119 Clerkenwell Road, EC1R 5BY (7242 9503, www.magmabooks.com). Chancery Lane tube or Farringdon tube/rail. **Open** 10am-7pm Mon-Sat. Map p150 B2 ㉕

If you can visualise it, this art and design specialist has probably got a book about it. Mags, DVDs, trendy toys, T-shirts and limited-edition posters and cards are also sold.

Pure Groove Records

6-7 West Smithfield, EC1A 9JX (7778 9278, www.puregroove.co.uk). Farringdon tube/rail. **Open** noon-7pm Mon-Fri. Map p150 C3 ㉖

A stylish, multimedia treasure trove of vinyl, poster art and CD gems, covering all things indie, alternative and cutting edge in guitar and electronic music. The rear, housing T-shirts, bags and posters, doubles as a stage for the regular live sets and film screenings.

Nightlife

Fabric
77A Charterhouse Street, EC1M 3HN (7336 8898, www.fabriclondon.com). Farringdon tube/rail. **Open** 10pm-6am Fri; 11pm-8am Sat; 11pm-6am Sun. **Map** p150 C3 ❷❼
Fabric is the club most party people come to see in London: the main room has the stomach-wobbling Bodysonic dancefloor, the second is a rave-style warehouse, the third is where the cool stuff happens. Fridays belong to the bass: highlights include DJ Hype, who takes over all three rooms once a month for his drum 'n' bass and dubstep night Playaz. Saturdays rock to techy, minimal, deep house sounds.

Volupté
7-9 Norwich Street, EC4A 1EJ (7831 1622, www.volupte-lounge.com). Chancery Lane tube. **Open** 5pm-1am Tue, Wed; 5pm-3am Thur, Fri; 2pm-2am Sat. **Map** p150 B3 ❷❽
Expect to suffer extreme wallpaper envy as you enter the ground-floor bar, then descend to the club proper. Punters enjoy some of the best cabaret talent in town from tables set beneath absinthe-inspired vines. Wednesday nights are Cabaret Salon and once a month the Black Cotton Club turns back the clock to the 1920s.

The City

Fewer than 10,000 souls live within the Square Mile (1.21 square miles, in fact), but every working day the population increases tenfold, as bankers, brokers, lawyers and traders storm into their towering office blocks. The City still holds to boundaries set by the 2nd-century walls of Roman Londinium (a few sections of which remain), although it then had six times more residents than now. Apart from two crowd-pullers – **St Paul's** and the **Tower of London** – the City might not seem to have much to offer casual visitors, but in fact the streets are full of historic gems.

For nightlife, head north-east of the City proper, where the pleasure zones of **Shoreditch** soak up bankers' loose change. The area's edginess and artiness have begun to follow cheaper rents further east, but the bars and clubs are still lively – on Friday and Saturday nights, often unpleasantly so.

Sights & museums

The art gallery at the **Barbican Centre** (£8, £4-£7 reductions; p169) has good exhibitions of pop culture, design and architecture, while the free Curve space shows excellent commissions. Of the City's three classic skyscrapers – **Lloyd's** (p161), the **Gherkin** (30 St Mary Axe, p162) and the NatWest Tower (Tower 42) – only Tower 42's bar, **Vertigo 42** (p167), is open to the public. However, **Heron Tower** (p161), now the City's tallest building, is to open a rooftop bar-restaurant.

Bank of England Museum
Entrance on Bartholomew Lane, EC2R 8AH (7601 5545, www.bankofengland.co.uk/museum). Bank tube/DLR. **Open** 10am-5pm Mon-Fri. **Admission** free. *Tours* free. **Map** p151 E4 ❷❾
Housed in the bank's former Stock Offices, this engaging museum explores the history of the national bank. As well as a rare chance to handle a 13kg gold bar, you can learn about Kenneth Grahame: the author of *The Wind in the Willows* was a long-term employee here.

The all-new story of London

The Museum of London catches up with the 20th century.

Over the last five years, the **Museum of London** (opposite) has received a top-to-bottom £20-million refurbishment, the high point of which was the spring 2010 unveiling of a superbly remodelled lower-ground-floor gallery covering the city from 1666 to the present day. Previously, the modern London gallery ended before World War I, but the new space features everything from an unexploded World War II bomb to a multimedia display on the Brixton riots and an outfit by the late Alexander McQueen.

The architects Wilkinson Eyre have increased gallery space by a quarter, enabling the museum to focus on the city's relationship with the rest of the world and how it was changed by trade, war and empire. There are displays and brilliant interactives on poverty, finance, shopping and 20th-century fashion, including a lovely recreation of a Georgian pleasure garden, with mannequins sporting Philip Treacy masks and hats.

The museum's biggest obstacle has always been its tricky location: the entrance is two floors above street level, hidden behind a grim wall. To solve this, a new space was created on the ground floor, allowing one key exhibit – the Lord Mayor's gold coach – to be seen from the outside.

Some of the displays are grand flourishes – the ever-changing suspended installation in the Sackler Hall (pictured above), a printing press gushing newsheets, a debtors' prison cell – but others ingeniously deal with difficulties. One key issue was what to do with the sheer wealth of artefacts the museum owns but has never been able to show. The solution? To put them in glass cases in the floor.

So now, when you visit the Museum of London, the city's fascinating history is, quite literally, under your feet.

Bunhill Fields

Old Street tube/rail. **Admission** free.
Map p151 E2 ③⓪
An important nonconformist burial
ground until the 19th century, Bunhill
contains memorials to John Bunyan,
Daniel Defoe and William Blake. It's a
moving little place, hemmed in by
office walls. Opposite, the former home
and chapel of John Wesley are now a
museum of Methodism (49 City Road,
7253 2262, www.wesleyschapel.org.uk).

Guildhall Art Gallery & Clockmakers' Museum

*Guildhall Yard, off Gresham Street,
EC2P 2EJ (7332 3700, www.guildhall-
art-gallery.org.uk). St Paul's tube, Bank
tube/DLR, or Moorgate tube/rail.* **Open**
10am-5pm Mon-Sat; noon-4pm Sun.
Admission £2.50; free-£1 reductions.
Free to all from 3.30pm daily, all day
Fri. **Map** p151 D4 ③①
The City of London's gallery contains
dull portraits of royalty and long-gone
mayors, and some wonderful surprises,
including a brilliant Constable, a few
high-camp Pre-Raphaelites and various absorbing paintings of London
through the ages. A sub-basement has
the scant remains of a 6,000-seat Roman
amphitheatre, built around AD 70. The
one-room Clockmakers' Museum (www.
clockmakers.org, closed Sun, free admission) is a symphony of ticking, chiming
clocks and watches.

Heron Tower

NEW *110 Bishopsgate, EC2M 4AY
(www.herontower.com). Liverpool
Street tube/rail.* **Map** p151 E3 ③②
Having become the tallest building in
the City in December 2009, Heron
Tower topped out at 755ft (including a
radio mast) in spring 2010. There are
plans for a restaurant and bar on the
top three floors (a bit under 600ft up),
but they won't open until spring 2011.

Lloyd's of London

*1 Lime Street, EC3M 7HA (www.lloyds.
com). Monument tube.* **Map** p151 E4 ③③

Lord Rogers' high-tech building has all
its mechanical services (ducts, stair-
wells, lift shafts) on the outside, a
design that still looks very modern 20
years later. The original Lloyd's
Register, with bas-reliefs of sea mon-
sters and nautical scenes, is on nearby
Fenchurch Street. No public access.

Monument

*Monument Street, EC3R 8AH
(7626 2717, www.themonument.info).
Monument tube.* **Open** 9.30am-5pm
daily. **Admission** £3; £2 reductions;
free under-5s. No credit cards. **Map**
p151 E5 ③④
Reopened after a £4.5m refurbishment,
the world's tallest free-standing stone
column was designed by Sir
Christopher Wren and his (often overlooked) associate Robert Hooke as a
memorial to the Great Fire of London.
It measures 202ft from the ground to
the tip of the golden flame on the orb
at its top, exactly the distance east to
Farriner's bakery in Pudding Lane,
where the fire is supposed to have
begun on 2 September 1666. You can
climb up the inside for fine City views.

Museum of London

NEW *150 London Wall, EC2Y
5HN (0870 444 3851, www.museum
oflondon.org.uk). Barbican or St
Paul's tube.* **Open** 10am-6pm daily.
Admission free; suggested donation
£2. **Map** p151 D3 ③⑤
This expansive museum (set in the middle of a roundabout) tells the history of
London – with assistance from newer
east London sibling, the Museum of
London Docklands (p179). Themes
include 'London Before London' – flint
axes, fossils, grave goods – and 'Roman
London', which has a reconstructed dining room complete with mosaic floor.
Sound effects and audio-visual displays
illustrate the medieval city, as well as
cases of shoes and armour, and there's
also the glittering Cheapside Hoard. But
the most glittering aspect of the museum is its new galleries; see box opposite.

LONDON BY AREA

Postman's Park

St Paul's tube. **Map** p151 C3 ③⑥
This peaceful, fern-filled park contains the Watts Memorial to Heroic Sacrifice: a wall of Victorian ceramic plaques, each of which commemorates a fatal act of bravery by an ordinary person.

St Paul's Cathedral

Ludgate Hill, EC4M 8AD (7236 4128, www.stpauls.co.uk). St Paul's tube.
Open 8.30am-4pm Mon-Sat. *Galleries, crypt & ambulatory* 9.30am-4.15pm Mon-Sat. **Admission** £11; free-£10 reductions; £25 family. *Tours* £3; £1-£2.50 reductions. **Map** p150 C4 ③⑦
A £40m restoration project has left the main façade of St Paul's looking as brilliant as it must have when the first Mass was celebrated here in 1710. The vast open spaces of the interior contain memorials to national heroes such as Wellington and Lawrence of Arabia, as well as superb mosaics and gilt added by the Victorians. The Whispering Gallery, inside the dome, is reached by 259 steps from the main hall (the acoustics are so good a whisper can be clearly heard across the dome). Stairs continue up to the first the Stone Gallery (119 steps), with its high external balustrades, then outside to the Golden Gallery (152 steps), with its giddying views. Head down to the crypt to see Nelson's grand tomb and the small tombstone of Sir Christopher Wren himself, inscribed: 'Reader, if you seek a monument, look around you.'

30 St Mary Axe

www.30stmaryaxe.com. Liverpool Street tube/rail. **Map** p151 F4 ③⑧
Completed only in 2004, Lord Foster's skyscraper has already become a cherished icon of modern London, its 'Erotic Gherkin' nickname plainly apt. Sadly, there's no public access.

Tower Bridge Exhibition

Tower Bridge, SE1 2UP (7403 3761, www.towerbridge.org.uk). Tower Hill tube or Tower Gateway DLR. **Open** *Apr-Sept* 10am-6.30pm daily. *Oct-Mar* 9.30am-6pm daily. **Admission** £7; free-£5 reductions; £15.50 family. **Map** p151 F5 ③⑨
Opened in 1894, this is the 'London Bridge' that wasn't sold to America. Originally powered by steam, the drawbridge is now opened by electric rams when big ships need to venture this far upstream (you can check when the bridge is next due to be raised on the website). An entertaining exhibition on the history of the bridge is displayed in the old steamrooms and on the west walkway, which provides a crow's-nest view along the Thames.

Tower of London

Tower Hill, EC3N 4AB (0844 482 7777, www.hrp.org.uk). Tower Hill tube or Tower Gateway DLR. **Open** *Mar-Oct* 10am-5.30pm Mon, Sun; 9am-5.30pm Tue-Sat. *Nov-Feb* 10am-4.30pm Mon, Sun; 9am-4.30pm Tue-Sat. **Admission** £17; free-£14 reductions; £47 family. **Map** p151 F5 ④⓪
Despite the exhausting crowds and long climbs up narrow stairways, this is one of Britain's finest historical attractions. Who wouldn't be fascinated by a close-up look at the crown of Queen Victoria or the armour (and prodigious codpiece) of King Henry VIII? The buildings of the Tower span 900 years of history and the bastions and battlements house a series of interactive displays on the lives of British monarchs – and excruciatingly painful deaths of traitors. The highlight has to be the Crown Jewels, viewed from a slow-moving travelator, but the other big draw is the Royal Armoury in the White Tower: four floors of swords, armour, pole-axes, halberds and other gruesome tools for chopping up human beings. Executions of noble prisoners were carried out on the green in front of the Tower – the site is marked by a glass pillow, sculpted by poet and artist Brian Catling in 2006.

Tickets are sold in the kiosk just to the west of the palace and visitors enter through the Middle Tower, but there's

Tower of London

also a free audio-visual display in the Welcome Centre outside the walls. There's plenty here to fill a whole day, but you can skip to the highlights using the audio tour, or by joining one of the highly recommended and entertaining free tours led by the Yeoman Warders (Beefeaters), who also care for the Tower's ravens.

Event highlights 'Fit for a King: five centuries of Royal Armour'.

Eating & drinking

Charlie Wright's (p168) is a great spot for drinks, whether or not jazz is playing. Cinnamon Club (p79) has a City sibling: **Cinnamon Kitchen** (9 Devonshire Square, EC2M 4YL, 7626 5000, www.cinnamonkitchen.co.uk).

Bar Kick

127 Shoreditch High Street, E1 6JE (7739 8700, www.cafekick.co.uk). Old Street tube/rail or Shoreditch High Street rail. **Open** *noon-11pm Mon-Wed; noon-midnight Thur-Sat; noon-10.30pm Sun.* **Table football bar.** Map p151 F1 ㊶

A big square room with a bar, open kitchen, flags of all nations tacked to the ceiling and foosball tables under TVs that silently screen international football. Cool and excellently boisterous, Kick takes enough of a hint from European cafés (quality food, a curated selection of drinks) to draw in nearly as many women as men. The busy staff remain calm and friendly under the onslaught of twirl-crazed party groups.

Black Friar

174 Queen Victoria Street, EC4V 4EG (7236 5474). Mansion House tube or Blackfriars rail. **Open** *10am-11pm Mon-Fri; 11am-11pm Sat; noon-10pm Sun.* **Pub.** Map p150 C4 ㊷

This curiously wedge-shaped pub at the north end of Blackfriars Bridge offers a handful of real ales, a dozen or so wines by the glass, the standard

lagers, and pub nosh (from steak pie to goat's cheese tart) that's more than adequate. But, if you can manage to push your way inside, it's the extraordinary Arts & Crafts interior, resplendent with carvings of Dominican monks and odd mottos, that you'll want to visit for. A bit unhinged, but great.

Bodean's

16 Byward Street, EC3R 5BA (7488 3883, www.bodeansbbq.com). Tower Hill tube. **Open** *noon-3pm, 6-10pm Mon-Fri; 6-10pm Sat.* **££. American.** Map p151 E5 ㊸

Across Bodean's five branches – Soho, Westbourne Grove, Fulham, Clapham and, handily, here – the shtick remains unchanged: Kansas City barbecue, with a small informal upstairs and bigger, smarter downstairs with US sport on TV. The food is decent, generously portioned and very meaty.

Book Club

NEW *100-106 Leonard Street, EC2A 4RH (7684 8618, www.wearetbc.com). Old Street tube/rail.* **Open** *8am-midnight Mon-Wed; 8am-2am Thur, Fri; 10am-2am Sat; 10am-midnight Sun.* **Admission** *free-£5.* **Bar/café.** Map p151 E2 ㊹

The lovely-looking, open and airy Book Club fuses lively creative events with late-night drinking seven nights of the week. Locally themed cocktails include The Shoreditch Twat (tequila, Jagermeister, vermouth, vanilla sugar and egg), and food is served all day. There's also free Wi-Fi, a pool table, ping pong and lots of comfy seats. The programme includes live art battle-cum-hip hop party Secret Wars and tranny superstar Jonny Woo's Dance Class – check the website for details.

Butcher at Leadenhall

NEW *Leadenhall Market, EC3V 1LR (7283 1662, www.butcheratleadenhall. com). Bank tube/DLR.* **Open** *7.30am-3pm Mon-Fri.* **££. Café.** Map p151 E4 ㊺

In the glorious Victorian surrounds of Leadenhall Market, one side of this small arcade unit is a butcher's shop, selling free-range meat, the other a small kitchen. The bulk of the menu comprises grilled cuts with chips and salad: beef, lamb, pork, veal, poultry. It's not cheap: a one-kilo 'City Boy Rib' costs £50, but chorizo with piquillo peppers (£6.50) and a changing dish of the day at £9.50 (Hungarian sausage and bean stew) are good value. Takeaway is popular, but there are also a few tables on the cobbles.

Callooh Callay

65 Rivington Street, EC2A 3AY (7739 4781). Shoreditch High Street rail or Old Street tube/rail. **Open** 5-11pm Mon, Thur, Sun; 4pm-1am Fri; 5pm-1am Sat. **Bar**. **Map** p151 F1 ⑯
All warm and whimsical, the neo-Victorian decor here is as eclectic as *Jabberwocky*, the Lewis Carroll nonsense poem from which the bar gets its name. The quirkiest touch is the hoodwinking oak Narnia wardrobe, through which you'll find a lounge, mirrored bar and loos tiled in old cassettes. The 'Mad Hatter Tiki Punchbowl' is served up in a gramophone speaker trumpet.

Eyre Brothers

70 Leonard Street, EC2A 4QX (7613 5346, www.eyrebrothers. co.uk). Old Street tube/rail. **Open** noon-2.45pm, 6.30-10.45pm Mon-Fri; 7-11pm Sat. **££**. **International**. **Map** p151 E2 ⑰
News has got around: Eyre Brothers does everything exceptionally well. Hence, it can be hard to book a table. It's a labour of love for brothers David and Robert, who evidently spend as much time crafting the changing menu as fashioning the clean-lined, sophisticated decor – chic leather furniture, designer lamps and divided dining areas. Authentic Portuguese dishes reflect the brothers' upbringing in Mozambique, while Spanish and French flavours add range and luxury.

Fish Central

149-155 Central Street, EC1V 8AP (7253 4970). Old Street tube/rail or bus 55. **Open** 11am-2.30pm Mon-Sat; 5-10.30pm Mon-Thur; 5-11pm Fri, Sat. **£**. **Fish & chips**. **Map** p151 D1 ⑱
This area was hardly residential in 1968, when Fish Central took a unit in the shopping precinct. Now it spans four units – rather stylishly, with etched glass and pale white and mint tones – but still serves simple fish to enthusiastic locals.

Restaurant at St Paul's

NEW *St Paul's Cathedral, St Paul's Churchyard, EC4M 8AD (7248 2469, www.restaurantatstpauls.co.uk). St Paul's tube.* **Open** noon-4.30pm daily. **££**. **British**. **Map** p150 C4 ⑲
This is a handsome, light-filled space in the cathedral crypt, with sensuous and textural decor – great for a restaurant, surprising in a place of worship. The food is excellent – asparagus and poached duck egg, prettily pink barnsley chop, portobello mushroom wellington and a gooseberry cobbler for pudding revealed deft hands in the kitchen – and well-priced at £16 for two courses, £20 for three. Restaurant is closed in the evening, so try the good-value set dinner at Sauterelle (Royal Exchange, EC3V 3LR, 7618 2483, www.danddlondon.com).

Saf

152-154 Curtain Road, EC2A 3AT (7613 0007, www.safrestaurant.co.uk). Old Street tube/rail. **Open** noon-11pm daily. **£££**. **Vegetarian**. **Map** p151 F1 ⑳
Saf sets new standards for vegan and raw food restaurants. It's almost a shame to eat meals this pretty; remarkable when you realise the vivid colours, varied textures and unusual flavours are created almost entirely from uncooked fruit and veg (a few items are cooked, at low temperatures). A must-visit for vegetarians bored of mushroom risotto every time they go out.

LONDON BY AREA

Black Friar p164

Sweetings

*39 Queen Victoria Street, EC4N 4SA
(7248 3062). Mansion House tube.*
Open 11.30am-3pm Mon-Fri. **£££**.
Fish & seafood. Map p151 D4 ⑤1
In these days of makeovers and global
menus, Sweetings is that rare thing –
a traditional British restaurant that
clings to its traditions as if the Empire
depended on it. It opens only for lunch,
takes no bookings, and is full soon after
noon, so order a silver pewter mug of
Guinness and enjoy the wait.

Vertigo 42

*Tower 42, 25 Old Broad Street, EC2N
1HQ (7877 7842, www.vertigo42.co.
uk). Bank tube/DLR or Liverpool Street
tube/rail.* **Open** noon-3pm, 5.30-11pm
Mon-Fri. **££££**. **Champagne bar**.
Map p151 E4 ⑤2
Short of introducing iris-recognition
scanning, the process of going for a
drink in Tower 42 (book in advance,
then get X-rayed and metal-detected on
arrival) could scarcely be more MI5.
But it's worth it: the 42nd floor location
delivers stupendous views. There are
nibbles and the champagne list offers
eight labels by the flute (from £12.75).

Shopping

East and north-east of Liverpool
Street station are some of London's
liveliest shopping areas, especially
on Sunday when **Spitalfields** and
Brick Lane markets are on the go.

Bordello

*55 Great Eastern Street, EC2A 3HP
(7503 3334, www.bordello-london.com).
Old Street tube/rail or Shoreditch High
Street rail.* **Open** 11am-7pm Tue-Sat;
1-5pm Sun. Map p151 E2 ⑤3
Seductive yet welcoming, Bordello
stocks luxurious lingerie by Damaris,
Buttress & Snatch, Myla and Pussy
Glamore, and swimwear by Jemma
Jube and Flamingo Sands. The edgy
vibe appeals to first-daters, East End
glamazons and burlesque stars.

A Child of the Jago

*10 Great Eastern Street, EC2A 3NT
(7377 8694, www.childofthejago.
blogspot.com). Old Street tube/rail or
Shoreditch High Street rail.* **Open**
11am-7pm Mon-Sat; noon-5pm Sun.
Map p151 F2 ⑤4
Joe Corre (Vivienne Westwood's son)
and the designer Simon 'Barnzley'
Armitage's eclectic boutique is about as
far from the high street as it gets, com-
bining modern and vintage. Barnzley's
cashmere hooded tops are handmade in
Scotland, and you'll find Westwood's
World's End collection upstairs.

One New Change

NEW *www.onenewchange.com.
St Paul's tube.* Map p150 C4 ⑤5
See box p168.

Three Threads

*47-49 Charlotte Road, EC2A 3QT
(7749 0503, www.thethreethreads.com).
Old Street tube/rail.* **Open** 11am-7pm
Mon-Sat; noon-5pm Sun. Map p151
F2 ⑤6
Free beer, a jukebox well stocked with
dad rock and conveniently placed bar
stools around the till… the Three
Threads tempts even the most shop-
phobic male. Exclusive, cult labels such
as Japan's Tenderloin, Fjall Raven,
Danish label Won Hundred and New
York's Built by Wendy are here, but the
vibe is more like a pal's house. It now
also stocks womenswear from Carhartt
and YMC, and bags from Mimi.

Nightlife

Book Club (p164) has a terrific
range of unusual night-time events.

Bathhouse

NEW *7-8 Bishopsgate Churchyard,
EC2M 3TJ (7920 9207, www.the
bathhousevenue.com). Liverpool Street
tube/rail.* **Open** 5pm-midnight Mon-
Wed; 5pm-2am Thur; 5pm-5am Fri;
9pm-5am Sat. **Admission** £5-£8.
Map p151 E3 ⑤7

LONDON BY AREA

Starchitect shopping

The City's on a mission to make you shop.

The City is no longer a ghost town out of working hours. Bars and cafés stay open in the evenings and at weekends, with Paternoster Square (beside St Paul's Cathedral, p162) busy all week. Hotels increased from two to ten in the last decade alone. Visitors now pour across the Millennium Bridge all week – and the City authorities are keen to make sure there's plenty for them to do when they get here.

Due to open in late 2010, just opposite the cathedral in the corner of New Change and Cheapside, the biggest of many projects is **One New Change** (p167), the first major building in London by 64-year-old French modernist starchitect Jean Nouvel (www.jeannouvel.com). Designer of the Arab World Institute in Paris and the Lyon Opera House, he is creating a 'ground scraper' (a building of monumental scale that isn't all that tall) that responds to the historic route of Watling Street. One New Change will feature dramatic views of St Paul's with its most distinctive feature: a kind of fissure driven through to the atrium at the heart of the building. As well as offices for 3,500 people, it will house leisure facilities, some 70 high-end shops, roof gardens and a rooftop restaurant providing views at about the same level as the cathedral's Stone Gallery.

■ www.onenewchange.com

This Victorian Turkish bathhouse is a now fresh party space. All marble and gilt mirrors, it seems almost too appropriate for decadent Sunday happening the Boom Boom Club and its showgirl burlesque and young neo-cabaret stars. Dress to the nines in vintage, then drink wildly to fit in. Saturday sees Rock-a-Billy Rebels draw dressed-up fans of '50s rock 'n' roll.

Charlie Wright's International Bar
45 Pitfield Street, N1 6DA (7490 8345, www.myspace.com/charliewrights). Old Street tube/rail. **Open** noon-1am Mon-Wed, Sun; noon-4am Thur, Fri; 6pm-4am Sat. **Map** p151 E1 ⑱
When Zhenya Strigalev and Patsy Craig began programming the line-up here, London's jazz fans were given a reason to visit. Now this agreeably scruffy venue stages a fine jazz programme every night except Saturday. Gigs don't usually start until 10pm, and run late on Thursday and Friday.

Comedy Café
66-68 Rivington Street, EC2A 3AY (7739 5706, www.comedycafe.co.uk). Old Street tube/rail or Shoreditch High Street rail. **Map** p151 F2 ⑲
Comedy Café is a purpose-built club, with the emphasis on inviting bills and satisfied punters. The atmosphere is fun and food is an integral part of the experience. Admission's free on Wednesday.

East Village
89 Great Eastern Street, EC2A 3HX (7739 5173, www.eastvillageclub.com). Old Street tube/rail. **Open** 5pm-midnight Tue, Wed; 5pm-1am Thur; 5pm-1am Fri; 9pm-4am Sat; 2-11pm Sun. **Map** p151 E2 ⑳
Local lad Stuart Patterson, promoter of all-day house-music parties since 1999, created this two-floor, 'real house' bar-club in 2008. The top-notch DJs should suit any sophisticated clubber; expect the likes of Chicago house don Derrick Carter and London's own Mr C.

Last Days of Decadence

*145 Shoreditch High Street, E1
6JE (7729 2896, www.thelastdaysof
decadence.com). Shoreditch High Street
rail.* Map p151 F1 ⑥①
Shoreditch High Street isn't going to
win awards for being pretty, but it's
pleasing to see boarded-up venues getting a new lease of life. The people
behind Last Days completely remodelled this two-floor bar, bringing in a bit
of art deco glamour. Despite cocktails
drolly served in teacups, this isn't just a
retro club: electro DJs jostle on the ros-
ter with burlesque performers.

Old Blue Last

*38 Great Eastern Street, EC2A 3ES
(7739 7033, www.theoldbluelast.com).
Old Street tube/rail or Shoreditch High
Street rail.* **Open** noon-midnight Mon-
Wed; noon-12.30am Thur, Sun; noon-
1.30am Fri, Sat. Map p151 F2 ⑥②
This shabby two-floor Victorian pub
was transformed by hipster handbook
Vice in 2004. Amy Winehouse, Arctic
Monkeys and Lily Allen have all
played secret shows in the sauna-like
upper room, but its high-fashion rock
'n' rollers also dig regular club nights
from the likes of girlie indie DJ troupe
My Ex Boyfriend's Records.

Plastic People

*147-149 Curtain Road, EC2A 3QE
(7739 6471, www.plasticpeople.co.uk).
Old Street tube/rail or Shoreditch High
Street rail.* **Open** 9pm-2am 2nd Thur of
mth; 10.30pm-4am Fri, Sat; 9pm-1.30am
Sun. Map p151 F1 ⑥③
The long-established, long-popular
Plastic People subscribes to the old-
school line that all you need for a party
is a dark basement and a kicking
sound system. The programming
remains true to form: deep techno to
house, all-girl DJ line-ups and many a
star arriving to play a secret gig.

T Bar

*18-22 Houndsditch, EC3A 7LP
(www.tbarlondon.com). Aldgate tube*
or Liverpool Street tube/rail.
Map p151 F4 ⑥④
When the first T Bar opened on
Shoreditch High Street, many said it
was too far from Old Street to succeed.
And how could it survive with superstar DJs playing, but no fee for entry?
Cue queues up the street. Still free
entry, T Bar has moved to a new location but still offers brilliant deep house
and techno nights. Fridays are most
popular with the artfully minded. It can
now stay open much later too.

Arts & leisure

Barbican Centre

*Silk Street, EC2Y 8DS (7638 4141,
7638 8891 box office, www.barbican.
org.uk). Barbican tube or Moorgate
tube/rail.* Map p151 D3 ⑥⑤
The Barbican is a prime example of
1970s brutalism, softened by rectangu-
lar ponds of friendly resident ducks.
The complex houses a cinema, theatre,
concert hall and art galleries, a
labyrinthine array of spaces that isn't
all that easy to navigate. The programming, however, is first class. At the
core of the classical music store, performing 90 concerts a year, is the brilliant London Symphony Orchestra
(LSO), supplemented by top jazz,
world-music and rock gigs. The annual BITE season cherry-picks exciting
theatre and dance from around the
globe, and the cinema shows art-house,
mainstream and international films.
Event highlights 'The Whale Watching
Tour' (27 Sept 2010); 'Only Connect' (until
15 Dec 2011); BITE11 (mid Jan-Apr).

LSO St Luke's

*161 Old Street, EC1V 9NG (7490
3939, 7638 8891 box office, www.lso.
co.uk/lsostlukes). Old Street tube/rail.*
Map p151 D2 ⑥⑥
The London Symphony Orchestra's
conversion of this fine Hawksmoor-
designed church into a 370-seat concert
hall cost £20m, but the gigs here have
proved it was worth every penny.

ZSL London Zoo p172

Neighbourhood London

LONDON BY AREA

Like many a modern metropolis, London is really two different cities. The centre is for work, play and lucky tourists, with most locals living where the rent is cheaper. This means restaurants and bars are often more vital – and exciting scenes more apt to develop – on the city's periphery. In **Greenwich**, the **Royal Botanic Gardens** at Kew and **Hampton Court**, however, neighbourhood London has tourist attractions that each easily fill a sightseeing day on their own.

North London

The key destinations in north London are Islington and Camden. The gentrification of **Islington**'s Georgian squares and Victorian terraces has attracted boutiques and cafés, especially along Upper Street. Gentrifying **Camden** – famous for its market and situated

beside London Zoo – is one of London's liveliest nightlife areas. West of Camden, snooty **St John's Wood** is the spiritual home of cricket, while further to the north, **Hampstead** and **Highgate** are prettily leafy, well-off villages either side of the lovely heath.

Sights & museums

Hampstead Heath
Hampstead tube or Hampstead Heath rail.
The trees and grassy hills of the heath make it a surprisingly wild patch of the metropolis. Aside from the pleasure of walking, sitting and even swimming in the ponds, you can visit Kenwood House/Iveagh Bequest (Hampstead Lane, 8348 1286, www.english-heritage. org.uk), every inch the stately pile. Built in 1616, it was purchased by brewing magnate Edward Guinness, who donated his brilliant art collection

to the nation in 1927. Highlights include Vermeer's *The Guitar Player* and a fine Rembrandt self-portrait.

Jewish Museum

NEW *Raymond Burton House, 129-131 Albert Street, Camden, NW1 7NB (8371 7373, www.jewishmuseum.org.uk). Camden Town tube.* **Open** 10am-5pm Mon-Wed; 10am-9pm Thur; 10am-2pm Fri; 10am-5pm Sun. **Admission** £7; free-£6 reductions; £17 family.

This expanded museum reopened in 2010, and it's a brilliant exploration of Jewish life since 1066. Access is free to the downstairs café, beside an ancient ritual bath, and shop. You must pay to go upstairs, but there you can wield the iron in a tailor's sweatshop, sniff chicken soup and pose for a wedding photo. There's a powerful Holocaust section, focused on a single survivor, Leon Greenman. Opposite, a beautiful room of religious artefacts, including a 17th-century synagogue ark and centrepiece chandelier of Hanukkah lamps, introduces Jewish ritual.

Keats House

NEW *Keats Grove, Hampstead, NW3 2RR (7332 3868, www.keatshouse.city oflondon.gov.uk). Hampstead tube or Hampstead Heath rail, or bus 24, 46, 168.* **Open** Mid Apr-Oct 1-5pm Tue-Sun. Nov-mid Apr 1-5pm Fri-Sun. **Admission** £5; free-£4 reductions. *Garden* free.

Recently reopened after careful restoration, this was home to the Romantic poet John Keats from 1818 until 1820, when he left for Rome in the doomed hope of alleviating his TB. There are events, talks and poetry readings, as well as a display on Keats's sweetheart and neighbour Fanny Brawne. The garden has been redesigned to reflect different themes in Keats' poetry.

Lord's & MCC Museum

St John's Wood Road, NW8 8QN (7616 8595, www.lords.org). St John's Wood tube. **Tours** Nov-Mar noon, 2pm

Clubbing in pubs

Big tunes and great pints.

When a whole gang of major clubs (the Cross, the Key, Canvas, Turnmills, the End) closed for good in 2008 and 2009, it was declared the end of clubbing era. Few bothered to point out that a new era was beginning at the same time.

As the bigger venues closed, pubs stealthily took up much of the slack, with a host of ace boozers providing cutting-edge entertainment for savvy clubbing folk. 'Proper' clubs often have a short time-frame in which to make their bucks (six hours a night, three nights a week), but pubs don't suffer such limitations. And their many small rooms provide a cheap testing ground for promoters who want to try different things.

Brixton has long had the **Dogstar** (p188), the watering hole referenced in the Streets' 'Too Much Brandy', and pint-quaffing party heads still skip about in Islington's **Old Queen's Head** (p173), but north-west London is suddenly leading the pack with **Paradise by Way of Kensal Green** (p192). East London's **Star of Bethnal Green** (p184) has top rave credentials thanks to Mulletover's promoter Rob Star. Decked out in wild murals, great sound system, free admission every night – Star is pretty much the perfect pub-club. Hands-in-the-air rave? Swap party? Queer disco-a-thon? Sunday roast? You've come to the right place, young hedonist.

daily. *Apr-Oct* 10am, noon, 2pm daily. **Admission** £12; £6-£7 reductions; £31 family; free under-5s.

Lord's is more than just a famous cricket ground – as the headquarters of the Marylebone Cricket Club (MCC), it is official guardian of the rules of cricket. As well as staging test matches and internationals, the ground is home to the Middlesex County Cricket Club (MCCC). Visitors can take an organised tour round the futuristic, pod-like NatWest Media Centre and august, portrait-bedecked Long Room.

ZSL London Zoo

Regent's Park, Camden, NW1 4RY (7722 3333, www.zsl.org/london-zoo). Baker Street or Camden Town tube then 274, C2 bus. **Open** *Sept, Oct, Feb-mid July* 10am-5.30pm daily. *Mid July-Aug* 10am-6pm daily. *Nov-Jan* 10am-4pm daily. **Admission** £17.20-£19.80; free-£18.30 reductions; £55.60-£65 family. London Zoo has been open in one form or another since 1826. Spread over 36 acres and containing more than 600 species, it cares for many of the endangered variety – as well as your nippers at the new children's zoo. The emphasis throughout is on upbeat education. Exhibits are entertaining – we especially like the recreation of a kitchen overrun with large cockroaches. The 'Meet the Monkeys' attraction allows visitors to walk through an enclosure that recreates the natural habitat of black-capped Bolivian squirrel monkeys.

Eating & drinking

In Camden, **Proud** (p174) is great for rock 'n' roll boozing, while the original **Haché** (24 Inverness Street, 7485 9100, www.hacheburgers.com; see also p95) provides sustenance.

Bull & Last

168 Highgate Road, Kentish Town, NW5 1QS (7267 3641). Kentish Town tube/rail then bus 214, C1, or Gospel Oak rail then bus C11. **Open** noon-

11pm Mon-Thur; noon-midnight Fri, Sat; noon-10.30pm Sun. **££**.
Gastropub.
You'll get seriously good yet informal cooking here: braised ox cheek with parsley risotto and roast marrow and cassoulet perhaps; or Cornish hake served with broad bean, shallot and potato salad. Even the bar snacks – sausage roll with black pudding, or a steak sandwich – are firmly in the gourmet bracket, and several real ales are on draught. Worth booking ahead.

Gilgamesh

Stables Market, Chalk Farm Road, Camden, NW1 8AH (7482 5757, www. gilgameshbar.com). Camden Town tube. **Open** 6pm-2.30am Mon-Thur; noon-2.30am Fri-Sun. **Bar-restaurant**.
A Babylonian theme bar and restaurant so screamingly over the top that it makes Kubla Khan's palace look like a bouncy castle. The restaurant's retractable glass roof and inspired pan-Asian cuisine is similarly unexpected, although by the time you've weaved a path to the lapis lazuli bar you'll probably be prepared for the cocktail menu.

Market

43 Parkway, Camden, NW1 7PN (7267 9700, www.marketrestaurant. co.uk). Camden Town tube. **Open** noon-2.30pm, 6-10.30pm Mon-Sat; 1-3.30pm Sun. **££**. **British**.
Camden's other Market is a utilitarian but excellent British restaurant. Stripped-back hardly covers it: brick walls are ragged and raw; zinc-topped tables are scuffed; old-fashioned wooden chairs look like they were once used in a classroom. Food is similarly pared down, reliant on the flavours of high-quality seasonal produce.

Masala Zone

25 Parkway, Camden, NW1 7PG (7267 4422, www.masalazone.com). Camden Town tube. **Open** noon-11pm Mon-Sat; 12.30-10.30pm Sun. **££**. **Indian**.

This branch of the Masala Zone chain is especially popular with hip youngsters who come for the buzzy vibe, reasonable prices and decent pan-Indian food. The eye-catching decor is themed round colourful 1930s-style posters, retro artefacts and bright lampshades. The menu is notable for its earthy curries, thalis and zesty street snacks.

Old Queen's Head

44 Essex Road, Islington, N1 8LN (7354 9993, www.theoldqueenshead. com). Angel tube. **Open** noon-midnight Mon-Wed, Sun; noon-1am Thur; noon-2am Fri, Sat. **Pub**.
See box p171.

Ottolenghi

287 Upper Street, Islington, N1 2TZ (7288 1454, www.ottolenghi.co.uk). Angel tube or Highbury & Islington tube/rail. **Open** 8am-11pm Mon-Sat; 9am-7pm Sun. **££. Bakery-café**.
This is more than an inviting bakery. Behind the pastries piled in the window is a slightly prim deli counter with lush salads, available day and evening, eat-in or take away. As a daytime café, Ottolenghi is brilliant, but the long canteen-style central table, slow-footed service and bright decor aren't for special occasions.

Shopping

Alfie's Antique Market

13-25 Church Street, Marylebone, NW8 8DT (7723 6066, www.alfiesantiques. com). Edgware Road tube or Marylebone tube/rail. **Open** 10am-6pm Tue-Sat. No credit cards.
The far side of Regent's Park from Camden, Church Street is now probably London's most important area for antiques shops, with a cluster centred on the estimable Alfie's Antique Market. Alfie's has more than 100 dealers in vintage furniture and fashion, art, accessories, books, maps and quite a lot more. Look out for The Girl Can't Help It (7724 8984, www.thegirl

canthelpit.com), for example, a wonderful, sparkling cache of vintage Hollywood kitsch.

Camden Market

Camden Lock *Camden Lock Place, off Chalk Farm Road, NW1 8AF (www. camdenlockmarket.com).* **Open** 10am-6pm Mon-Fri (reduced stalls); 10am-6pm Sat, Sun.
Camden Market *Camden High Street, at Buck Street, NW1 (www.camdenmarkets.org).* **Open** 9.30am-6pm daily.
Stables Market *off Chalk Farm Road, opposite Hartland Road, NW1 8AH (7485 5511, www.stablesmarket. com).* **Open** 10.30am-6pm Mon-Fri (reduced stalls); 10am-6pm Sat, Sun.
All *Camden Town or Chalk Farm tube.* Amid T-shirts, corsets and chintz, between the thousands of tourists who want a snap of themselves with a genuine British punk, there are treats to be found by the discerning visitor. Our advice? Go later in the afternoon during the week, when it's quieter. 'Camden Market' is a collective name for several areas. Camden Market itself sells garish neon sunglasses and slogan T-shirts. Almost next door is the listed Electric Ballroom, which sells vinyl on weekends. Inverness Street Market opposite sells similar garb to the Camden Market, as well as a diminishing supply of fruit and veg. North, you'll find crafts, clothes, trinkets and small curiosities with a Japanese pop culture influence at Camden Lock and Camden Lock Village, the latter having opened after major fire damage to the market in spring 2009. North again is the Stables Market, with its Horse Hospital section, selling vintage clothing, snacks and classic designer furniture. Here too is Cyberdog, with its 'rave toys' and day-glo clubware.

Camden Passage

Off Upper Street, Islington, N1 (7359 0190, www.camdenpassageantiques. com). Angel tube.

Some of the quirky antiques dealers who first brought shoppers here remain, especially in characterful Pierrepont Arcade, but they have been joined by wonderful boutiques. Paul A Young Fine Chocolates (no.33) is one gorgeous example, with almost everything made in the downstairs kitchen. Kirt Holmes (no.16) does elegant handmade jewellery, Frost French (nos.22-26) is full of wearable and desirable clothes, including cute knits, while Equa (no.28) proves that eco-friendly clothes can be fashionable. Upper Street itself has loads of independent shops, covering both fashion and design.

Nightlife

For great weekend vibes, get down to the **Old Queen's Head** (p173).

Barfly

49 Chalk Farm Road, Chalk Farm, NW1 8AN (7688 8994 information, 0844 847 2424 box office, www.barflyclub.com). Chalk Farm tube. No credit cards.
As other similarly sized venues (200 capacity) open with smarter decor and less conventional programming, this venue's star has begun to fade. Still, it's part of the indie-rock fabric and the capital's original indie-electro nexus.

EGG

200 York Way, King's Cross, N7 9AP (7609 8364, www.egglondon.net). King's Cross tube/rail then free shuttle from York Way.
With three Ibiza-styled floors, a garden and a huge terrace (complete with small pool), EGG is big enough to lose yourself in but manages to feel intimate. The upstairs bar in red ostrich leather is rather elegant, but the main dancefloor downstairs has a warehouse rave feel.

Jazz Café

5 Parkway, Camden, NW1 7PG (7688 8899 information, 0844 847 2514 box office, www.jazzcafe.co.uk). Camden Town tube.

There's some jazz on the schedule here, but this two-floor club deals more in soul, R&B and hip hop these days, and has become the first port of call for soon-to-be-huge US acts (Mary J Blige and the Roots played early dates here).

KOKO

1A Camden High Street, Camden, NW1 7JE (0870 432 5527, 0844 847 2258 box office, www.koko.uk.com). Mornington Crescent tube.
Avoid standing beneath the sound-muffling overhang downstairs and you may find that this one-time music hall is one of London's finest venues. The 1,500-capacity hall stages weekend club nights and gigs by indie rockers, from cultish to those on the up.

Luminaire

311 Kilburn High Road, Kilburn, NW6 7JR (7372 7123 information, 0844 477 1000 box office, www.theluminaire.co.uk). Kilburn tube or Brondesbury rail.
The booking policy is fantastically broad, taking in everything from the Young Gods to Scritti Politti via Acoustic Ladyland. The sound system is up to scratch, the decor stylish and the staff really approachable.

Proud

Horse Hospital, Stables Market, Chalk Farm Road, Camden, NW1 8AH (7482 3867, www.proudcamden.com). Chalk Farm tube.
North London guitar slingers do rockstar debauchery at this former Horse Hospital, whether draping themselves – cocktail in hand – over the luxurious textiles in the individual stable-style booths, sinking into deck chairs on the terrace, or spinning round in the main band room to trendonista electro, indie and other alt-sounds.

Roundhouse

Chalk Farm Road, Camden, NW1 8EH (7424 9991 information, 0844 482 8008 box office, www.roundhouse.org.uk). Chalk Farm tube.

Camden Passage p173

Grandstand view

The View Tube is where to watch London 2012 develop.

Container Café

View Tube

If you wanted contemporary east London packed up in a box, this would be it – and what a brightly coloured box it is. Made out of recycled metal shipping containers and painted a vivid yellow-green, the View Tube (www.theviewtube.co.uk) is carefully placed on a ridge a short walk from Pudding Mill Lane DLR to provide the best possible vantage on the rapidly developing Olympic Park.

Almost in touching distance is the Sir Peter Cook/Populous Olympic Stadium, on your right Zaha Hadid's low-slung Aquatics Centre, and between them a copse – nay, forest – of busy cranes with a foreground of trucks, all busy about their summer 2011 deadline for completion.

View Tube combines its amazing setting with a commitment to social enterprise (cycle hire from Bikeworks, 'Classroom with a View' for school trips) and local producers (Beetroot & Culture veg, H Forman smoked salmon in the cream cheese bagels), which supply the excellent café.

Appropriately named, the Container Café is furnished with blue stools that echo the angular London 2012 motif, a pair of cute globe ceiling lights and, dividing the single room, a pot plant trellis with a hard hat hung off it. Even soon after opening, all East End life was here. A charming, lightly bearded Antipodean barista, a psychogeographically inclined couple with their urban sociology books, various merchandisers, an ad exec on his mobile, and, nose to the French windows, daily visitor David Doyle, an illustrator who has been patiently developing pencil sketches of the site. The view could hardly be bettered.

Getting here from the DLR stop is easy, but you'll need the courage of your convictions to weave through construction hoardings that are discreetly marked as a pedestrian walkway. Do so: this place is a lot of fun.

■ View Tube, the Greenway, Marshgate Lane, E15 2PJ. Pudding Mill Lane DLR. **Open** 9am-4.30pm daily.

or Hoxton rail. **Open** 10am-5pm Tue-Sat; noon-5pm Sun. **Admission** free; donations appreciated.

Housed in a set of 18th-century almshouses, the Geffrye Museum offers a vivid physical history of the English interior. Displaying original furniture, paintings, textiles and decorative arts, the museum recreates a sequence of typical middle-class living rooms from 1600 to the present – a fascinating take on domestic history.

Event highlights 'Christmas Past' (23 Nov 2010-2 Jan 2011).

Museum of London Docklands

No.1 Warehouse, West India Quay, Hertsmere Road, Docklands, E14 4AL (7001 9844, www.museumindocklands. org.uk). Canary Wharf tube or West India Quay DLR. **Open** 10am-6pm daily. **Admission** free.

Housed in a 19th-century warehouse (itself a Grade I-listed building), this huge sibling of the Museum of London (p161) explores the complex history of London's docklands and the river. Displays spreading over three storeys take you from the arrival of the Romans all the way to the docks' 1980s closure and the area's redevelopment. A haunting new exhibition sheds light on London's shameful involvement in the transatlantic slave trade.

Olympic Park

NEW *www.london2012.com*.

The View Tube offers the best vantage point on the key facilities for London 2012; see box opposite. We've also included a cycle route on pp48-50.

One Canada Square

Canary Wharf tube/DLR.

Cesar Pelli's dramatic office block, the country's tallest habitable building since 1991 (although soon to be overtaken by various competitors), remains an icon of our last period of financial overconfidence, instantly recognisable from all over London.

Ragged School Museum

46-50 Copperfield Road, Mile End, E3 4RR (8980 6405, www.raggedschool museum.org.uk). Mile End tube. **Open** 10am-5pm Wed, Thur; 2-5pm 1st Sun of mth. **Admission** free; donations appreciated.

Ragged schools were an early experiment in public education: they provided tuition, food and clothes for destitute children. This one was the largest in London, and Dr Barnardo himself taught here. It's now a sweet local museum with a complete mock-up of a classroom and an Edwardian kitchen.

V&A Museum of Childhood

Cambridge Heath Road, Bethnal Green, E2 9PA (8983 5235, www.museumof childhood.org.uk). Bethnal Green tube/ rail or Cambridge Heath rail. **Open** 10am-5.45pm daily. **Admission** free; donations appreciated.

Home to one of the world's finest collections of kids' toys, dolls' houses, games and costumes, the Museum of Childhood shines brighter than ever after extensive refurbishment, which has given it an impressive entrance. Part of the Victoria & Albert (p85), the museum has been amassing child-related objects since 1872 and continues to do so, with *Incredibles* figures complementing Barbie Dolls and Victorian praxinoscopes. There are plenty of interactive exhibits and a decent café too.

Event highlights 'Food Glorious Food' (29 Jan-8 May 2011).

Whitechapel Gallery

NEW *77-82 Whitechapel High Street, E1 7QX (7522 7888, www.whitechapel gallery.org). Aldgate East tube*. **Open** 11am-6pm Tue, Wed, Fri-Sun; 11am-9pm Thur. **Admission** free.

This East End stalwart has enjoyed a major redesign that saw the Grade II-listed building expand into the equally historic former library next door – rather brilliantly, the architects left the two buildings stylistically distinct rather than trying to smooth out their differences. As well as nearly tripling its exhibition space, the Whitechapel gave itself a research centre and archives room, as well as a proper restaurant and café. It looks set to improve a stellar reputation as a contemporary art pioneer built on shows of Picasso (*Guernica* was shown here in 1939), Pollock, Rothko and Frida Kahlo. With no permanent collection, there's a rolling programme of shows. **Event highlights** The Bloomberg Commission: Claire Barclay (until 2 May 2011); 'Social Sculpture' (ongoing).

Eating & drinking

Beside Old Spitalfields Market, **St John Bread & Wine** (94-96 Commercial Street, 7251 0848, www.stjohnbreadandwine.com) is the fine offshoot of St John (p157).

Albion at the Boundary Project

2-4 Boundary Street, Shoreditch, E2 7DD (7729 1051, www.albioncaff.co.uk). Old Street tube/rail or Shoreditch High Street rail. **Open** 8am-midnight daily. **£**. **Café**.
Boundary Project is a terrific operation in otherwise dishevelled Shoreditch. Albion is the ground-floor 'caff' (their description), food shop and bakery; Boundary is the smarter French restaurant in the basement, while a rooftop bar-grill and hotel rooms top off the operation (p206). Everything from Albion's British nostalgia menu tastes delicious, from a little appetiser of perfect crackling to a proper Irish stew.

Brick Lane Beigel Bake

159 Brick Lane, E1 6SB (7729 0616). Liverpool Street tube/rail or Shoreditch High Street rail. **Open** 24hrs daily. **£**. No credit cards. **Bagel bakery**.
This charismatic little East End institution rolls out perfect bagels both plain and filled (egg, cream cheese, mountains of salt beef), superb bread

and moreish cakes. Even at 3am, fresh baked goods are being pulled from the ovens at the back; no wonder the queue trails out the door when the innumerable local bars and clubs begin to close.

Chaat

36 Redchurch Street, Shoreditch, E2 7DP (7739 9595, www.chaatlondon. co.uk). Liverpool Street tube/rail then bus 8, 388, or Shoreditch High Street rail. **Open** 6.30-11pm Mon-Sat. **££**. **Bangladeshi**.
Chaat, which means 'snack food', is a welcoming, home-style Bangladeshi kitchen just beyond the northern end of London's most famous – and now frankly over-egged – curry corridor. Unpretentious, affordable comfort food is served up here in sparsely decorated but cheerful surroundings.

Dreambagsjaguarshoes

34-36 Kingsland Road, Hoxton, E2 8DA (7729 5830, www.dreambags jaguarshoes.com). Hoxton rail. **Open** 5pm-midnight Mon; noon-1am Tue-Fri; 5pm-1am Sat; noon-12.30am Sun. **Bar**.
Still as trendy as the day it first opened, this bar offers a fast-track education in what makes Shoreditch cool. Grungey but glam scruffs lounge in decor that changes, regularly and completely – artists are commissioned at intervals to give the place a makeover. The background music is self-consciously edgy and decent pizzas are available from next door.

E Pellicci

332 Bethnal Green Road, Bethnal Green, E2 0AG (7739 4873). Bethnal Green tube/rail or bus 8. **Open** 7am-4pm Mon-Sat. **£**. No credit cards. **Café**.
Not just a caff, but a social club, cabbies meeting room and unofficial match-making service, E Pellicci has been warmly welcoming customers since 1900. The marquetry-panelled interior is cramped and sharing tables for the trad English and Italian dishes is to be expected – in fact, relished.

One Canada Square p179

Rosa's

*12 Hanbury Street, Spitalfields, E1
6QR (7247 1093, www.rosaslondon.
com). Aldgate East tube or Liverpool
Street tube/rail.* **Open** *11am-10.30pm
Mon-Thur, Sun; 11am-1am Fri, Sat.*
££. Thai.

Rosa's is good-looking for a cheap eats,
shared-tables place, with wooden
architraves cunningly turned into wall
sculptures and attractive lighting. The
dishes are (mostly) the familiar Thai
roll-call, but there's a freshness and
honesty about the cooking.

Sông Quê

*134 Kingsland Road, Shoreditch,
E2 8DY (7613 3222). Old Street
tube/rail then bus 243, or Hoxton rail.*
Open *noon-3pm, 5.30-11pm Mon-Sat;
12.30pm-11pm Sun.* **£. Vietnamese**.

North-east London retains its monop-
oly on the capital's most authentic
Vietnamese restaurants, and Sông
Quê is still the benchmark. It's an efficient, canteen-like operation to which
diners of all types are attracted – be
prepared to share tables at busy times.

Tayyabs

*83 Fieldgate Street, Whitechapel,
E1 1JU (7247 9543, www.tayyabs.
co.uk). Aldgate East or Whitechapel
tube.* **Open** *noon-11.30pm daily.* **£.**
Pakistani.

Tayyabs is the East End equivalent of
the caffs favoured by truckers in
South Asia. It has been around since
the 1970s, and although the interior
has been extended, it's still a challenge
to bag a table. Cooking is big, bold and
sassy. The place gets crowded, but
service is swift and prices low.

Viajante

NEW *Patriot Square, Bethnal Green,
E2 9NF (7871 0461, www.viajante.co.
uk). Bethnal Green tube or Cambridge
Heath rail.* **Open** *noon-midnight daily.*
££££. Modern European.

Fêted young chef Nuno Mendes has
opened his own restaurant in a former

town hall – and it's rather different to
most places in this down-at-heel neighbourhood. A stint at El Bulli informs
Mendes's cooking: the six-, nine- or 12-
course tasting menus (£60-£85, with
matched wines for extra £30-£60) are
firmly in the 'experimental' camp.
Expect culinary fireworks. Inventive
tapas are served at the bar and there's
a more affordable three-course lunch.

Shopping

On Sundays, the whole area from
Old Spitalfields Market (below)
east to Brick Lane is a hectic
shopper's paradise.

Brick Lane Thrift Store

*68 Sclater Street, Spitalfields, E1 6HR
(7739 0242). Liverpool Street tube/rail
or Shoreditch High Street rail.* **Open**
noon-7pm daily.

At this second-hand shop, almost
everything is £10 or less. Across two
levels is a refined collection of popular
lines and best-sellers, such as checked
Western shirts, from the East End
warehouse. It's worth getting the tube
along to Stepney Green too, for Brick
Lane's predecessor the East End Thrift
Store (Unit 1A, Watermans Building,
Assembly Passage, 7423 9700).

Broadway Market

*www.broadwaymarket.co.uk. London
Fields rail, or bus 236, 394.*

Broadway Market has huge fashion
kudos, but it's high-quality produce
(this is primarily a specialist food market), well-edited vintage clothing and
independent boutiques that make it
really worth a visit. The market was-
n't always like this: after years of
decline, in 2004 volunteers from the
local traders' and residents' association
set about transforming their ailing fruit
and veg market. Now, it is one of
London's most successful local markets – the problem is making your
mind up between buying clothes,
books or tasty treats.

Caravan

NEW *3 Redchurch Street, Shoreditch, E2 7DJ (7033 3532, www.caravan style.com). Shoreditch High Street rail.* **Open** 11am-6.30pm Tue-Fri; noon-6pm Sat, Sun.

Quirky and romantic, Caravan is the brainchild of nostalgic stylist Emily Chalme, full of cute bygone finds such as a lamp in the shape of a duck or hand-printed wallpaper. Ignore the Brick Lane trendies – they're just part of the furniture – and get stuck into the beautifully curated homewares.

Cheshire Street

Aldgate East tube or Shoreditch High Street rail.

It doesn't look impressive, but this street off the northern section of Brick Lane is a haven for independent shops and vintage threads: artist Katy Hackney and costume designer Jane Petrie's gift shop-cum-gallery Shelf (no.40); Labour & Wait (no.18), paying homage to timeless, unfaddy domestic goods that combine beauty with utility; and Beyond Retro (no.112), an enormous bastion of second-hand clothing and accessories, give you a feel for the range on offer.

Columbia Road Market

Columbia Road, Bethnal Green, E2. Old Street tube/rail then bus 243, or Hoxton rail. **Open** 8am-2pm Sun.

On Sunday mornings, this unassuming East End street is transformed into a swathe of fabulous plant life and the air is fragrant with blooms. But it's not just about flora: alongside the market is a growing number of shops selling everything from pottery and Mexican glassware to cupcakes and perfume. Get there early for the pick of the crop, or around 2pm for the bargains; refuel at Jones Dairy (23 Ezra Street).

Jeanette's

NEW *64-66 Redchurch Street (entrance on Club Row), Shoreditch, E2 7DP (no phone, http://jeanettesshop.blogspot. com). Shoreditch High Street rail.* **Open** 11am-7pm Wed-Fri; 11am-5pm Sat, Sun.

The former glitter-encrusted host of fashion club night Boombox, Jeanette (aka James Main) stocks one-offs pinched from his designer friends like Christopher Kane and east London-based label New Power Generation. The antithesis of London's iconic-yet-stuffy boutiques.

Old Spitalfields Market

Commercial Street, between Lamb Street & Brushfield Street, Spitalfields, E1 6AA (7247 8556, www.visit spitalfields.com). Liverpool Street tube/rail. **Open** 9.30am-5pm Thur, Fri, Sun. *Antiques* 8.30am-4.30pm Thur. *Food* 10am-5pm Fri-Sun. *Fashion* 9.30am-5pm Fri. *Records & books* 10am-4pm 1st & 3rd Fri of the mth.

Since the 2003 renovation and total overhaul of the much-loved Spitalfields Market, it's a leaner, cleaner affair, bulked out with slightly soulless boutiques. A pitch here is expensive, so expect gastro-nibbles, wittily sloganed baby T-shirts and leather bags. If you want to avoid the crowds and make more idiosyncratic finds, forget the busy Sunday market and come on a Thursday for heaps of vintage fashion.

Old Truman Brewery

91-95 Brick Lane, Spitalfields, E1 6RF. Liverpool Street tube/rail or Shoreditch High Street rail.

The great brick buildings of this old brewery are home to a formidable array of funky retailers: Junky Styling (no.12) for innovative reworkings of second-hand clothes; Gloria's (no.6) for retro and up-to-the-minute sneakers; or denim and brogues from A Butcher of Distinction (no.11). Despite the fading fortunes of many record shops, Rough Trade East even chose to open a big, new, warehouse-style store, café and gig space here. Open only one day a week, the Sunday (Up)Market (7770 6100, www.sundayupmarket.co.uk) is

LONDON BY AREA

a buzzy collection of 140 stalls selling edgy fashion from fresh young designers, vintage gear, art and crafts, and well-priced jewellery. It's more relaxed, cheaper and all-round hipper than near neighbour Old Spitalfields Market.

123 Boutique

NEW *123 Bethnal Green Road, Shoreditch, E2 7DG (www.123bethnal greenroad.co.uk). Shoreditch High Street rail.* **Open** noon-7pm Tue, Wed, Fri, Sat; noon-8pm Thur; 11am-6pm Sun.

This eye-rollingly avant-garde, four-storey mini department store opened in spring 2010 in a Grade II-listed warehouse that used to prepare dodgy shooters for the London underworld. It's new mission? To sell recycled clothing with, as co-owner Ross Barry pointed out, 'the emphasis on fashion rather than the sustainable bit'. The first floor is a sort of rambling bazaar and the second floor hosts the store's own label, 123 – slick, sharp and, yes, sustainable.

Nightlife

Bardens Boudoir

36-44 Stoke Newington Road, Dalston, N16 7XJ (7249 9557, www.bardens boudoir.co.uk). Dalston Junction rail, or bus 67, 76, 149, 243. No credit cards. Located in the heart of Turkish Dalston below a disused furniture store, the 300-capacity Boudoir is something of a shambles – but that doesn't bother the often out-there line-ups nor the hipsters that love them. Hungry? 19 Numara Bos Cirrik (next door at no.34) is one of the city's best Turkish restaurants.

Bethnal Green Working Men's Club

42-44 Pollard Row, Bethnal Green, E2 6NB (7739 7170, www.workers playtime.net). Bethnal Green tube. The sticky red carpet and broken lampshades perfectly suit the programme of quirky lounge, retro rock 'n' roll and fancy-dress burlesque parties from spandex-lovin' dance husband-and-wife Duotard or Grind a Go Go. The mood is friendly, the playlist upbeat and the air always full of artful, playful mischief.

Café Oto

18-22 Ashwin Street, Dalston, E8 3DL (7923 1231, www.cafeoto.co.uk). Dalston Junction rail, or bus 30, 38, 67, 76, 149, 56, 277, 242. No credit cards. This 150-capacity café and music venue can't easily be categorised, though its website offers the tidy definition: 'creative new music that exists outside of the mainstream'. That means Japanese noise rockers, electronica pioneers, improvising noiseniks and artists from the strange ends of the rock, folk and classical spectrums.

Dalston Superstore

NEW *117 Kingland High Street, Dalston, E8 2PB (7254 2273). Dalston Junction rail.*
The opening of this gay arts-space-cum-bar cemented Dalston's status as the final frontier of east London's gay scene. It's a confidently cool, New York-style dive bar split between two floors, clad in cement, brick and steel vents, but enlivened with fluoro flashes, graffiti and art installations. During the day there's café grub and Wi-Fi; at night, expect queues for the impressive and eclectic guest DJs.

Star of Bethnal Green

359 Bethnal Green Road, Bethnal Green, E2 6LG (07932 869705, www. starofbethnalgreen.com). Bethnal Green tube. **Open** 11.30am-midnight Mon-Thur, Sun; 11.30am-2am Fri, Sat. See box p171.

Vortex Jazz Club

Dalston Culture House, 11 Gillet Street, Dalston, N16 8JN (7254 4097, www.vortexjazz.co.uk). Dalston Kingsland rail.
The Vortex is on the first floor of a handsome new building, with a restaurant on the ground floor. The space can

feel a bit sterile but the programming is superb, packed with left-field talent from Britain, Europe and the US. London's most exciting jazz venue.

South London

South London's attractions are many, but not always immediately obvious. Due south you'll find buzzing residential districts such as boisterous **Brixton**, with its lively nightlife, and the excellent bars and restaurants of **Clapham** and **Battersea**. South-east is **Greenwich**, laden with centuries of royal and maritime heritage. South-west are further headline attractions: **Kew** and **Hampton Court Palace**.

Sights & museums

Discover Greenwich & the Old Royal Naval College

NEW *Greenwich, SE10 9LW (8269 4747, www.oldroyalnaval college.org.uk). Cutty Sark DLR/ Greenwich DLR/rail.* **Open** 10am-5pm daily. **Admission** free.
Designed by Wren in 1694, with Hawksmoor and Vanbrugh helping to complete the project, the Old Royal Naval College is a superb collection of buildings originally built as a hospital for the support of seafarers and their dependants. The public can visit the rococo chapel, where there are free organ recitals, and the Painted Hall, a tribute to William and Mary that James Thornhill took a dedicated 19 years to complete. But start at the new attraction, Discover Greenwich (see box p187), which pulls the entire World Heritage Site together – including the several attractions run by the National Maritime Museum (p186).

Dulwich Picture Gallery

Gallery Road, Dulwich, SE21 7AD (8693 5254, www.dulwichpicture gallery.org.uk). North Dulwich or West Dulwich rail. **Open** 10am-5pm Tue-Fri; 11am-5pm Sat, Sun. **Admission** £5; free-£4 reductions.
This bijou gallery – the first to be purpose-built in the UK – was designed by Sir John Soane in 1811. It's a beautiful space that shows off Soane's ingenuity with and interest in lighting effects. The gallery displays a small but outstanding collection of work by Old Masters, offering a fine introduction to the baroque era through work by Rubens, Rembrandt and Poussin.
Event highlights 'Salvator Rosa: Bandits, Wilderness & Magic' (15 Sept-28 Nov 2010).

Hampton Court Palace

East Molesey, Surrey KT8 9AU (0844 482 7777, www.hrp.org.uk). Hampton Court rail, or riverboat from Richmond or Westminster to Hampton Court Pier (Apr-Oct). **Open** *Palace* Apr-Oct 10am-6pm daily; Nov-Mar 10am-4.30pm daily. *Park* dawn-dusk daily.
Admission *Palace, garden & maze* £14; free-£11.50 reductions; £38 family. *Maze* £3.50; free-£2.50 reductions. *Gardens* Apr-Oct £4.60; free-£4 reductions; Nov-Mar free.
It's a half-hour train ride from central London, but this spectacular palace, once owned by Henry VIII, is well worth the trek. It was built in 1514 and for the next 200 years became a focal point of English history: Shakespeare gave his first performance to James I here in 1604; and, after the Civil War, Oliver Cromwell was so besotted by the building he ditched his puritanical principles and moved in. Centuries later, the rosy walls of the palace still dazzle. Its vast size can be daunting, so it's a good idea to take advantage of the costumed guided tours. The Tudor Kitchens are great fun, with their giant cauldrons, fake pies and blood-spattered walls. More spectacular sights await outside, where the exquisitely landscaped gardens – on a scale to rival Versailles – contain fine topiary, peaceful Thames views and the famous Hampton Court maze.

LONDON BY AREA

National Maritime Museum

Romney Road, Greenwich, SE10 9NF (8858 4422, 8312 6565 recorded information, www.nmm.ac.uk). Cutty Sark DLR or Greenwich DLR/rail. **Open** 10am-5pm daily. **Admission** free; donations appreciated.

The world's largest maritime museum contains a huge store of creatively organised art, cartography, models and regalia. 'Explorers' covers great sea expeditions back to medieval times, while 'Maritime London' contains Nelson's uniform, complete with fatal bullet-hole; it moves to the Sammy Ofer Wing when it opens in 2013. The interactives are upstairs: the Bridge has a ship simulator, All Hands lets children load cargo, and you can try your hand as a ship's gunner. From the museum a colonnaded walkway leads to the Queen's House (8312 6565), designed by Inigo Jones and holding art by the likes of Hogarth and Gainsborough. Up the hill in the park, the Royal Observatory and Planetarium (8312 6565, www.rog.nmm.ac.uk) are also part of the museum – here you can straddle the Prime Meridian Line or take in a star show (£6.50, £4.50 reductions) in the Planetarium.

Royal Botanic Gardens (Kew Gardens)

Kew, Richmond, Surrey TW9 3AB (8332 5655, 8940 1171 information, www.kew.org). Kew Gardens tube/rail, Kew Bridge rail or riverboat to Kew Pier. **Open** *Apr-Aug* 9.30am-6.30pm Mon-Fri; 9.30am-7.30pm Sat, Sun. *Sept, Oct* 9.30am-6pm daily. *Nov-Jan* 9.30am-4.15pm daily. *Feb-Mar* 9.30am-5.30pm daily. **Admission** £13; free-£12 reductions.

The unparalleled collection of plants at Kew was begun by Queen Caroline, wife of George II, with exotic plants brought back by voyaging botanists (Charles Darwin among them). In 1759, Lancelot 'Capability' Brown was employed by George III to improve on the work of his predecessors, setting the template for a garden that today attracts thousands of visitors every year. Head straight for the 19th-century greenhouses, filled to the roof with tropical plants, and next door the Waterlily House's quiet and pretty indoor pond (closed in winter). Brown's Rhododendron Dell is at its best in spring, while the Xstrata Treetop Walkway, some 60ft above the ground, is terrific fun among autumn leaves.

Wimbledon Lawn Tennis Museum

Museum Building, All England Lawn Tennis Club, Church Road, SW19 5AE (8946 6131, www.wimbledon.org/ museum). Southfields tube or bus 39, 493. **Open** 10.30am-5pm daily; ticket holders only during championships. **Admission** £18; free-£15 reductions.

Highlights at this popular museum on the history of tennis include a 200° cinema screen that allows you to find out what it's like to play on Centre Court and a re-creation of a 1980s men's dressing room, complete with a 'ghost' of John McEnroe. Included in the ticket price is a behind-the-scenes tour. On Centre Court itself the big news is the retractable roof, which permits extended evening play – as well as bringing to an end those irritatingly predictable rain delays.

Eating & drinking

Franco Manca

4 Market Row, Electric Lane, Brixton, SW9 8LD (7738 3021, www.franco manca.co.uk). Brixton tube/rail. **Open** noon-5pm Mon-Sat. **Pizza**.

Franco Manca is the sort of discreet place you might walk past while ogling the Afro-Caribbean goodies in the surrounding market. Don't. It uses well-sourced, quality ingredients (many organic), top-notch equipment and good sourdough bases, quickly baked at high temperatures in the Neopolitan manner to seal in the flavour and lock in the moisture of the crust.

Discover Greenwich

The best thing in Greenwich since Sir Christopher Wren.

Maritime Greenwich is a superb cluster of historical attractions – it celebrated a decade as a UNESCO World Heritage Site a few years back – but it has always felt a little unfocused. There are the National Maritime Museum (opposite page) and Queen's House at the bottom of Greenwich Park, and the Royal Observatory and Greenwich Meridian Line at the top of the park's steep hill. There's the *Cutty Sark* and the fabulous colonnades of Wren's Old Royal Naval College by the DLR station. Worse, they're run by three different organisations.

So the opening of **Discover Greenwich** (p185) in the Old Royal Naval College is cause for celebration. It doesn't only do a fantastic job of tying the whole site together, with focused, informative sections on architecture and building techniques, the life of Greenwich pensioners, Tudor royalty and so forth, but also does so with a real sense of fun. While you're reading about coade stone

or scagliola (popular fake stone building materials), for example, the nippers can be busy building their own chapel with soft bricks or trying on a heavy knight's helmet.

The corner that describes Henry VIII's Chapel Royal is especially lovely. A reconstructed stained-glass window divides this section from the rest of the room, and when you open the flap that conceals a titchy model of the chapel itself there's a waft of incense and the strains of 16th-century choral music to give you atmosphere. There are also tremendous artefacts: shop tokens that were used by traders instead of money, for example, or the clay 'witch bottle', which X-rays prove contains bits of metal, nail clippings… and urine.

Next door, the superb **Old Brewery** (p188), a café, restaurant and micro-brewery, serves good food and superlative ale, while the other side of the building has a well-stocked shop and a Tourist Information Centre.

Lounge

NEW *55-58 Atlantic Road, Brixton, SW2 8PZ (7733 5229, www.lounge brixton.co.uk).* **Open** 11am-11pm Tue, Wed; 11am-midnight Thur-Sat; 11am-5pm Sun.

'Original urban retreat' is its subtitle, and such is Lounge. Ten paces from the Dogstar (below), its open windows facing Front Line Brixton Ltd, Lounge offers quality lunches by day (organic beefburgers, toasted paninis) and, by night, cocktails (£5.50, including a Lounge Martini of Grand Marnier, Bourbon and fresh lime). Monthly Brixton-themed film nights, rotating exhibitions and unplugged music sessions provide entertainment.

Old Brewery

NEW *Pepys Building, Old Royal Naval College, SE10 9LW (3327 1280, www. oldbrewerygreenwich.com). Cutty Sark DLR.* **Open** *Café* 10am-5pm daily. *Restaurant* 6-11pm Mon-Sat; 6-10.30pm Sun. *Bar* 11am-11pm Mon-Sat; noon-10.30pm Sun. **££. Modern British/microbrewery**.

The Meantime Brewing Company, creator of unusual artisan beers that have won international awards, has opened a microbrewery, pub and café-diner in Discover Greenwich (see box p187), on the site of a 1717 brewery. Here you can enjoy authentic, historical brews – such as the London Porter (p159) – from a selection of around 50 beers on draught or bottled, listed by style, and a menu that runs from pickled herring with a vinegary spring vegetable and mussel accompaniment or neck of mutton with purple sprouting broccoli, boiled new potatoes and salty anchovy sauce.

Nightlife

Dogstar

389 Coldharbour Lane, Brixton, SW9 8LQ (7733 7515, www.antic-ltd.com/dogstar). Brixton tube/rail. **Open** 4pm-2am Mon-Thur; 4pm-4am Fri; noon-4am Sat; noon-2am Sun.

A Brixton institution from back when Coldharbour Lane was somewhere people feared to go, Dogstar is a big street-corner pub exuding the urban authenticity loved by clubbers. The atmosphere can be intense, but it's never less than vibrant. See also box p171.

Fire/Lightbox

South Lambeth Road, Vauxhall, SW8 1UQ (www.myspace.com/firelondon). Craving clubs full of shirts-off muscle boys going at night-and-day techno? For a number of years the 'Vauxhall Village' has been destination of choice for hardcore gay clubbers, the sort who think nothing of starting on Friday and finding themselves still dancing on Monday. Key venues such as Fire are now also hosting mixed nights from the likes of Durr and Bugged Out. The Lightbox here is an all-round LED sensation.

O2 Arena, IndigO2 & Matter

Millennium Way, North Greenwich, SE10 0BB (8463 2000, 0844 856 0202 box office, www.theo2.co.uk). North Greenwich tube. Since its launch in 2007, this conversion of the Millennium Dome has been a huge success. The O2 Arena – a state-of-the-art, 23,000-capacity enormodome with good acoustics and sightlines – hosts the headline rock and pop acts. Its little brother, Indigo2, isn't actually that little (capacity 2,350) but is a good fit for big soul, funk and pop-jazz acts (Roy Ayers, Stacey Kent), knackered old pop stars (Gary Numan, Ultravox) and all points in-between. The newest addition to the nightlife portfolio, though, is a mighty collaboration with superclub Fabric (p159). The 2,600-capacity Matter (7549 6686, www.matterlondon.com) was designed by architect William Russell to operate as a concert venue, club, performing arts space or VIP club, and has good sightlines and magnificent sound. Thames Clippers (p214) operate half hourly boats back to central London.

RVT

Royal Vauxhall Tavern, 372
Kennington Lane, Vauxhall, SE11 5HY
(7820 1222, www.rvt.org.uk). Vauxhall
tube/rail. **Open** 7pm-midnight Mon-Fri;
9pm-2am Sat; 2pm-midnight Sun.
Admission £5-£7.

If you're seeking a very London gay
experience, this is where to start. The
pub-turned-legendary-gay-venue
operates an anything-goes booking
policy. The most famous fixture is
Saturday's queer performance night
Duckie (www.duckie.co.uk), with
Amy Lamé hosting turns at midnight
that range from strip cabaret to porn
puppets; Sunday's Dame Edna
Experience drag show, from 5pm, is
also absolutely essential, drawing
quasi-religious devotees.

Arts & leisure

BAC (Battersea Arts Centre)

Lavender Hill, Battersea, SW11 5TN
(7223 2223, www.bac.org.uk). Clapham
Common tube, Clapham Junction rail or
bus 77, 77A, 345.

Housed in the old Battersea Town Hall,
the forward-thinking BAC hosts young
theatre troupes; expect quirky, fun and
physical theatre from the likes of cult
companies Kneehigh and 1927. There
are also exciting festivals that combine
theatre and performance art, or showcase stand-up comedy, often leading
the way for the rest of London.

West London

Notting Hill Gate, **Ladbroke
Grove** and **Westbourne Park**
tube stations form a triangle that
contains lovely squares, grand
houses and fine gardens, along
with shops, bars and restaurants
to serve the kind of bohemian
who can afford to live here. Off
Portobello Road are the boutiques
of **Westbourne Grove** and
Ledbury Road.

Sights & museums

Museum of Brands, Packaging & Advertising

Colville Mews, Lonsdale Road, Notting
Hill, W11 2AR (7908 0880, www.
museumofbrands.com). Notting Hill
Gate tube. **Open** 10am-6pm Tue-Sat;
11am-5pm Sun. **Admission** £5.80;
free-£3.50 reductions.

Robert Opie began collecting the things
most of us throw away when he was 16.
Over the years the collection has grown
to include milk bottles, vacuum clean-
ers and cereal packets. The emphasis is
on British consumerism through the last
century, though there are items as old
as an ancient Egyptian doll.

Eating & drinking

Le Café Anglais

8 Porchester Gardens, Bayswater,
W2 4DB (7221 1415, www.lecafe
anglais.co.uk). Bayswater tube.
Open noon-3.30pm, 6.30-11pm
Mon-Thur; noon-3.30pm, 6.30-11.30pm
Fri; 11am-3.30pm, 6.30-11.30pm Sat;
noon-3.30pm, 6.30-10.15pm Sun. **£££**.
Modern European.

Chef-proprietor Rowley Leigh's fine
restaurant opened to great acclaim in
2007 and is still very popular. The
white, art deco-style room is big, with
floor-to-ceiling leaded windows on one
side, the open kitchen, rotisserie grill
and bar opposite. It's a see-and-be-seen
place with a long menu that's a mix-
and-match delight.

Kiasu

48 Queensway, Bayswater, W2 3RY
(7727 8810). Bayswater or Queensway
tube. **Open** noon-11pm daily. **£**.
Malaysian.

A cheerful, cheap, all-day restaurant
frequented by South-east Asians. Glass
mugs of sweet teh tarik, Malaysia's
favourite blend of tea and condensed
milk, help to soothe the chilli heat of
dishes such as soft-shell crab, served in
the Singapore chilli crab style.

LONDON BY AREA

Franco Manca p186

Ledbury

127 Ledbury Road, Westbourne Grove, W11 2AQ (7792 9090, www.the ledbury.com). Westbourne Park tube. **Open** noon-2.30pm, 6.30-10.30pm Mon-Sat; noon-3pm, 7-10pm Sun. **£££**.

French.

Notting Hillites flock to this elegant gastronomic masterpiece, where the food is as adventurous and accomplished as any, but less expensive than many. Flavours are delicate but intense, often powerfully earthy. It is possible to spend only £20-£30 on wine, but it's worth pushing the boat out.

River Café

Thames Wharf, Rainville Road, Hammersmith, W6 9HA (7386 4200, www.rivercafe.co.uk). Hammersmith tube. **Open** 12.30-3pm, 7-9.30pm Mon-Sat; 12.30-3pm Sun. **££££. Italian**. Despite the sad death of co-founder Rose Gray, the River Café's popularity shows no sign of waning. A refit hasn't transformed the winning formula, but did add a cheese room and a bar near the entrance. The wine list and staff are friendlier and more relaxed here than in most upmarket restaurants, but the food is excellent.

Taqueria

139-143 Westbourne Grove, Notting Hill, W11 2RS (7229 4734, www. taqueria.co.uk). Notting Hill Gate tube. **Open** noon-11pm Mon-Thur; noon-11.30pm Fri; noon-10.30pm Sat, Sun. **£. Mexican**. With its tortilla-making machine from Guadalajara, this place shows what Mexican street food is about: masa (maize dough) is flattened into soft tortillas for tacos, fried crisp for tostadas and shaped into thick patties for griddled sopes. Masks, movie posters and gorgeous staff make the place as easy on the eye as on the taste buds.

Westbourne House

65 Westbourne Grove, Westbourne Grove, W2 4UJ (7229 2233, www. westbournehouse.net). Bayswater or Royal Oak tube. **Open** noon-11.30pm Mon-Thur; noon-midnight Fri; 9.30am-midnight Sat; 9.30am-10.30pm Sun.

Cocktail bar.

This big, handsome pub has swapped nicotine stains and pint glasses for shiny surfaces, gilding on the mirrors and faux-French furniture, made all the more twinkly by low lighting and candles. The cocktail list is the work of drinks supremo Mat Perovetz: there are seven 'proper' martinis, spirits are premium and the delivery is pristine.

Shopping

Ledbury Road

Westbourne Park tube.
This strip of boutiques is shopping catnip for yummy mummies. They flock for chi-chi French fashion at Paul & Joe (nos.39-41), swimwear at Odabash (no.48B), designer jewellery at Ec one (no.56) and super chocolates at Keith Hurdman's Melt (no.59).

Portobello Road Market

Portobello Road, Notting Hill, W10 & W11 (www.portobelloroad.co.uk). Ladbroke Grove or Notting Hill Gate tube. **Open** 8am-6.30pm Mon-Wed, Fri, Sat; 8am-1pm Thur. *Antiques* 4am-4pm Fri, Sat.
Portobello is super-busy, but fun. Antiques start at the Notting Hill end, further down are food stalls, and emerging designer and vintage clothes congregate under the Westway and along the walkway to Ladbroke Grove on Fridays (usually marginally quieter) and Saturdays (invariably manic). Portobello also has fine shops, such as Honest Jon's 30-year-old record emporium (no.278) and Jasmine Guinness's hip kids' shop Honeyjam (no.267).

Rellik

8 Golborne Road, Ladbroke Grove, W10 5NW (8962 0089, www.rellik london.co.uk). Westbourne Park tube. **Open** 10am-6pm Tue-Sat.

LONDON BY AREA

This celeb fave was set up in 2000 by three Portobello market stallholders: Fiona Stuart, Claire Stansfield and Steven Philip. The trio have different tastes, which means there's a mix of pieces by the likes of Vivienne Westwood, Halston, Christian Dior and the ever-popular Ossie Clark.

Westfield London

Ariel Way, Shepherd's Bush, W12 7GF (7333 8118, www.westfield.com/london). White City or Wood Lane tube, or Shepherd's Bush tube/rail. **Open** 10am-10pm Mon-Wed, Fri; 10am-10pm Thur; 9am-9pm Sat; noon-6pm Sun.

Occupying 46 acres and nine different postcodes, Westfield London became Europe's largest shopping centre when it opened in 2008. The centre, which is on the site the London 1908 Games, cost around £1.6bn to build, and it houses more than 250 shops. Popular labels that have never had stand-alone stores in the UK, such as Hollister and Ugg, have shops here. Highlights from the boutique-like labels include Sienna Miller's Twenty8Twelve, Tabio, Myla and COS. Michelin-starred chefs Pascal Aussignac and Vincent Labeyrie can soothe away any shopping induced stress with their gastronomic creations at Croque Gascon.

Nightlife

Notting Hill Arts Club

21 Notting Hill Gate, Notting Hill, W11 3JQ (7460 4459, www.nottinghillarts club.com). Notting Hill Gate tube.

Cool west London folk are grateful for this small basement club. It isn't much to look at, but somehow almost single-handedly keeps this side of town on the radar thanks to nights like Thursday's YoYo – for fans of crate-digging, from funk to 1980s boogie.

O2 Empire Shepherd's Bush

Shepherd's Bush Green, W12 8TT (8354 3300, 0844 477 2000 box office, www.o2shepherdsbushempire.co.uk). *Shepherd's Bush Market tube or Shepherd's Bush tube/rail.*

This former BBC theatre is a great mid-sized venue, holding 2,000 standing or 1,300 seated. The sound is decent (with the exception of the alcove behind the stalls bar) and the staff are lovely. Bookings range from Steve Winwood to the Ting Tings.

Paradise by Way of Kensal Green

19 Kilburn Lane, Kensal Green, W10 4AE (8969 0098, www.theparadise. co.uk). Kensal Green tube or Kensal Rise rail. **Open** noon-midnight Mon-Wed; noon-1am Thur; noon-2am Fri, Sat; noon-11.30pm Sun.

Another fine exponent of the new art of pub-clubbing. See box p171.

Arts & leisure

Cinéphilia West

NEW *171 Westbourne Grove, Notting Hill, W11 2RS (7792 4433, www. cinephilia.co.uk). Notting Hill Gate tube.* **Open** 9.30am-6.30pm Tue-Sat; 11am-6.30pm Sun.

Cinéphilia West combines every conceivable filmic interest under one roof. Here you'll find a gallery with rare film posters, a good bookshop and a café, along with seminars and, of course, a programme of screenings.

Lyric Hammersmith

King Street, Hammersmith, W6 0QL (0871 221 1722, www.lyric.co.uk). Hammersmith tube.

Artistic director Sean Holmes launched his tenure in 2009 with a pledge to bring writers back into the building, making space for neglected modern classics and new plays alongside the cutting-edge physical and devised work for which the Lyric is best known. An inviting prospect, which should complement the Lyric's great track record as a breeding ground for young, experimental companies.

Essentials

Hotels 194
Getting Around 211
Resources A-Z 217
Index 220

Boundary p206

Hotels

Given general gloom about the economy, London's hotel sector remains surprisingly busy with openings, perhaps excited about the London 2012 Games. Two very different new hotels should be up and running on central Leicester Square (see box p202) by the time you read this. At the top end of the price range, huge refurbishment of the **Savoy** should be complete, and the Renaissance London St Pancras Marriott – in the amazing Victorian red-brick edifice that fronts the new Eurostar terminal – could open in 2011. Mid-range business hotels are also thriving: **Apex** has opened a second City hotel, while the monstrous Park Plaza Westminster Bridge has sprung up in front of its sister **Park Plaza County Hall**.

The sheer amount of activity is pushing hoteliers into new parts of town and driving steady improvements in quality. Pressure may even be beginning to build on prices: the stylish budget category, in which the **Hoxton** has had few credible competitors outside an Earl's Court cadre – **Base2Stay**, the **Mayflower** trio, **Stylotel** – may well be getting a shake-up: **Bermondsey Square**'s standard rooms start at £129 and the 'Tiny' rooms (their own, and justified, description) at the superb **Dean Street** go from £95. Still, you can't expect bargains in London: there is good value to be found, but to get a room that's genuinely cheap you'll either have to book months in advance or drop your standards.

One trend we've enjoyed in the last couple of years has been what you might term 'B&B deluxe'. **40 Winks** is only the artiest addition to a field that already includes **Rough Luxe** and the **Fox & Anchor**.

Money matters

When visitors moan about London prices (you know you do), their case is strongest when it comes to hotels. The average room rate has dipped recently, but we still reckon any decent double averaging under £120 a night is good value: hence, **£** in the listings below represents a rack rate of £100 or less. Hotels do offer special deals, though, notably at weekends; check their websites or ask when you book, and also look at discount websites such as www.london-discount-hotel.com and www.alpharooms.com.

The South Bank

All Seasons London Southwark Rose

47 Southwark Bridge Road, SE1 9HH (7015 1480, www.southwarkrosehotel. co.uk). London Bridge tube/rail. **££**.
The five-year-old Rose declares itself as sleekly modern with giant, domed, brushed aluminium lampshades and smart metal-framed cube chairs in a lobby hung with the work of Japanese photographer Mayumi. The rooms feature the dark woods, panelled headboards and crisp white linens of most 'contemporary' London hotels – but hey, who's knocking it? Fully wired up, there are even electric blackout blinds.

Bermondsey Square Hotel

Bermondsey Square, Tower Bridge Road, SE1 3UN (0870 111 2525, www.bespokehotels.com). Borough tube or London Bridge tube/rail. **££**.
This is a deliberately kitsch new-build on a newly developed square. Suites are named after the heroines of psychedelic rock classics (Lucy, Lily and so on), there are classic discs on the walls, and you can kick your heels from the suspended Bubble Chair at reception. But, although occupants of the Lucy suite get a multi-person jacuzzi (with a great terrace view), and anyone can get

SHORTLIST

Best new
- Apex London Wall (p206)
- Dean Street Townhouse & Dining Room (p203)
- 40 Winks (p208)

Most exciting prospects
- St John Hotel (see box p202)
- Savoy (see box p207)

All-round winners
- Claridge's (p201)
- Covent Garden Hotel (p202)
- Dean Street Townhouse & Dining Room (p203)

Best new takes on old London
- Connaught (p202)
- Fox & Anchor (p206)
- Hazlitt's (p203)

Best eating & drinking
- Albion at Boundary (p206)
- Connaught at the Connaught (p202)
- York & Albany (p209)

Best bargains
- Weekend suites at City Inn Westminster (p197)
- 'Tiny' rooms at Dean Street Townhouse & Dining Room (p203)
- Weekend stays at the Fox & Anchor (p206)
- Advance bookings at the Hoxton Hotel (p206)

Budget style
- B+B Belgravia (p198)
- Bermondsey Square Hotel (left)
- Hoxton Hotel (p206)
- Lux Pod (p199)
- Mayflower Hotel (p209)

Cheap & cheerful
- Clink Hostel (p201)

ESSENTIALS

sex toys from reception, the real draw isn't the gimmicks – it's well-designed rooms for competitive prices. The Brit food restaurant-bar is a bit hit-or-miss, but the hotel's pretty and the cheerful staff are helpful.

Park Plaza County Hall

1 Addington Street, SE1 7RY (7021 1800, www.parkplaza.com). Lambeth North tube or Waterloo tube/rail. **££.**
From the tube the approach is rather grimy, but this enthusiastically – if somewhat haphazardly – run hotel is well located just behind County Hall. Each room has its own kitchenette (microwave, sink), room sizes aren't bad (floor-to-ceiling windows help them feel bigger) and there's a handsomely vertiginous atrium, into which you peer down on the restaurant from infrequent glass lifts. The huge new Park Plaza Westminster Bridge has now opened just across the road.

Premier Inn London County Hall

County Hall, Belvedere Road, SE1 7PB (0870 238 3300, www.premierinn.com). Waterloo tube/rail. **£.**
A position right by the London Eye (p63) and friendly, efficient staff make this refurbished chain hotel the acceptable face of budget convenience. Check-in is quick; rooms are spacious, clean and warm, with comfortable beds and decent bathrooms with good showers, although some are quite dark. Buffet-style breakfast is extra and wireless internet access costs £10 a day.

Westminster & St James's

City Inn Westminster

30 John Islip Street, Westminster, SW1P 4DD (7630 1000, www.cityinn.com). Pimlico tube. **£££.**
There's nothing particularly flashy about this chain, but it is neatly designed, well run and obliging: the rooms have all the added extras you'd want (iMacs, CD/DVD library for your in-room player, free broadband, flatscreen TVs) and the floor-to-ceiling windows mean that river-facing suites on the 12th and 13th floors have superb night views – when the business people go home for the weekend you might grab one for £125.

Haymarket Hotel

1 Suffolk Place, St James's, SW1Y 4BP (7470 4000, www.firmdale.com). Piccadilly Circus tube. **££££.**
A terrific addition to Kit Kemp's Firmdale portfolio, this block-size building was designed by John Nash, the architect of Regency London. The public spaces are a delight, with Kemp's trademark combination of contemporary arty surprises (a giant light-bulb over the library's chessboard, a gothic little paper-cut of layered skulls above the free afternoon canapés) and impossible-to-leave, acid green, plump, floral sofas. Wow-factors include the bling basement swimming pool and bar (shiny sofas, twinkly roof) and the couldn't-be-more central location.

Trafalgar

2 Spring Gardens, Westminster, SW1A 2TS (7870 2900, www.thetrafalgar.com). Charing Cross tube/rail. **£££.**
In an imposing building, the Trafalgar is a Hilton – but you'd hardly notice. The mood is young and dynamic at what was the chain's first 'concept' hotel. To the right of the open reception is the cocktail bar, with DJs most nights, while breakfast downstairs is accompanied by gentle live music. The good-sized rooms (a few corner suites look into Trafalgar Square) have a masculine feel, with white walls and walnut furniture.

Windermere Hotel

142-144 Warwick Way, Westminster, SW1V 4JE (7834 5163, www.windermere-hotel.co.uk). Victoria tube/rail. **££.**

Heading a procession of small hotels, the Windermere is a comfortable, traditionally decked-out London hotel with no aspirations to boutique status. The decor may be showing its age a bit in the hall, but you'll receive a warm welcome and excellent service – there are over a dozen staff for just 20 rooms.

South Kensington & Chelsea

Aster House

3 Sumner Place, South Kensington, SW7 3EE (7581 5888, www.aster house.com). South Kensington tube. **££**.
On a swish, white-terraced street, the Aster triumphs through great attention to detail (impeccable housekeeping, the mobile phone guests can borrow) and the warmth of its managers. It's all low-key, soothing creams with touches of dusty rose and muted green. Breakfast in a lovely plant-filled conservatory.

B+B Belgravia

64-66 Ebury Street, Belgravia, SW1W 9QD (7823 4928, www.bb-belgravia. com). Victoria tube/rail. **££**.
B+B Belgravia have taken the B&B experience to a new level, although you pay a bit more for the privilege of staying somewhere with a cosy lounge that's full of white and black contemporary furnishings. It's sophisticated and fresh without being hard-edged, and there are all kinds of goodies to make you feel at home: an espresso machine for 24/7 caffeine, an open fireplace, newspapers and DVDs.

Blakes

33 Roland Gardens, South Kensington, SW7 3PF (7370 6701, www.blakes hotels.com). South Kensington tube. **££££**.
As original as when Anouska Hempel opened it in 1983 – the scent of oranges and the twittering of lovebirds fill the dark, oriental lobby – Blakes and its maximalist decor have stood the test of time, a living casebook for interior design students. Each room is in a different style, with antiques from Italy, India, Turkey and China. Downstairs is the Eastern-influenced restaurant, complemented by a gym and wireless internet for a celebrity clientele enticed by the discreet, residential location.

Gore

190 Queen's Gate, South Kensington, SW7 5EX (7584 6601, www.gorehotel. com). South Kensington tube. **££££**.
This fin-de-siècle period piece was founded by descendants of Captain Cook in two grand Victorian town houses. The lobby and staircase are close hung with old paintings, and the bedrooms all have carved oak beds, sumptuous drapes and old books. The suites are spectacular: the Tudor Room has a huge stone-faced fireplace and a minstrels' gallery; tragedy queens love the Venus room, with Judy Garland's old bed and replica ruby slippers.

Halkin

Halkin Street, Belgravia, SW1X 7DJ (7333 1000, www.halkin.como.bz). Hyde Park Corner tube. **££££**.
Gracious and discreet behind a Georgian-style façade, Christina Ong's first hotel (sister to the more famous Metropolitan) was ahead of the East-meets-West design trend when it opened in 1991 and its subtle marriage of European luxury and oriental serenity looks more current than hotels half its age. Off curving black corridors, each room has a touchscreen bedside console to control everything from the 'Do not disturb' sign to the air-con.

Lanesborough

1 Lanesborough Place, Knightsbridge, SW1X 7TA (7259 5599, www. lanesborough.com). Hyde Park Corner tube. **££££**.
Considered one of London's historic luxury hotels, the Lanesborough was in fact impressively redeveloped only

Gore

in the 1990s. Occupying an 1820s Greek Revival hospital building, its luxurious guest rooms are traditionally decorated (antique furniture, Carrera-marble bathrooms) but with electronic keypads to change the air-con or call on the superb 24hr room service. Rates include high-speed internet, movies and calls within the EU and to the US; complimentary personalised business cards state you are resident here.

Lux Pod

38 Gloucester Road, South Kensington, SW7 4QT (7460 3171, www.theluxpod. com). Gloucester Road tube. **££**.
This little hideaway is the pride and joy of its owner, Judith Abraham, with many of the features purpose-designed. Little is the operative word: it's a tiny space that ingeniously packs in a bathroom, slide-top kitchenette and lounge, with the comfy bed high up above the bathroom and accessible only by ladder. All is shiny and modern, and the room is packed with gadgets and high-style details. The tight space is ideal for one, a little fiddly to get round for two,

but terrific fun for any design fan, tech-geek or traveller bored of samey hotels.

Morgan House

120 Ebury Street, Belgravia, SW1W 9QQ (7730 2384, www.morganhouse.co. uk). Pimlico tube or Victoria tube/rail. **£**.
The Morgan has the understated charm of the old family home of a posh but unpretentious English friend: a pleasing mix of nice old wooden or traditional iron beds, pretty floral curtains and coverlets in subtle hues, the odd chandelier or big gilt mirror over original mantelpieces, padded wicker chairs and sinks in every bedroom. Though there's no guest lounge, guests can sit in the little patio garden.

Myhotel Chelsea

35 Ixworth Place, Chelsea, SW3 3QX (7225 7500, www.myhotels.com). South Kensington tube. **£££**.
The Chelsea Myhotel feels a world away from its sleekly modern Bloomsbury predecessor (11-13 Bayley Street, 7667 6000), its aesthetic softer and more feminine. Pink walls, a floral sofa and a plate of scones in the lobby offer a posh English foil to the mini-chain's signature feng shui touches and aquarium. The modernised country farmhouse feel of the bar-restaurant works better for breakfast than a boozy cocktail, but the conservatory-style library is wonderful.

Number Sixteen

16 Sumner Place, South Kensington, SW7 3EG (7589 5232, www.firmdale. com). South Kensington tube. **£££**.
This may be Firmdale's most affordable hotel, but there's no slacking in style – witness the fresh flowers and origami-ed birdbook decorations in the comfy drawing room. Bedrooms are generously sized, bright and light, and carry the Kit Kemp trademark mix of bold and traditional. By the time you finish breakfast in the sweet conservatory, looking out on the delicious back garden with its central water feature, you'll have forgotten you're in the city.

ESSENTIALS

Connaught p202

Vicarage Hotel

10 Vicarage Gate, Kensington, W8 4AG (7229 4030, www.londonvicarage hotel.com). High Street Kensington or Notting Hill Gate tube. **££**.

Devotees return regularly to this tall Victorian townhouse, tucked in a leafy square by Kensington Gardens (p85). It's comfortable and resolutely old-fashioned. There's a grand entrance hall with red-and-gold striped wallpaper, a chandelier and a huge gilt mirror, as well as a sweeping staircase that ascends to an assortment of good-sized rooms furnished in pale florals and nice old pieces of furniture.

West End

Academy Hotel

21 Gower Street, Bloomsbury, WC1E 6HG (7631 4115, www.the etoncollection.com). Goodge Street tube. **£££**.

Comprising five Georgian townhouses, the Academy has a restrained country-house style – decor in most rooms is soft, summery florals and checks; the eight suites look more sophisticated. Guests are cocooned from the busy streets and those in the split-level doubles get plenty of breathing space at decent rates. The library and conservatory open on to walled gardens where drinks and breakfast are served in summer.

Arosfa

83 Gower Street, Bloomsbury, WC1E 6HJ (7636 2115, www.arosfalondon. com). Goodge Street tube. **£**.

Given the reasonable room rates, the trendy swishness of the public areas in this amiable budget hotel comes as a pleasant surprise. You're treated to Philippe Starck chairs, mirrored chests and a huge New York skyline in the lounge; more stylish embellishments in the halls; and tasteful, neutral tones in the well-equipped bedrooms. Recent improvements include flatscreen TVs, free wireless internet and the wherewithal for hot drinks in the rooms.

Charlotte Street Hotel

15-17 Charlotte Street, Fitzrovia, W1T 1RJ (7806 2000, www.firmdale.com). Goodge Street or Tottenham Court Road tube. **££££**.

This gorgeous Firmdale hotel is a fine exponent of Kit Kemp's fusion of traditional and avant-garde – you won't believe it was once a dental hospital. Public rooms contain Bloomsbury Set paintings (Duncan Grant, Vanessa Bell), while the bedrooms mix English understatement with bold decorative flourishes. The huge beds and trademark polished granite bathrooms are suitably indulgent, and some rooms have unbelievably high ceilings. The bar-restaurant buzzes with media types, for whom the screening room must feel like a home comfort.

Claridge's

55 Brook Street, Mayfair, W1K 4HR (7629 8860, www.claridges.co.uk). Bond Street tube. **££££**.

Claridge's is sheer class and pure atmosphere, its signature art deco redesign still dazzling. Photographs of Churchill and sundry royals grace the grand foyer, as does an absurdly over-the-top Dale Chihuly chandelier. Without departing too far from the traditional, Claridge's bars and restaurant are actively fashionable – Gordon Ramsay is the in-house restaurateur, and the A-listers can gather for champers and sashimi in the bar. The rooms divide evenly between deco and Victorian style, with period touches balanced by high-tech bedside panels.

Clink Hostel

78 King's Cross Road, King's Cross, WC1X 9QG (7183 9400, www.clink hostel.com). King's Cross tube/rail. **£**.

In a former courthouse, the Clink sets the bar high for hosteldom. There's the setting: the original wood-panelled lobby and courtroom where the Clash stood before the beak (now filled with backpackers surfing the web). Then there's the urban chic ethos, from the

Sleep off your eats

Pioneer restaurant St John is opening its first hotel.

St John (p157) is the London restaurant that revolutionised modern British cooking, so the announcement it was opening a West End hotel has raised optimistic eyebrows. Why? Co-owner Trevor Gulliver put it succinctly: 'It will be that rare thing – a hotel where people would actually want to eat.'

The first floor, ground floor and basement of the **St John Hotel** (1-2 Leicester Street, WC2H 7BL) will contain a bar and restaurant, then 15 rooms and a suite are to be arranged above. 'Just as you feel well fed and well taken care of when you eat at St John, we'll take that spirit into the hotel,' says Gulliver. In keeping with the white, masculine, minimalist style of the original Smithfield eaterie, converted from a derelict smokehouse, the decor here won't smother visitors with cushions and curtains.

The plans suggest the hotel-restaurant should open as this guide hits the shelves, just north of Leicester Square, a location noted for neither gustatory delicacies nor good hotels. Interestingly, Starwood Hotels are opening one of their excellent **W Hotels** (www. starwoodhotels.com/whotels) this year, a few hundred yards south of the St John Hotel – 192 rooms of competition and a renaissance of sorts, in a bit of town that sorely needs both.

streamlined red reception counter to the dining area's chunky wooden tables and Japanese-style 'pod' beds. Clink's cosier sister, Ashlee House (261-265 Gray's Inn Road, 7833 9400, www.ashleehouse.co.uk) is nearby.

Connaught

Carlos Place, Mayfair, W1K 2AL (7499 7070, www.the-connaught.co.uk). Bond Street tube. **££££**.
It isn't the only London hotel to provide butlers, but there can't be many that offer 'a secured gun cabinet room' for hunting season. This is traditional British hospitality for those who love 23-carat gold leaf and stern portraits in the halls, but all mod cons in their room, down to free wireless and flatscreens in the en suite. Both of the bars – gentleman's club cosy Coburg and cruiseship deco Connaught (p108) – and the Hélène Darroze restaurant are impressive. In the new wing, which doubled the guestrooms, there's a spa and 60sq m swimming pool.

Covent Garden Hotel

10 Monmouth Street, Covent Garden, WC2H 9LF (7806 1000, www. firmdale.com). Covent Garden or Leicester Square tube. **££££**.
On the ground floor, the 1920s Paris-style Brasserie Max and its retro zinc bar have been cunningly expanded – testament to the continuing popularity of Firmdale's snug and stylish 1996 establishment. Its location and tucked-away screening room ensure it continues to attract starry customers, and guests needing a bit of privacy can retreat upstairs to the lovely panelled private library. In the individually styled guest rooms, pinstriped wallpaper and floral upholstery are mixed with bold, contemporary elements.

Cumberland

Great Cumberland Place, off Oxford Street, W1H 7DL (0870 333 9280, www.guoman.com). Marble Arch tube. **£££**.

Perfectly located (turn the right way out of Marble Arch tube and you're there in seconds), the Cumberland is a monster. There are 900 rooms, plus 119 in an annexe, and an echoing, chaotic lobby with dramatic modern art and a waterfall sculpture. The rather small rooms are minimalist and nicely designed (acid-etched headboards, neatly modern bathrooms, plasma TVs). Dine at exclusive Rhodes W1 (7616 5930, www.rhodesw1.com) or the bar-brasserie, or brave the late-night, trash-industrial-style DJ bar.

Dean Street Townhouse & Dining Room

NEW 69-71 Dean Street, Soho, W1D 3SE (7434 1775, www.sohohouse.com). Leicester Square or Piccadilly Circus tube. £££.
This is the latest winning enterprise from the people behind Soho House members' club. To one side of a buzzy ground-floor restaurant (p132) are four floors of bedrooms that run from full-size rooms with early Georgian panelling and reclaimed oak floors to half-panelled 'Tiny' rooms that are barely bigger than their double beds – but available for from £95. The atmosphere is gentleman's club cosy (there are cookies in a cute silver Treats container in each room), but modern types also get rainforest showers, 24hr service, Roberts DAB radios, free wireless internet and big flatscreen TVs.

Dorchester

53 Park Lane, Mayfair, W1K 1QA (7629 8888, www.thedorchester.com). Hyde Park Corner tube. ££££.
A Park Lane fixture since 1931, the Dorchester's interior is opulently classical, but its attitude is cutting-edge, with a terrific level of personal service. With one of the grandest lobbies in town, amazing park views, state-of-the-art mod cons and a magnificently refurbished (to the tune of £3.2 million) spa, it's small wonder the hotel welcomes movie stars (the lineage runs from Elizabeth Taylor to Tom Cruise) and political leaders (Eisenhower planned D-Day here). You're not likely to be eating out, either: the Dorchester employs 90 chefs at the Grill Room, Alain Ducasse and China Tang.

Harlingford Hotel

61-63 Cartwright Gdns, Bloomsbury, WC1H 9EL (7387 1551, www. harlingfordhotel.com). Russell Square tube or Euston tube/rail. ££.
An affordable hotel with bundles of charm in the heart of Bloomsbury, the Harlingford has light airy rooms with boutique aspirations. Decor is lifted from understated sleek to quirky with the help of vibrant colour splashes from the glass bathroom fittings and the mosaic tiles. The crescent it's set in has a lovely, leafy private garden.

Hazlitt's

6 Frith Street, Soho, W1D 3JA (7434 1771, www.hazlittshotel.com). Tottenham Court Road tube. £££.
Four Georgian townhouses comprise this absolutely charming place, named after William Hazlitt, the spirited 18th-century essayist who died here in abject poverty. With flamboyance and staggering attention to detail the rooms evoke the Georgian era, all heavy fabrics, fireplaces, free-standing tubs and exquisitely carved half-testers, yet modern luxuries – air-conditioning, TVs in antique cupboards, free wireless internet and triple-glazed windows – have also been subtly attended to. It gets creakier and more crooked the higher you go, culminating in enchanting garret single rooms.

Montagu Place

2 Montagu Place, Marylebone, W1H 2ER (7467 2777, www.montagu-place. co.uk). Baker Street tube. £££.
A stylish small hotel in a pair of Grade II-listed Georgian townhouses, catering primarily for the midweek business traveller. All rooms have pocket-sprung beds, as well as cafetières and flatscreen

TVs (DVD players are available from reception). The look is boutique-hotel sharp, except for an uneasy overlap of bar and reception – though you can simply get a drink and retire to the graciously modern lounge.

Morgan
24 Bloomsbury Street, Bloomsbury, WC1B 3QJ (7636 3735, www.morgan hotel.co.uk). Tottenham Court Road tube. **££**.

This brilliantly located, comfortable budget hotel looks better than it has for a while after recent renovations. The rooms have ditched floral for neutral, and are equipped with free wireless, voicemail, air-con and flatscreen tellies with Freeview. A slap-up English breakfast is served in a good-looking room with wood panelling, London prints and blue-and-white china plates. The spacious flats are excellent value.

No.5 Maddox Street
5 Maddox Street, Mayfair, W1S 2QD (7647 0200, www.living-rooms.co.uk). Oxford Circus tube. **£££**.

A bit different, this: for your money, you get a chic, self-contained apartment. Shut the discreet brown front door, climb the stairs and flop into a well-furnished home from home with all mod cons, including new flatscreen TVs. Each apartment has a fully equipped kitchen, but room service will shop for you in addition to the usual hotel services. The East-meets-West decor is classic 1990s minimalist, but bright and clean after refurbishment.

One Aldwych
The Strand, WC2B 4RH (7300 1000, www.onealdwych.com). Covent Garden or Temple tube, or Charing Cross tube/rail. **££££**.

You only have to push through the front door and enter the breathtaking Lobby Bar to know you're in for a treat. Despite its weighty history – the 1907 building was designed by the men behind the Ritz – One Aldwych is thoroughly modern, from Frette linen through bathroom mini-TVs to environmentally friendly loo flushes. The location is perfect for Theatreland, but

Rough Luxe

the cosy screening room and swimming pool may keep you indoors.

Piccadilly Backpackers

12 Sherwood Street, Soho, W1F 7BR (7434 9009, www.piccadillybackpackers. com). Piccadilly Circus tube. **£.**
You couldn't be more central than at this enormous hostel plonked right behind Piccadilly Circus. The almost invisible entrance gives way to several floors of accommodation and facilities like a travel shop, laundry, internet café and TV lounge. Sure, it's basic, but it's relaxed, bright and airy. Try for the third floor – here's where you'll find dorms of pod beds quirkily decorated by graphic art students.

Rough Luxe

1 Birkenhead Street, King's Cross, WC1H 8BA (7837 5338, www.rough luxe.co.uk). King's Cross tube/rail. **££.**
In a bit of King's Cross that's choked with ratty B&Bs, this Grade II-listed property has walls artfully distressed, torn wallpaper, signature works of art, old-fashioned TVs that barely work and even retains the sign for the hotel that preceded Rough Luxe: 'Number One Hotel'. Each room has free wireless internet, but otherwise have totally different characters. It's all rather hip and fun. The owners are more than happy to chat over a bottle of wine in the back courtyard where a great breakfast is served.

Sanctum Hotel

20 Warwick Street, Soho, W1B 5NF (7292 6100, www.sanctumsoho.com). Oxford Circus or Piccadilly Circus tube. **£££.**
Sanctum is Soho club cool with its dark colours, bling room handles and deco lamps, sexed up with a handful of rotating beds and a no-questions-asked policy. The rooms follow one of four colour schemes, broadly deco or powder-puff boudoir in style, with plenty of mirrors and an unspeakable number of TV channels. The residents-only,

24hr-means-24hr bar is small but funky, opening on to a two-level terrace outside, which is topped off with a multi-person jacuzzi.

Sanderson

50 Berners Street, Fitzrovia, W1T 3NG (7300 1400, www.morganshotelgroup. com). Oxford Circus tube. **££££.**
This Schrager/Starck statement creation takes clinical chic to new heights. The only touch of colour in our room was a naïve landscape painting nailed to the ceiling over the silver sleigh bed. Otherwise, it's all flowing white net drapes, glass cabinets and retractable screens. The residents-only Purple Bar sports a button-backed purple leather ceiling and fabulous cocktails; the 'billiard room' has a purple-topped pool table and weird tribal adaptations of classic dining-room furniture.

Savoy

NEW *The Strand, WC2R 0EU (7836 4343, www.fairmont.com). Covent Garden or Embankment tube, or Charing Cross tube/rail.* **££££.**
See box p207.

Sherlock Holmes Hotel

108 Baker Street, Marylebone, W1U 6LJ (7486 6161, www.sherlockholmes hotel.com). Baker Street tube. **£££.**
Park Plaza transformed a dreary Hilton into this hip boutique hotel a few years back. Guests now mingle with local office workers in the casually chic bar (extending to a lounge in the style of a glossed-up gentlemen's club) and organic restaurant. The bedrooms resemble hip bachelor pads: beige and brown colour scheme, leather headboards and spiffy bathrooms. Split-level 'loft' suites take advantage of the first floor's double-height ceilings, and there's a gym with sauna.

22 York Street

22 York Street, Marylebone, W1U 6PX (7224 2990, www.22yorkstreet.co.uk). Baker Street tube. **££.**

Imagine one of those bohemian French country houses you see in *Elle Decor* – all pale pink lime-washed walls, wooden floors and quirky antiques. That's the feel of this graceful, unpretentious bed and breakfast. There's no sign on the door and the sense of staying in a hospitable home continues when you're offered coffee in the spacious breakfast room-cum-kitchen with its curved communal table. Many of the rooms have en suite baths.

The City

Andaz Liverpool Street

40 Liverpool Street, EC2M 7QN (7961 1234, www.london.liverpool street.andaz.com). Liverpool Street tube/rail. **££££**.

A faded railway hotel until its £70m Conran overhaul in 2000, this is now one of Hyatt's boutique brand. The new approach offers well-informed, down-to-earth service and eco-friendliness. The bedrooms still wear style-mag uniform – Eames chairs, Frette linens – but free services (local calls, wireless internet, healthy minibar) and savvy efforts to connect with the vibey local area are appreciated: witness the temporary Summer Garden, installed at the base of the breathtaking atrium as a place to lounge over cocktails, and entertainments in the Freemasons' Temple.

Apex London Wall

NEW *7-9 Copthall Avenue, EC2R 7NJ (0845 365 0000, www.apexhotels.co.uk). Tower Hill tube.* **££**.

The mini-chain's newest London hotel shares the virtues of its predecessor (Apex City of London, 1 Seething Lane, 7702 2020). The service is obliging, the rooms are crisply designed with all mod cons, and there are comforting details – rubber duck in the impressive bathrooms, free jelly beans, free local calls. From the suites, a terrace peers into offices, but the view from the restaurant – of a flamboyantly sculpted business institute – is as good.

Boundary

2-4 Boundary Street, E2 7DD (7729 1051, www.theboundary.co.uk). Shoreditch High Street rail or bus 8, 26, 48. **£££**.

In a converted warehouse, Conran's latest combines restaurant, rooftop bar, ground-floor café (p180) and excellent hotel rooms, the whole establishment clearly a labour of love. Each room has a wet room and hand-made bed, but is otherwise coolly individual, with classic furniture and original art. The five split-level suites range in style from the bright and sea-salt fresh Beach to a new take on Victoriana, while the remaining rooms are themed by design style: Mies van der Rohe, Shaker and so on. Good rates too on a Sunday.

Fox & Anchor

115 Charterhouse Street, EC1M 6AA (0845 347 0100, www.foxandanchor. com). Barbican tube or Farringdon tube/rail. **££**.

No more than a few atmospheric, well-appointed and luxurious rooms above a bustling, darkly panelled pub, this was one of our most enjoyable stays of 2008. Each en suite room differs, but the high-spec facilities (big flatscreens, clawfoot bath, drench shower) and quirky attention to detail (bottles of ale in the mini-bar, 'Nursing hangover' signs to hang out if you want some privacy) are common throughout. Expect some clanking market noise in the early mornings.

Hoxton Hotel

81 Great Eastern Street, EC2A 3HU (7550 1000, www.hoxtonhotels.com). Old Street tube/rail. **£**.

Everything you've heard is true. First, there's the hip location. Then there are the great design values: the foyer is a sort of postmodern country lodge (with stag's head) and rooms that are small but well thought-out and full of nice touches (Frette linens, free fresh milk in the mini-fridge). Above all, it's the budget-airline pricing system, by which you might catch a £1-a-night room.

An old stager reborn

The Savoy's complex renovation approaches an end.

If you're planning to do big-money luxury in London, this should be a great year to get traditional: the superluxed **Savoy** (p205) is due to have reopened in summer 2010 – after numerous delays. Built in 1889 to put up theatre-goers from Richard D'Oyly Carte's Gilbert & Sullivan shows, the Savoy is the hotel from which Monet painted the Thames, where Vivien Leigh met Laurence Olivier, where Londoners learned to love the martini. Long known for its discreet mix of Edwardian neo-classical and art deco, the Grade II-listed hotel will have undergone more than £100m of renovations.

An impressive £2.5m is being dropped on the fifth-floor Royal Suite alone: two bedrooms (plus an optional third, if you've extra guests), a kitchen (for your chef, silly, you're not expected to cook) and eight bay windows overlooking the river can cost that kind of dosh. The famous cul-de-sac at the front entrance gets a garden of new topiary and a centrepiece crystal fountain (Lalique, of course), but the welcome will begin before you even arrive with a phone call to check out your particular needs. 'Anything that needs doing for a guest will be done in advance,' says General Manager Kiaran MacDonald.

There will be a new tearoom, with glass-roofed conservatory, while the leather counter of the new champagne bar is set on a stage that once hosted big bands for dinner dances. Be reassured, though: the Savoy Grill (to be run by Gordon Ramsay), the American Bar and the rooftop swimming pool will remain in place. It's tradition, you know.

Malmaison

Charterhouse Square, EC1M 6AH
(7012 3700, www.malmaison.com).
Barbican tube or Farringdon tube/rail.
£££.

It's part of a chain, but the Malmaison is a charming hotel, beautifully set in a cobblestone square near the lively restaurants and bars of Smithfield Market. The reception is stylish with its lilac-and-cream checked floor, exotic plants and petite champagne bar; purples, dove-grey and black wood dominate the rooms, where you'll find free broadband and creative lighting. The gym and a subterranean brasserie complete the picture.

Rookery

12 Peter's Lane, Cowcross Street,
EC1M 6DS (7336 0931, www.rookery
hotel.com). Farringdon tube/rail. **£££**.
The front door of the Rookery is satisfyingly hard to find, especially when the streets are teeming with Fabric (p159) devotees (the front rooms can be noisy on these nights). Once inside, guests enjoy a warren of creaky rooms, individually decorated in the style of a Georgian townhouse: clawfoot baths, elegant fourposters. The split-level Rook's Nest suite has views of St Paul's (p162).

Zetter

86-88 Clerkenwell Road, EC1M 5RJ
(7324 4444, www.thezetter.com).
Farringdon tube/rail. **£££**.
Zetter is a fun, laid-back, modern hotel with interesting design notes, a refreshing lack of attitude, friendly staff and firm eco-credentials (such as occupancy detection systems in the bedrooms). The rooms, stacked up on five galleried storeys overlooking the intimate bar area, are smoothly functional, but cosied up with choice home comforts like hot-water bottles and old Penguin paperbacks, as well as having walk-in showers with Elemis smellies. The arrival of Bistrot Bruno Loubet (p156) should keep the place popular with not-quite-young creatives.

Fox & Anchor p206

Neighbourhood London

Base2Stay

25 Courtfield Gardens, Earl's Court,
SW5 0PG (0845 262 8000, www.base2
stay.com). Earl's Court tube. **££**.
Base2Stay looks good, with its modernist limestone and taupe tones, and keeps prices low by removing inessentials: no bar, no restaurant. Instead, there's a 'kitchenette' (microwave, sink, silent mini-fridge, kettle), with all details carefully attended to (plenty of kitchenware, including corkscrew and can opener). The rooms, en suite (with power showers) and air-conditioned, are as carefully thought-out, with desks, free wireless and flatscreens, but the single/bunkbed rooms are barely wider than the beds themselves.

40 Winks

NEW *109 Mile End Road, Stepney,*
E1 4UJ (7790 0259, 07973 653944
mobile, www.40winks.org). Stepney
Green tube. **££**. No credit cards.

Opposite a housing estate and cheap Somali diners, the flamboyantly camp and fashionable family home of an interior designer has become the B&B of choice for movie stars and fashion movers. The 'micro-boutique hotel' 40 Winks looks extraordinary (kitchen frescoes, a music room with Beatles drumkit, a lion's head tap in the bath), but each stay is made thoroughly individual by owner David Carter's commitment to his guests. You'll feel like you're staying with an ingenious friend, rather than just renting a room.

Mayflower Hotel
26-28 Trebovir Road, Earl's Court, SW5 9NJ (7370 0991, www.mayflower-group.co.uk). Earl's Court tube. **£.**
The Mayflower Group – the other properties are New Linden (59 Leinster Square, Bayswater, 7221 4321, www.newlinden.co.uk) and Twenty Nevern (20 Nevern Square, Earl's Court, 7565 9555, www.twentynevernsquare.co.uk) – has been leading the budget style revolution for years, but here's where the lushly contemporary house style evolved, proving affordability can be opulently chic and perfectly equipped. Cream walls and sleek dark woods are an understated background for richly coloured fabrics and intricate wooden architectural fragments, like the lobby's imposing Jaipuri arch.

Pavilion
34-36 Sussex Gardens, Paddington, W2 1UL (7262 0905, www.pavilion hoteluk.com). Edgware Road tube or Marylebone or Paddington tube/rail. **£.**
Behind a deceptively modest façade is what could be the city's funkiest, most original hotel. A voluptuously exotic paean to excess and paint effects, the Pavilion's madly colourful themed rooms ('Highland Fling', 'Afro Honky Tonk', 'Casablanca Nights') have become a celeb-magnet and are often used for fashion shoots. Not for lovers of minimalism and 'facilities' – though it's got most of the usual necessities.

Rockwell
181-183 Cromwell Road, Earl's Court, SW5 0SF (7244 2000, www.therockwell.com). Earl's Court tube. **££.**
The Rockwell aims for relaxed contemporary elegance – and succeeds magnificently. There are no identikit rooms here: they're all individually designed with gleaming woods and glowing colours alongside creams and neutrals. Each has a power shower, Starck fittings and bespoke cabinets in the bathrooms. Garden rooms have tiny patios, complete with garden furniture.

Stylotel
160-162 Sussex Gardens, Paddington, W2 1UD (7723 1026, www.stylotel.com). Marylebone tube or Paddington tube/rail. **£.**
Stylotel is a retro-futurist dream: metal floors and panelling, lots of royal blue (the hall walls, the padded headboards) and pod bathrooms. But the real deal is its new bargain-priced studio and apartment (respectively, £120-£150 and £150-£200, including breakfast), designed – like the hotel – by the owner's son. These achieve real minimalist chic with sleek brushed steel or white glass wall panels and simply styled contemporary furniture upholstered in black or white.

York & Albany
127-129 Parkway, Camden, NW1 7PS (7387 5700, www.gordonramsay.com). Camden Town tube. **£££.**
Overcommitment to TV enterprises might have knocked some gloss off Gordon Ramsay's restaurants, but his only hotel is great. Housed in a grand John Nash building that was designed as a coach-house, York & Albany consists of a split-level restaurant, bar and deli downstairs; above them are ten rooms, handsomely designed in mellow shades by Russell Sage. The decor is an effective mix of ancient and modern, quietly charismatic furniture and modern technology (free wireless). Two rooms have Regent's Park views.

ESSENTIALS

Getting Around

Airports

Gatwick Airport

0844 335 1802, www.gatwickairport. com. About 30 miles south of central London, off the M23.

The quickest rail link to London is the **Gatwick Express** (0845 850 1530, www.gatwickexpress.com) to Victoria; it runs 3.30am-12.30am daily and takes 30mins. Tickets cost £16.90 single or £28.80 open return (valid for 30 days).

Southern (0845 748 4950, www. southernrailway.com) also runs trains to Victoria, every 5-10mins (every 25mins 1am-4am). It takes about 35mins, and costs £10.90 single and £23.80 open return (valid for one month).

Thameslink trains (0845 748 4950, www.firstcapitalconnect.co.uk) run to St Pancras. Tickets cost £8.90 single or £17 for a 30-day open return.

By road, **National Express** (0871 781 8178, www.nationalexpress.com) runs a regular coach service for £7.50 each way, taking 65-110mins, while **taxi** to central London takes a bit over an hour and costs around £100.

Heathrow Airport

0870 000 0123, www.heathrowairport. com. About 15 miles west of central London, off the M4.

The **Heathrow Express** (0845 600 1515, www.heathrowexpress.co.uk) runs to Paddington every 15mins (5.10am-11.25pm daily) and takes 15-20mins. The train can be boarded from Terminals 1, 2 and 3 (Heathrow Central tube station) or Terminal 5 (which has its own tube station); from Terminal 4, get a shuttle to Heathrow Central. Tickets are £16.50 single, £32 return (£1 less online, £2 more on board).

The journey by **tube** into central London is longer but cheaper. The 50-60min Piccadilly Line ride into central London costs £4 one way. Trains run every few minutes from about 5am to 11.57pm daily (6am-11pm Sun).

The **Heathrow Connect** (0845 678 6975, www.heathrowconnect.com) rail service offers direct access to stations including Ealing Broadway and Paddington. The trains run every half-hour, with stops at Heathrow Central and Terminal 4; there's a shuttle from T4 station to T5. A single to Paddington is £7.40, an open return £14.80.

By road, **National Express** (0871 781 8181, www.nationalexpress.com) runs coaches daily to London Victoria (90mins, 5am-9.35pm daily) from Heathrow Central bus terminal every 20-30mins. It's £5 for a single or £9 for a return. A **taxi** to central London costs £40-£75 and takes 30-60mins.

London City Airport

7646 0000, www.londoncityairport.com. About 9 miles east of central London.

The **Docklands Light Railway** now has a stop for London City Airport, which is often less chaotic than the city's other airports. The journey to Bank station in the City takes around 20mins, and trains run 5.30am-12.30am Mon-Sat or 7am-11.30pm Sun. A **taxi** costs roughly £30 to central London, but less to the City or Canary Wharf.

Luton Airport

01582 405100, www.london-luton.com. About 30 miles north of central London, J10 off the M1.

A short bus ride links the airport to Luton Airport Parkway station, from which **Thameslink** trains (0845 748 4950, www.firstcapitalconnect.co.uk) depart for stations including St Pancras and City, taking 35-45mins. Trains leave every 15mins or so (at least hourly through the night) and cost £11.50 single and £20.50 return.

By coach, Luton to Victoria takes 60-90mins. **Green Line** (0870 608 7261, www.greenline.co.uk) runs a 24hr service (£11 single, £16 return). A taxi to central London costs £70-£80.

Stansted Airport

0870 000 0303, www.stanstedairport. com. About 35 miles north-east of central London, J8 off the M11.

The **Stansted Express** (0845 748 4950, www.stanstedexpress.com) runs to Liverpool Street station, taking 40-45mins and leaving every 15-45mins. Tickets are £19 single, £28.80 return.

The **Airbus** (0871 781 8181, www. nationalexpress.com) is one of several coach services; it takes at least 80mins to reach Victoria, with coaches running roughly every 30mins (24hrs daily), more frequently at peak times. A single is £10, a return is £17. A taxi to central London costs around £100.

Arriving by coach

Coaches run by National Express (0871 781 8181, www.nationalexpress.com), the biggest coach company in the UK, arrive at **Victoria Coach Station** (164 Buckingham Palace Road, SW1W 9TP, 7730 3466, www.tfl.gov.uk).

Arriving by rail

Trains from mainland Europe run by Eurostar (0870 518 6186, www. eurostar.com) arrive at **St Pancras International** station (0870 518 6186, www.stpancras.com).

Mainline stations

For times and prices, call 0845 748 4950 or visit www.nationalrail.co.uk. All the major stations are served by the tube.

Public transport

Travel Information Centres give help with the tube, buses and Docklands Light (DLR; opposite). Call 0843 222 1234 or visit www.tfl.gov.uk/ journeyplanner for more information.

Camden Direct *Camden Town Hall, Argyle Street (opposite King's Cross St Pancras).* **Open** 9am-5pm Mon-Fri.
Euston rail station Open 7.15am-9.15pm Mon-Fri; 7.15am-6.15pm Sat; 8.15am-6.15pm Sun.
Heathrow Terminals 1, 2 & 3 tube station Open 7.15am-9pm daily.
Liverpool Street tube station Open 7.15am-9.15pm Mon-Sat; 8.15am-8.15pm Sun.
Piccadilly Circus tube station Open 9.15am-7pm daily.
Victoria rail station Open 7.15am-9.15pm Mon-Sat; 8.15am-8.15pm Sun.

London Underground

Delays are fairly common, with lines closing most weekends for engineering works. Trains are hot and crowded in rush hour (8-9.30am, 4.30-7pm Mon-Fri). Even so, the colour-coded lines of the Underground ('the tube') are the quickest way to get about. Underground, Overground and DLR lines are shown on the **tube map** on the back flap.

Using the Underground

Tube and DLR fares are based on a system of six zones, stretching 12 miles from the centre of London. A flat **cash fare** of £4 per journey applies across zones 1-4 on the tube, £4.50 for zones 1-6; customers save up to £2.50 per journey with a pre-pay Oyster card (opposite). Anyone caught with neither ticket nor Oyster will be fined £25 (£50 if you fail to pay within three weeks).

To enter and exit the tube using an **Oyster card**, touch it to the yellow reader, which opens the gate. Make sure you also touch the card to the reader when you exit, or you'll be charged a higher fare when you next use your card to enter a station. On certain lines, you'll see a pink reader (the 'validator') – touch it in addition to the yellow entry/exit readers and on some routes it will reduce your fare.

To enter using a **paper ticket**, place it in the slot with the black magnetic strip facing down, then pull it out of the top to open the gates. Exit in the same way; tickets for single journeys will be retained by the gate on final exit.

Oyster cards

A pre-paid smartcard, Oyster is the cheapest way of getting around on buses, tubes and the DLR. You can get Oyster cards from www.tfl.gov.uk/oyster, Travel Information Centres, tube stations, some rail stations and newsagents, or by calling 0870 849 9999. A £3 refundable deposit is payable on new cards. A tube journey in zone 1 using Oyster pay-as-you-go costs £1.80; single journeys from zones 1-6 using Oyster are £4.20 (7am-7pm Mon-Fri) or £2.40 (all other times).

Travelcards

If you're only taking the tube, DLR, buses and trams, using Oyster to pay as you go will always be capped at the same price as an equivalent Day Travelcard. However, if you're also using National Rail services, Oyster may not be accepted: opt instead for a Day Travelcard, a ticket that allows travel across all the London networks. **Anytime Day Travelcards** can be used all day. They cost £7.20 for zones 1-2. Tickets are valid for journeys started by 4.30am the next day. The **Off-Peak Day Travelcard** is only for travel after 9.30am Mon-Fri (all day for weekends and public holidays). It costs £5.60 for zones 1-2.

Travelling with children

Under-5s travel free on buses and trams without the need to provide any proof of identity. **Under-11s** can also travel free, but need to obtain a 5-10 Oyster photocard. An 11-15 Oyster photocard is needed by **under-16s** to pay as they go on the tube/DLR and to

buy 7-Day, monthly or longer period Travelcards. For details, see www.tfl.gov.uk/fares or call 0845 330 9876.

Visitors can apply for a **photocard** (www.tfl.gov.uk/photocard) in advance. Photocards are not required for adult rate 7-Day Travelcards, Bus Passes or for any adult rate Travelcard or Bus Pass charged on an Oyster card.

Underground timetable

Tube trains run daily from around 5am (except Sunday, when they start an hour or so later depending on the line, and Christmas Day, when there's no service). You shouldn't have to wait more than ten minutes for a train; during peak times, services should run every two or three minutes. Times of last trains vary; they're usually around 12.30am (11.30pm on Sun). The tube runs all night only on New Year's Eve; otherwise, get the night bus (p214).

Docklands Light Railway

DLR trains (7363 9700, www.tfl.gov.uk/dlr) run from Bank station (on the Central tube line) or Tower Gateway, close to Tower Hill tube (Circle and District lines). At Westferry station, the line splits east and south via Island Gardens to Greenwich and Lewisham; a change at Poplar can take you north to Stratford. The easterly branch forks after Canning Town either to Beckton or, via London City Airport, to Woolwich Arsenal. Trains run 5.30am-12.30am daily. With very few exceptions, adult single **fares** on the DLR are the same as the Underground (opposite).

Rail & Overground

Independently run commuter services coordinated by National Rail (0845 748 4950, www.nationalrail.co.uk) leave from the city's main rail stations. Visitors heading to south London, or to more remote destinations such as Hampton Court, will need to use these overground services. Travelcards are valid within the right zones, but not all routes accept Oyster pay-as-you-go.

The orbital **London Overground** line continues to open piecemeal. It already runs through north London from Stratford in the east to Richmond in the south-west, and new spurs connect Willesden Junction in the north-west to Clapham Junction in the south-west, Gospel Oak in the north to Barking in the east, and New Cross to Shoreditch High Street in the south-and north-east. Trains run about every 20mins. We've listed Overground stations as 'rail', but the trains all accept Oyster and prices are, almost always, the same as on the Underground (p212).

Buses

All London buses are now low-floor vehicles that are accessible to wheelchair-users and passengers with buggies. The only exceptions are Heritage Route 9 and 15 Routemasters (p76).

You must have a ticket or valid pass before boarding any bus in zone 1 and articulated, single-deckers ('bendy buses') anywhere in the city. You can buy a **ticket** (or 1-Day Bus Pass) from machines at bus stops, but they're often not working; it's better to travel with an Oyster or Travelcard (p213). Using Oyster pay-as-you-go costs £1.20 a trip; your total daily payment, regardless of how many journeys, will be capped at £3.90. Paying cash costs £2 single. Under-16s travel for free (using an Oyster photocard; p213). A 1-Day Bus Pass gives unlimited bus and tram travel for £3.80. Inspectors patrol buses at random; if you don't have a ticket, you may be fined £50.

Many buses operate 24 hours a day, seven days a week. There are also some special **night buses** with an 'N' prefix, which run from about 11pm to 6am. Most night services run every 15-30mins, but busier routes run a service around every 10mins. They all feel a lot less frequent after a heavy night.

Water transport

Most river services operate every 20-60mins between 10.30am and 5pm, but run more frequently and later in the summer months; for details, see www.tfl.gov.uk. Thames Clippers (0870 781 5049, www.thamesclippers.com), which runs a service between Embankment Pier and Royal Arsenal Woolwich Pier, boarded at Blackfriars, Bankside, London Bridge, Canary Wharf and Greenwich, offers Oyster cardholders 10% off fares and a third off to Travelcard holders.

Taxis & minicabs

If a **black cab**'s orange 'For Hire' sign is lit, it can be hailed. If it stops, the cabbie must take you to your destination if it's within seven miles. It can be hard to find an empty cab, especially just after the pubs close. Fares rise after 8pm on weekdays and at weekends. You can book black cabs from the 24hr **Taxi One-Number** (0871 871 8710; a £2 booking fee applies, plus 12.5% on credit cards), **Radio Taxis** (7272 0272) and **Dial-a-Cab** (7253 5000; credit cards only, booking fee £2).

Minicabs (saloon cars) are often cheaper than black cabs, but only use licensed firms (look for a disc in the front and rear windows), and avoid those who illegally tout for business in the street: drivers may be unlicensed, uninsured and dangerous. Trustworthy, fully licensed firms include **Addison Lee** (7387 8888), which will text you when the car arrives, and **Lady Cabs** (7272 3300), **Ladybirds** (8295 0101) and **Ladycars** (8981 7111), which employ only women drivers. Otherwise, text HOME to 60835 ('60tfl'; 35p plus standard call rate) for the numbers of the two nearest licensed minicab operators and the number for Taxi One-Number, which provides licensed black cabs. No matter who you choose, always ask the price when you book and confirm it with the driver.

Driving

Congestion charge

Driving into central London 7am-6pm Mon-Fri have costs £8; the restricted area is shown at www.cclondon.com, but watch for signs and roads painted with a white 'C' on a red circle. Expect a fine of £50 if you fail to pay (£100 if you delay payment). Passes can be bought from garages, newsagents and NCP car parks; you can also pay at www.cclondon.com, on 0845 900 1234 or (after pre-registering on the website) by SMS. You can pay any time during the day or, for £2 more, until midnight on the next charging day.

Parking

Parking on a single or double yellow line, a red line or in residents' parking areas during the day is illegal, and you may be fined, clamped or towed. In the evening (from 7pm in much of central London) and at various weekend times parking on single yellow lines is legal and free. If you find a clear spot on a single yellow during the evening, look for a sign giving local regulations. During the day meters cost around £1.10/15mins, limited to two hours, but they are free at certain evening and weekend times. Parking on double yellows and red routes is always illegal.

NCP 24hr **car parks** (0845 050 7080, www.ncp.co.uk) are numerous but cost £2-£7.20/120mins: try Arlington House, Arlington Street, in St James's, W1; Snowsfields in Southwark, SE1; and 4-5 Denman Street in Soho, W1.

Vehicle removal

If your car has disappeared, it's either been stolen or, if it was illegally parked, towed to a car pound. A release fee of £200 is levied for removal, plus £40 per day from the first midnight after removal. You'll also probably get a parking ticket of £60-£100 when you collect the car (£30-£50 if paid within 14 days). To find out how to retrieve your car, call 7747 4747.

Vehicle hire

Alamo (0870 400 4562, www.alamo. co.uk), **Budget** (0844 544 3439, www. budget.co.uk) and **Hertz** (0870 844 8844, www.hertz.co.uk) all have airport branches. Shop around for the best rate and always check the level of insurance.

Cycling

London isn't the friendliest town for cyclists, but the **London Cycle Network** (www.londoncyclenetwork. org.uk) and **London Cycling Campaign** (7234 9310, www.lcc.org. uk) help to keep things improving, and **Transport for London** (0843 222 1234, www.tfl.gov.uk) has been giving riders some great support, including online and printable route-finders.

Cycle hire

A City Hall-sponsored bike rental scheme should have launched in late 2010, with 6,000 bikes available from 400 self-service docking stations in central London. Users rent bikes with a credit card and are charged based on how long they take before parking the bike at another dock. For details, see www.tfl.gov.uk/cycling. South Bank's **London Bicycle Tour Company** (7928 6838, www.londonbicycle.com) and, in Fitzrovia, **Velorution** (7637 4004, www.velorution.biz) are handy for longer rentals.

Walking

The best way to see London is on foot, but the city's street layout is complicated – even locals often carry maps. There are street maps of central London in the By Area chapters (pp58-169). There's also route advice at www.tfl.gov.uk/gettingaround.

ESSENTIALS

LIMERICK

e travel ap

vers have

aiting for.

nd maps work

o roaming ch

ime Out Guides' in tl

neout.com/iphonecityguide

Resources A-Z

For information on travelling to the United Kingdom from within the European Union, including details of visa regulations and healthcare provision, see http://europa.eu/travel.

Accident & emergency

In the event of a serious accident, fire or other incident, call **999** – free from any phone, including payphones – and ask for an ambulance, the fire service or police; the number from most mobile phones is **112**. If there is no current danger, call non-emergency number **0300 123 1212** instead. The listed hospitals have 24hr A&E departments.

Chelsea & Westminster *369 Fulham Road, Chelsea, SW10 9NH (8746 8000, www.chelwest.nhs.uk). South Kensington tube.*
Royal London *Whitechapel Road, E1 1BB (7377 7000, www.bartsand thelondon.nhs.uk). Whitechapel tube.*
St Thomas's *Lambeth Palace Road, SE1 7EH (7188 7188, www.guysand stthomas.nhs.uk). Westminster tube or Waterloo tube/rail.*
University College *235 Grafton Road, Bloomsbury, NW1 2BU (0845 155 5000, www.uclh.nhs.uk). Euston Square or Warren Street tube.*

Credit card loss

American Express *01273 696933, www.americanexpress.com.*
Diners Club *0870 190 0011, www.dinersclub.co.uk.*
MasterCard/Eurocard *0800 964767, www.mastercard.com.*
Visa/Connect *0800 891725, www.visa.co.uk.*

Customs

For allowances, see www.hmrc.gov.uk.

Dental emergency

Dental care is free for the under-18s, students resident in this country and people on benefits, but all other patients must pay (NHS-eligible patients at a subsidised rate).

Disabled

London is a difficult place for disabled visitors, although legislation is slowly improving access and general facilities. The bus fleet is now low-floor for easier wheelchair access, but the tube remains escalator-dependent. The *Tube Access Guide* booklet is free; call the Travel Information number (7222 1234) for more details.

Most major attractions and hotels have good accessibility, though provisions for the hearing- or sight-disabled are patchier. Enquire about facilities in advance. *Access in London* is an invaluable reference book for disabled travellers, available for a £10 donation from **Access Project** (www.access project-phsp.org). **Artsline** (21 Pine Court, Wood Lodge Gardens, Bromley, Kent BR1 2WA, 7388 2227, www. artsline.org.uk; 9.30am-5.30pm Mon-Fri) has handy information on disabled access to arts and cultural events.

Electricity

The UK uses 220-240V, 50-cycle AC voltage and three-pin plugs.

Embassies & consulates

American Embassy *24 Grosvenor Square, Mayfair, W1A 2LQ (7499 9000, http://london.usembassy.gov). Bond Street or Marble Arch tube. Open 8.30am-5.30pm Mon-Fri.*

Australian High Commission
*Australia House, Strand, Holborn,
WC2B 4LA (7379 4334, www.uk.
embassy.gov.au). Holborn or Temple
tube.* **Open** 9am-5pm Mon-Fri.
Canadian High Commission
*38 Grosvenor Street, Mayfair, W1K
4AA (7258 6600, www.canada.org.uk).
Bond Street or Oxford Circus tube.*
Open 8am-4pm Mon-Fri.
Embassy of Ireland *17 Grosvenor
Place, Belgravia, SW1X 7HR (7235
2171, 7225 7700 passports & visas,
www.embassyofireland.co.uk). Hyde
Park Corner tube.* **Open** 9.30am-
5.30pm Mon-Fri.
New Zealand High Commission
*New Zealand House, 80 Haymarket,
St James's, SW1Y 4TQ (7930 8422,
www.nzembassy.com). Piccadilly Circus
tube.* **Open** 9am-5pm Mon-Fri.

Internet

Most hotels have broadband and/or
wireless access, and there are cyber-
cafés dotted around town. Many normal cafés now have wireless access.

Left luggage

Security precautions have meant bus
and rail stations have left-luggage
desks rather than lockers; call 0845 748
4950 for details.

Gatwick Airport *01293 502014
South Terminal, 01293 569900
North Terminal.*
Heathrow Airport *8745 5301
Terminal 1, 8759 3344 Terminal 3,
8897 6874 Terminal 4, 8283 5073
Terminal 5.*
London City Airport *7646 0162.*
Stansted Airport *01279 663213.*

Opening hours

Banks 9am-4.30pm (some close at
3.30pm, some 5.30pm) Mon-Fri;
sometimes also Saturday mornings.
Businesses 9am-5pm Mon-Fri.

Post offices 9am-5.30pm Mon-Fri;
9am-noon Sat.
Pubs & bars 11am-11pm Mon-Sat;
noon-10.30pm Sun.
Shops 10am-6pm Mon-Sat; some to
8pm. Many are also open on Sunday,
usually 11am-5pm or noon-6pm.

Pharmacies

Branches of Boots (www.boots.com)
and larger supermarkets have a phar-
macy, and there are independents on
most high streets. Staff can advise on
over-the-counter medicines. Most phar-
macies open 9am-6pm Mon-Sat.

Police

Look up 'Police' in the phone book or
call 118 118, 118 500 or 118 888 if none
of these police stations are convenient.

Belgravia *202-206 Buckingham
Palace Road, Pimlico, SW1W 9SX
(7730 1212). Victoria tube/rail.*
Charing Cross *Agar Street, Covent
Garden, WC2N 4JP (7240 1212).
Charing Cross tube/rail.*
Chelsea *2 Lucan Place, SW3 3PB
(7589 1212). South Kensington tube.*
West End Central *27 Savile Row,
Mayfair, W1S 2EX (7437 1212).
Piccadilly Circus tube.*

Post

For general enquiries, call 0845 722
3344 or consult www.postoffice.co.uk.
Post offices are usually open 9am-6pm
Mon-Fri and 9am-noon Sat, although
the **Trafalgar Square Post Office**
(24-28 William IV Street, WC2N 4DL,
0845 722 3344) opens 8.30am-6.30pm
Mon-Fri and 9am-5.30pm Sat.

Smoking

Smoking is banned in all enclosed public spaces, including pubs, bars, clubs,
restaurants, hotel foyers, shops and
public transport.

ESSENTIALS

Telephones

London's dialling code is 020; standard landlines have eight digits after that. If you're calling from outside the UK, dial your international access code, then the UK code, 44, then the full London number, omitting the first 0 from the code (Australia 61, Canada 1, New Zealand 64, Republic of Ireland 353, South Africa 27, USA 1).

US cellphone users will need a tri- or quad-band handset.

Public payphones take coins and/or credit cards. International calling cards (bargain minutes via a freephone number) are widely available.

Tickets

It is well worth booking ahead – even obscure acts can sell out and the high-profile gigs and sporting events do so in seconds. It is usually cheaper to bypass ticket agents and go direct to the box office – the former will charge booking fees that could top 20 per cent. Should you have to use them, booking agencies include **Ticketmaster** (0870 277 4321, www.ticketmaster.co.uk), **Stargreen** (7734 8932, www.stargreen.com), **Ticketweb** (0844 477 1000, www.ticketweb.co.uk), **See Tickets** (0870 264 3333, www.seetickets.com) and **Keith Prowse** (0870 840 1111, www.keithprowse.com); **tkts** (p139) sells reduced price West End theatre tickets on the day of performance.

Time

London is on Greenwich Mean Time (GMT), five hours ahead of US Eastern Standard time. In autumn (31 Oct 2010, 30 Oct 2011) the clocks go back an hour to GMT; they go forward to British Summer Time on 27 Mar 2011.

Tipping

Tip in taxis, minicabs, restaurants (some waiting staff rely heavily on tips), hotels, hairdressers and some bars (not pubs). Ten per cent is normal, with some restaurants adding as much as 15%. Always check whether service has been included in your bill: some restaurants include a service charge, but also leave space for a tip on your credit card slip.

Tourist information

The new City of London Information Centre, beside St Paul's, offers tours with specialist City-trained guides as well as information.

City of London Information Centre *St Paul's Churchyard, EC4M 8BX (7332 1456, www.cityoflondon. gov.uk). St Paul's tube.* **Open** 9.30am-5.30pm Mon-Sat; 10am-4pm Sun.
Greenwich Tourist Information Centre *Discover Greenwich, Pepys House, 2 Cutty Sark Gardens, SE10 9LW (0870 608 2000, www.greenwich whs.org.uk). Cutty Sark DLR.* **Open** 10am-5pm daily.
London Information Centre *Leicester Square, WC2H 7BP (7292 2333, www.londontown.com). Leicester Square tube.* **Open** 8am-10pm daily. *Helpline* 8am-10pm Mon-Fri; 9am-8pm Sat, Sun.

Visas

Citizens of the EU don't require a visa to visit the UK; for limited tourist visits, citizens of the USA, Canada, Australia, New Zealand and South Africa can also enter the UK with only a passport. But *always* check the current situation at www.ukvisas.gov.uk well before you travel.

What's on

Time Out remains London's only quality listings magazine. Widely available every Tuesday, it gives listings for the week from Wednesday. For gay listings, look for freesheets *Boyz* and *QX*.

Index

Sights & Areas

30 St Mary Axe p162

a

Albert Memorial p84
All Saints p113
Apsley House p89

b

Bank of England Museum p159
Banqueting House p74
BBC Broadcasting House p113
Belgravia p92
Benjamin Franklin House p140
Bloomsbury p119
Borough Market p70
British Library p122
British Museum p119
Brompton Oratory p84
BT Tower p113
Buckingham Palace & Royal Mews p81
Bunhill Fields p161

c

Camden Market p173
Carlyle's House p93
Cartoon Museum p119
Charles Dickens Museum p120
Chelsea p93
Chelsea Physic Garden p93
Churchill War Rooms p74
City, The p159
City Hall p58
Clerkenwell p149
Columbia Road Market p183
Courtauld Gallery p149
Covent Garden p138
Covent Garden Piazza p140

d

Design Museum p58
Discover Greenwich & the Old Royal Naval College p185
Dr Johnson's House p149
Dulwich Picture Gallery p185

e

East London p177

f

Fashion & Textile Museum p59
Fitzrovia p113
Fleet Street p152
Florence Nightingale Museum p59
Fortnum & Mason p82
Foundling Museum p120

g

Garden Museum p59
Geffrye Museum p177
Golden Hinde p59
Guards Museum p81
Guildhall Art Gallery & Clockmakers' Museum p161

h

Hampstead Heath p170
Hampton Court Palace p185
Handel House Museum p107
Harrods p92
Hayward p59
Heron Tower p161
HMS Belfast p59
Holborn p149
Household Cavalry Museum p81
Houses of Parliament p76
Hunterian Museum p152
Hyde Park p89

i

Imperial War Museum p63

j

Jewish Museum p171

k

Keats House p171
Kensington Palace & Gardens p85
King's Cross p122
Knightsbridge p89

l

Leicester Square p127
Liberty p136
Lloyd's of London p161
London Bridge Experience p63
London Canal Museum p124
London Eye p63
London Film Museum p63
London Transport Museum p140
London Zoo p172
Lord's & MCC Museum p171

m

Madame Tussauds p98
Marylebone p98
Mayfair p107
Monument p161
Museum & Library of the Order of St John p152
Museum of Brands, Packaging & Advertising p189
Museum of London p161
Museum of London Docklands p179

n

National Army Museum p93
National Gallery p76
National Maritime Museum p186
National Portrait Gallery p76
Natural History Museum p85
North London p170

o

O2 Arena p188
Old Operating Theatre, Museum & Herb Garret p65
Old Spitalfields Market p183
Olympic Park p179
One Canada Square p179

p

Petrie Museum of Egyptian Archaeology p120
Photographers' Gallery p127
Pollock's Toy Museum p113
Portobello Road Market p191
Postman's Park p162

r

Ragged School Museum p179
Regent's Park p98
Ripley's Believe It or Not! p127
Ronnie Scott's p138
Routemaster buses p76
Royal Academy of Arts p107
Royal Botanic Gardens (Kew Gardens) p186
Royal Hospital Chelsea p95
Royal Institute of British Architects p113

Royal Institution & Faraday Museum p107

s

Saatchi Gallery p95
St Bartholomew-the-Great p152
St Bride's Church p155
St George's Bloomsbury p120
St James's p81
St James's Park p82
St James's Piccadilly p82
St Martin-in-the-Fields p76
St Paul's Cathedral p162
St Paul's Covent Garden p141
Science Museum p85
Sea Life London Aquarium p65
Selfridges p105
Serpentine Gallery p85
Shakespeare's Globe p65
Sir John Soane's Museum p155
Soho p127
Soho Square p127
Somerset House & the Embankment Galleries p155
South Bank p58
Southbank Centre p73
South Kensington p84
South London p185

t

Tate Britain p78
Tate Modern p65
Temple Church & Middle Temple p155
Topolski Century p66
Tower Bridge Exhibition p162
Tower of London p162
Trafalgar Square p78

v

V&A Museum of Childhood p179

w

Wallace Collection p101
Wellcome Collection p124
Wellington Arch p90
Westfield London p192
West London p189
Westminster p74
Westminster Abbey p78
Westminster Cathedral p79
Whitechapel Gallery p179
Wigmore Hall p107
Wimbledon Lawn Tennis Museum p186
Winston Churchill's Britain at War Experience p66

Eating & Drinking

a

Abeno Too p141
Albannach p79
Albion at the Boundary Project p180
All Star Lanes p120
Amaya p90
Anchor & Hope p66
Anglesea Arms p88
Arbutus p127
Artesian p101
Atelier de Joël Robuchon, L' p141
Autre Pied, L' p101

b

Baltic p66
Baozi Inn p130
Bar Kick p164
Barrafina p130
Ba Shan p130
Battersea Pie p141
Benito's Hat p113
Bi Bim Bap p130
Bistrot Bruno Loubet p156
Black Friar p164
Bob Bob Ricard p130
Bocca di Lupo p130
Bodean's p164
Boisdale of Belgravia p92
Book Club p164

ESSENTIALS

Bradley's Spanish Bar
  p116
Brasserie Max p141
Brick Lane Beigel Bake
  p180
Bull & Last p172
Busaba Eathai p130
Butcher at Leadenhall
  p164

c

Cadogan Arms p95
Café Anglais, Le p189
Callooh Callay p165
Cambio de Tercio p88
Camino & Bar Pepito
  p124
Canteen p66
Caravan p156
Chaat p180
Cha Cha Moon p132
Chisou p107
Cinnamon Club p79
Clerkenwell Kitchen
  p156
Comptoir Gascon, Le
  p156
Comptoir Libanais p101
Connaught Bar p108
Corrigan's Mayfair p108

d

Dean Street Townhouse
  & Dining Room p132
Dehesa p132
Dog & Duck p132
Dreambagsjaguarshoes
  p180
Driver p124
Dukes Hotel p82

e

Eagle p156
Empress of Sichuan
  p132
E Pellicci p180
Espresso Room p120
Eyre Brothers p165

f

Fairuz p101
Fernandez & Wells p132

Fish Central p165
Food for Thought p142
Franco Manca p186
French House p132
Fromagerie, La p101

g

Gallery Mess p95
Galvin at Windows
  p108
Galvin Bistrot de Luxe
  p101
Gaucho Piccadilly p108
Giaconda Dining Room
  p142
Gilgamesh p172
Gladstone Arms p69
Golden Eagle p103
Golden Hinde p103
Gordon's p142
Great Queen Street
  p142

h

Haché p95
Hakkasan p116
Hibiscus p108
Hix & Mark's Bar p133
Hummus Bros p121

i

Imli p133
Inn The Park p82

j

Jerusalem Tavern p156

k

Kiasu p189
Konstam at Prince Albert
  p125

l

LAB p133
Lamb p121
Lamb & Flag p142
Lantana p116
Ledbury p191
Library p90
Long Bar p116
Lounge p188
Lowlander p142

m

Madsen p88
Magdalen p69
Maison Bertaux p133
Marcus Wareing p90
Market p172
Masala Zone p172
Match Bar p116
Maze p108
Milk & Honey p133
M Manze p69
Modern Pantry p157
Momo p108
More p69
Moro p157
Museum Tavern p121

n

Nag's Head p92
Nahm p92
Napket p95
National Dining Rooms
  p79
Newman Arms p116
Nobu Berkeley Street
  p108
Nordic Bakery p133

o

Oddono's p88
Old Brewery p188
Old Queen's Head p173
Only Running Footman
  p109
Ottolenghi p173

p

Petite Maison, La p109
Polpo p133
Princi p135
Providores & Tapa Room
  p103

r

Racine p90
Rake p69
Restaurant at St Paul's
  p165
River Café p191
Roast p69
Rock & Sole Plaice
  p142

Roka & Shochu Lounge
  p116
Rosa's p182

s

Saf p165
St John p157
St Pancras Grand p125
St Stephen's Tavern p79
Sake No Hana p82
Salt Yard p117
Scandinavian Kitchen
  p117
Scoop p144
Scott's p109
Seven Stars p158
Sheekey, J p144
Sketch: The Parlour
  p109
Skylon p70
Sông Quê p182
Sweetings p167

t

Taqueria p191
Tayyabs p182
Terroirs p144
Texture p103
Three Kings of
  Clerkenwell p158
Tibits p109
Tini p89
Tom's Kitchen p96
Tsuru p70
Two Floors p135

v

Vertigo 42 p167
Viajante p182
Vinoteca p158

w

Wagamama p121
Wahaca p144
Westbourne House p191
Wild Honey p109
Wine Wharf p70
Wolseley p82

y

Yauatcha p135
Ye Old Mitre p158

z

Zuma p90

Arts & Leisure

a

Adelphi Theatre p146
Almeida p177
Arsenal Football Club
  p177

b

BAC (Battersea Arts
  Centre) p189
Barbican Centre p169
BFI Southbank p72

c

Cadogan Hall p97
Chelsea Football Club p97
Cinéphilia West p192
Coliseum p148
Curzon Soho p138

d

Donmar Warehouse p148

g

Gielgud Theatre p138

i

ICA (Institute of
  Contemporary Arts)
  p83

k

Kings Place p125

l

London Palladium p139
LSO St Luke's p169
Lyric Hammersmith p189

n

National Theatre p72
Noël Coward Theatre
  p148

o

Odeon Leicester Square
  p139
Old Vic p73

p

Palace Theatre p139
Place p125
Prince Charles Cinema
  p139
Prince Edward Theatre
  p139

r

Royal Albert Hall p89
Royal Court Theatre
  p97
Royal Opera House
  p148

s

Sadler's Wells p177
St John's, Smith Square
  p81
Savoy Theatre p148
Screen on the Green
  p177
Shaftesbury Theatre
  p148
Shunt p73
Siobhan Davies Dance
  Studios p73
Soho Theatre p139
Southbank Centre p73

t

tkts p139

v

Victoria Palace Theatre
  p81

w

Wembley Stadium p177
Wigmore Hall p107

Young Vic p73

ESSENTIALS